AGAINST SUCH THINGS

A Memoir of Trauma, Addiction, & Survival

Rachel K. Baldwin

Adolescent Bird Publishing House

OLYMPIA, WASHINGTON

Adolescent Bird Publishing House
P.O. Box 11982
Olympia, WA 98508-1982

www.rachelkbaldwin.com
www.facebook.com/againstsuchthings
www.instagram.com/calmbeforetherach

Publisher's Note: This is a work of nonfiction. The events and dialogue are recreated to the best of the author's memory. Some names have been changed to protect the privacy of those depicted. The views expressed in this memoir are solely those of the author.

Against Such Things/ Rachel K. Baldwin. -- 1st ed. Hardback Feb. 2021
ISBN 978-0-578-86204-0

Printed in the United States of America

For my father, who was the waves, and then the anchor
My children, the lighthouse in the storm
And finally, J, my port of safety, my shelter on the shore

(to suffer silence is penance self-imposed)

— PAIGE GREY, "HEART UNDRESSED"

CHAPTER ONE

The Prestige

YOU KNOW THE PART at the beginning of a social media post, or movie, or whatever that gives you a heads-up there will be triggers?

Like, a LOT of triggers?

Well, this is that.

If you are anything like me, you almost *always* skip through the prologue and go straight to the meat of the text: I'm hoping I tricked you into not doing that here.

This fake-out chapter is my attempt at getting your attention, so you don't do the whole jump forward thing, and then panic when you get hit head-fucking-on by a runaway train to Intensity-Ville.

So: Last call for trigger warnings. Triggers ahead; I repeat, triggers ahead.

(If you need specifics on which *kinds* of triggers—i.e., SPOILERS—please flip to the 'Resources' section at the back of the book.)

***

Okay, now that we've got THAT out of the way, let's discuss another super-salient point: This book does not—in any way—claim to be the objective, be-all-end-all, every-perspective-covered truth; it details MY perception, my experience, and illustrates my resulting decisions based on what I believed at any given point.

As with all situations anywhere ever, there are multiple sides to every story. The people and events depicted here are multifaceted; I only claim this to be an accurate portrayal of my point of view.

The stories, though: They are real. They are mine.

Most names are changed out of respect, innocence notwithstanding.

Although these are all MY stories, these are not ALL my stories: I've given you a slice, a sliver, a mere piece of the pie.

I sincerely hope what I've written here succinctly captures the over-arching message; no matter what you've been through, no matter what you've done:

Even Against Such Things, Healing IS Possible

Okay, then: The train is leaving the station. Hop on for the ride, if you dare.

SFORZANDO

CHAPTER TWO

Tortillas & Two Bad Men

"BUT DADDY *SAIIID*!"

I rub my tears away with one chubby, dimpled fist; the other clutches my favorite teddy bear—the one with the red apple stitched onto his blue bib—tighter in the crook of my arm. My mother's face twists into a grimace, and lines form across her otherwise smooth forehead as she glowers in frustration. "Your father, I swear! You have him wrapped around your little finger. I can't win with either of you."

I hiccup and snuggle my well-loved bear closer to the yellow floor-length party dress Daddy bought me: Not the usual naptime attire, no, but this is a special day.

"It's her birfday, Mommy. She gived me a party invitation and everyfing!"

We stand face-to-face like two cowboys in the old west at high noon. The living room lights of the historic Victorian house we call home are dimmed to set the mood for my nap.

"And—and Daddy *saiiid*!!" I howl, dissolving into sobs.

My mother leans over and hisses through clenched teeth. "Rachel Kay! That is *enough*! Stop it right now before you wake the baby!"

My sobs turn to whimpers, and she groans and throws up her hands in surrender.

"Fine. Go. But, just there and back," she says, exasperation running hot currents through her strained voice. "And no cake!"

I stare up at her with wide-eyed sincerity, my tears erased by a smile. "Otay, Mommy!"

***

My best friend's house is kitty-corner from ours—in a quiet neighborhood—and it is her fifth birthday. I won't be 5 years old until summer, and I've never been to a birthday party; never been allowed across the street unaccompanied before, either.

I approach the crosswalk as I was taught, looking both ways before venturing forward. I walk primly up the front porch steps balancing in both hands the present my mother threw together at the last minute, careful not to muss the wrapping. The tinkling of laughter and gaiety reaches me through the closed door. I ring the doorbell, and when it swings open, the heavenly aroma of fresh-baked tortillas wafts over me.

My friend's mother pulls me into a warm embrace, her soft, portly middle a stark contrast to her rough, flour-covered hands. "Hola, Mija! So glad you can come! We not think you make it. Bienvenidos!!"

She holds me out at arm's length, her face beaming. "You stay for sleepover with other ninitas?"

My face grows warm, and I scrape the toe of my new t-strap Mary Janes back-and-forth on the top step. "I can't. I just comed to drop off this pwesent and say happy birfday. I hafta take a nap."

She clucks and pulls me in for another hug. "No, no, Mija! You no leave without at least have cake!"

As she releases me from the embrace, I catch a glimpse of the dining room table behind her. On it stands a tall cake covered in sugar flowers and vibrant frosting. I hesitate and glance toward my house. I can't see my mother on the porch or peering out through the windows.

"Wellll, maybe just for a minute."

I step inside and into a bustle of activity: kids running and laughing, grown-ups chattering in a language I don't fully understand.

She leads me into the dining room, where I set down my gift. "I get you piece."

I marvel as she places a corner slice—topped with one of the mouth-watering frosting flowers—in a small dish.

"Fank you," I say through a mouthful of cake.

She laughs and motions toward the back door. "De nada! Rapida: Finish and come say hola to other ninos; they play party games in backyard."

I stuff the last few bites into my mouth and follow her outside. Beyond the screen door, swinging merrily in the branches of a broad, reaching elm is a dazzling, multicolored miniature donkey.

I crane my neck, and my jaw drops open. "What is *that*?"

She smiles down at me. "Is piñata! We fill with bombon—how you say, candy?—and take turns beating with stick. Then it burst, and candy rain down!"

My friend sees me and races over, tackling me with a hug. "Rachel, you came!! See my piñata? Isn't it great?" She takes my hand and pulls me toward a group of people on the other side of the yard. "Do you want to go first?"

I examine the unfamiliar faces, and my shyness comes rushing back. "No, fank you."

She shrugs and smiles. "Okay, me first, then!"

From the sidelines, I observe as young and old alike take turns attempting to loosen the promised prize from the festive piñata. When at last it breaks open and candy showers down like a ticker-tape parade, I am not quick enough to grab a piece from the bare lawn surrounding the tree. My friend's mother directs a pudgy boy of about 6 to share his bounty: He relinquishes a portion of his prize—a grape Jolly Rancher—begrudgingly from his sticky, overstuffed hands.

My face burning with guilt, I shove the forbidden sweet in my mouth and tuck it into the side of my cheek in hopes my mother won't notice. "Fank you, but I really hafta go now."

After hugs and promises to come visit again soon, I dart through the empty dining room and out the front door. From the porch, I search again for any sign of my mother. There is none.

This time, I dash across the street without even considering the rules. Once across, I hide behind one of two giant oaks that frame the front entrance of our walkway. I peek my head around the side of the tree, and when satisfied I have not been spotted, I lean back onto the rough bark and try to formulate an excuse to explain my extreme tardiness.

After a few desperate moments, my eyes land on a driveway two doors down. It slopes downhill at a steep angle and is full of shadows. My mother has deemed it strictly off-limits.

Perfect.

I take a deep breath and bound up the stairs and into my house. The living room is deserted.

"Mommy! Where are you?"

My mother hurtles in from the kitchen, fuming. "Where have you *been*, Rachel Kay! I said there and back; it's been nearly an hour!"

I've never seen her so angry. I wait—still and silent as one of my baby dolls—for a break in her tirade, then launch into my tale.

"Mommy, I was *kidnapped*! Two bad men comed and taked me down that old, scary driveway! I tried to scweam, but one of them covered my mouf so I couldn't. I waited 'til they weren't looking, then I runned away!"

The color drains from my mother's face, and she rushes across the room and gathers me in her arms. "Oh, my goodness!! My poor *girl!* Are you hurt? Are you all right?"

Like a Precious Moments figurine—all big eyes and holy adoration—I nod solemnly. "Yes, Mommy, I'm otay now."

In quick succession, my father is called home from work, and the police arrive. A towering detective asks question after question, and I dutifully recite my story, gravely repeating the details of my 'kidnapping' complete with descriptions of the 'two bad men.'

For the next several days, my mother is adamant about keeping me in her line of sight. Both she and my father shower me nonstop with love and attention.

But, I feel stifled during the day, longing to go outside and play with my friends. And at night, remorse weighs heavy on my conscience.

Finally, I can take it no longer: The burden of guilt outweighs the fear of punishment. One night after bedtime stories, I trudge into the living room where my parents are sitting together on the couch.

"I have somefing to tell you."

My mother holds up her hand to pause the conversation between my father and her and faces me. "What is it, honey?"

I fiddle with the button on my two-piece flannel pajamas and speak in a hushed tone. "I lied."

My father stands, crosses the room, and turns the television volume down. "What did you lie about, young lady?"

I stare up at him, then hang my head. "The bad men."

My parents look at each other, first in confusion, then understanding. For a long moment, no one speaks.

A muted whir comes from where my father stands, and I jerk my head in his direction. Confused, I work to comprehend what I am seeing: the snakeskin blur of his thick leather belt ripping through his belt loops. He doubles the until moment's ago benign serpent, then snaps it. The resounding crack echoes through the house.

"Into the bedroom. Now."

My father, a male Medusa, and me, a stone child.

"Wh-why, Daddy?" I choke out between shallow breaths.

"You heard me. Go. Now. Rita, you get her britches pulled down."

Like a bird jostled too early from the nest, my mother takes flight off her brand new, 1979 Sears & Roebucks sofa—takes flight, then hovers in place like a concussed, window-battered hummingbird.

"Victor, I don't know; isn't the bare bottom a little extreme?"

"Move. Both of you."

We both flinch at the razor edge in his voice; a cloud darkens his features, and the man I love seems hidden somewhere unreachable behind the storm. My mother stumbles and skitters like a frightened kitten, then steers me into a small bedroom off the main living area.

I sway at the edge of the bed, stiff with fear, pleading silently for her to intercede, to hug me close, to tuck me back into bed. Although she appears meek and centered, her irises widen and constrict in a frantic concerto in time with the thunderous pounding of my heart.

"Come on, Rachel. Be a good girl and listen. Pull your jammie bottoms down and lean over the edge of the bed."

I cling to my mother's sleeve, in near hysterics now. "But, Mommy, I'm *saw-wee*! I won't lie again: I *pwomise*!"

My father's looming figure in the doorway casts a cold shadow across our exchange, and a chill courses through my slight frame.

Snap—goes the belt.

No matter how much I will my muscles to obey, I cannot move. My mother spins me around by my shoulders, pulls my pajamas and purple cotton panties down around my ankles, and pushes me forward onto the bed to appease my father's growing rage.

SNAP.

My father's shadow swells as he steps into the room, and a stone child turns to ice.

"I don't want to hear a single peep from you, young lady. You lie still until I finish, or you will live to regret it!"

I nod my damp cheek against the stubbly, hobnail-chenille bedspread.

Snap—CRACK.

A searing hot, unimaginable pain shoots across my tender backside and radiates through every connected nerve ending. Sensations reminiscent of the time I touched the fiery-red stove burner coil envelop me from head to toe.

I wriggle away instinctively, forming a ball at the corner of the bed. "Owwww! Daddy, stop!"

"I told you to hold still! You're going to get another lash for every time you move!"

"But Daddy! It *hurts*!"

"It's for your own good, Daughter. It's about time you had some discipline. Now hold still!"

Snap—CRACK, CRACK, CRACK!

I roll out of the way just in time. The barest edge of the viper's metal head bites my lower thigh; my body is wracked with sobs.

"Rita, make yourself useful; hold her still!"

"But Vic—" Faint, unconvincing, ineffective.

"Do what I said, or you'll be sorry!"

My mother's cool, ropey hands are on my shoulders again, this time pinning me in place—immovable—against the ridges of the blanket.

"Just do what he says," she whispers into my ear. "The quicker we listen, the quicker this will all be over."

SNAP—and then:

I am floating—free—above us all. Below, I see my small body pressed onto the mattress, red welts blooming like opium poppies on my fair skin—blooming, blistering, bursting—but I am still. I don't move. How can I? Down below without myself to make me. I am so *very* still, such a good girl who listens.

***

I haven't been allowed outside to play since Daddy took his belt off. I'm not sure how long it's been, but I am so tired of Lincoln Logs and stuffed animals and my forever crying baby brother. I have been remanded to the kitchen table under my mother's watchful eye, with only my coloring books to keep me company. Not so much as an occasional break to watch Bible story cartoons on the Christian channel—the only cartoons I am ever allowed—even those are off-limits now.

My mother is making canned chicken noodle soup and tuna sandwiches—my least favorite meal—when there is a knock at the front door. I wait until she goes to answer it, then crawl across the soft shag carpeting and hide under a lamp table to see who is here. From my vantage point—scrunched criss-cross applesauce under the heavy wooden legs of the table—I can only see them from the knees down: my mother, in cotton shorts and terrycloth house slippers; my friend's brother wearing jeans, his dark toes peeping out through worn sandals.

I lean out as far as I dare and see my mother holding the screen door open with one hip, her arm braced against the doorframe, passively blocking the entrance.

She cuts him off before he can offer a greeting. "No, Rachel cannot come out to play. She is on restriction. You'll have to come back another day."

"No, ma'am. You misunderstand. I do not ask if your girl can play. I come to tell you a message from mi Madre."

The exasperation in her voice is plain—the conspicuous disdain.

"Oh, I didn't recognize you. You're Rachel's little friend's brother? Well, what is it then? And make it quick. I'm in the middle of making lunch."

"My sister, we take family trip to go on rides at Cedar Point, to have cotton candy. My sister love the cotton candy."

He stops speaking, and after a long pause, my mother sighs and twirls her free hand. "Yes, yes; get on with it."

"On way home, we drive next to cliff. Is hot, so window is down. She not wear harness."

"A seat belt, you mean. What exactly are you trying to say, young man?"

He sniffles and pauses again. "She die. Fly out window. Her head hit ground and break open like watermelon."

"Oh, dear Jesus!!"

"Yes. Mi Madre say she with Jesus now. Say to tell your girl 'thank you' for coming to party. She was very happy your girl come."

CHAPTER THREE

Gold Edition Faith

IT'S DARK OUT AND numbingly cold. My nose is sticking out of the covers, and it keeps waking me: as if Jack Frost himself flew by and bit it. I try to pull the blankets high enough to cut the chill, but then my breath gets all hot and foggy, and it wakes me again. I curl up tighter and snuggle closer to my teddy for warmth.

"Wake up! Be quick about it! It's time to go!"

I sit up, startled, and see my mother crouched next to my bed, flashlight in hand, my small suitcase open beside her.

I rub my bleary eyes and stare blankly. "But go where Mommy? It's nighttime!"

"Don't you worry about that; just do as I say. Put on your shoes, grab your Bible, and your teddy, and let's *go*!"

Shivering, I stumble out of bed: In the moonlight cast through the window, I can see my breath. I laugh at the sight. "Mommy, look! I can make clouds in the house! Isn't that silly?"

My mother turns from her haphazard packing and nods curtly. "Yes, Rachel. A house with no heat. Again. Silly is *not* the word.

"Come on, your father and brother are waiting in the car. You know the drill; get a move on before your father loses his temper!"

***

We curl up together in the backseat of the wood-paneled station wagon—my little brother, Jack, now almost 4, and me, nearly 8—and watch as another house fades into the distance. Our mother made us a nest of pillows and blankets, peppered generously with magnetic board games and stuffed animals, to keep us occupied as we hit the open road: destination elsewhere, once again.

After weeks of overnight rest stops and nondescript tent camping sites, we pull off the main highway and change over to winding backroads. The scent of southern magnolia and flowering dogwood floats in through the open windows. Cresting the top of a gentle hill, a large wooden sign with intricately carved, garish yellow font comes into view:

Heritage USA
Home of the PTL Television Network

And a little farther down:

Camp Meeting: 7:30 p.m.
Passion Play: 9 p.m.

My father pulls the station wagon to the side of the road and parks. "Okay, kids! We are here! We've reached the promised land! Get on out and stand in front of the sign so your mother can get a picture of you two."

The four of us tumble out of the car: my parents smiling and hugging, Jack and I huddled together and gawking at the unfamiliar surroundings.

My mother herds us over to flank the massive sign and snaps photos with her polaroid camera. "Oh, Vic! I can hardly believe we are *here*! It's a miracle this place even exists!"

My father nods, his sandy hair fluttering in the slight breeze, and his smug, hardened demeanor—a striking blend of Robert De Niro and John Goodman-esque features—softens into a mixture of staidness braided through with hope. "You're right, Rita. Everything is going to come together for us now. Just you wait."

Jack, having been woken from his nap for the required picture taking, is cranky and begins to whimper. No discernible words, though; his mouth firmly corked by his thumb, his pudgy little hand gripping the silky pillow he carries everywhere.

The cords on my father's neck raise and thicken like the ridges on a corrugated metal roof. "Shut that kid up! We still have to find a campsite and get settled for the night." He stomps back to the car, drops down into the driver's seat, and slams the door behind him.

I guide my little brother back to my side and coo softly, trying to settle him down. "It's okay, Jacky, it's okay. Daddy says it's all going to be okay now."

***

The campsites are easy enough to find: follow the yellow line. The yellow line traversing the park indicating where those registered in the campground are permitted to go—the places free of charge—the campground itself, the gift shop, the television studio to participate as audience members of Jim & Tammy Faye Bakker's *The PTL Club*. The rest of the compound—water park, restaurants, petting zoo—are accessible by following the blue line, which requires payment to access and a fancy plastic bracelet indicating you belong.

The campsites are the nicest we've seen all summer: There is a communal bathroom with hot water, and each site has electrical outlets. Jack and I can ride our bikes—strapped the whole trip to the luggage rack on top of the wagon—while our parents set up the tent, if we stay within view.

After a dinner of canned corned beef hash and too-crispy fried eggs, my mother helps me wriggle into my Strawberry Shortcake pajamas, my skin still damp from the shower.

I stick my lower lip out and pout. "It's not even dark yet, though."

"Just do as you are told, young lady! Tomorrow, we are getting up with the birds to learn about God. We get to see a TV show filmed live!

Maybe we'll even get to meet Pastor Jim and his wife in person; doesn't that sound exciting?"

I sigh and toss my braid over my shoulder. "I guess so."

"This is what your father needs, Rachel Kay. The Lord told him to bring us here, and The Lord always carries his flock through to the end."

I shrug and climb on top of the sleeping bag next to my brother, who snuggles up beside me. My mother leaves the tent and rejoins my father on the picnic bench outside.

"Want a story, Jacky?" I whisper, making sure my voice is low enough so only he can hear.

He snuggles closer. "'Bout the other world?"

I nod. "Okay," I begin. "Long ago, before we had parents or rules or Sunday School, we were MAGIC. You were the real, live Jack from "Jack & the Beanstalk," and we would climb all the way up to the clouds and eat sweets and dance with the *fairies*!"

He smiles up at me with his thumb plugging his mouth, his eyes full of stars. "More, Sissy! Tell more!"

I weave a tale of a secret fantasy world—a world to which we so often escape—and watch through the open tent flap as the boughs of the trees sway in the wind, waiting for the stars to come out for the night.

When I wake sometime later, the stars are out in full force, and the July air is thick and muggy.

My father is glowing with unbridled joy: a look I've never seen on him. "Come on, Daughter, let's get going! We want to get good seats; the line for the audience is sure to wrap around the studio."

Still half asleep, I fumble for my cast-off clothes, then help my mother locate Jack's silky pillow in a preemptive move to avoid a tantrum. In short order, we are all dressed and, with granola bars tucked in our pockets, ready for our adventure.

We stroll together up the steep hill, following the yellow line and signs toward the recording studio. My father hums a few bars of "Amazing Grace," and I run up next to him and swoop my hand into his. His smile is warm and golden, like the sunrise spilling over a hill, and all is right in the world.

***

We are one of the first families in line, and the set coordinator ushers us in and seats us second row, dead center. The televangelist—in his fancy powder blue, three-piece-suit, and handheld microphone—leaps out to thunderous applause and walks amongst the crowd, praising God, shaking hands, and kissing babies.

Edging past the knees and elbows of the sardine-packed audience members, he barrels down our row and grasps my father's hand tightly. "Praise Jesus! God has a plan for you, my son!"

My father beams with adulation, and his eyes glisten with moisture.

"I told you, Rita! The Lord meant for us to come!" He whispers over my head as Reverend Bakker continues to the next person in our row.

Opening credits come next, and a falsetto soprano rendition of "The Sun Will Shine Again," and then the star of the show: the new *PTL Parallel Gold Edition Bible*.

"Folks, this first edition, gen-u-ine 24k-gold-leaf-edged canon of the Word of God, can be *yours* to take home today!"

My father's eyes shine—enraptured—and he leans past me again, the pale curls on his muscular arm tickling my face, this time to take my mother's hand.

"That's right! *You* can be a part of the Kingdom of God! Why store up your treasures on Earth, when you can invest in eternal life?"

"Rita! It's happening! This is the sign I've been waiting for!"

My mother's brow furrows as she works to formulate a response. "I don't know, Vic…how much is it? We only have about $250 left to our name, and—"

Pastor Bakker paces in front of the audience, his voice rising as he waves the Bible over his head. "Don't let the devil take away your power flock! Don't let him mock you! Money is no object when it comes to the prosperity God will bestow on those who walk in faith!"

My father throws my mother a knowing glance and sits straighter in his chair, grasping the edge of the seat in front of him.

"Who will be the first to pledge! Who will step forward in faith, and for a mere $100, secure a future for his household in the Hereafter?"

My father jumps up and bolts down the aisle and up the stage steps, waving two crumpled fifties in his outstretched hand. "I will; praise Jesus! I stand in faith, Pastor!"

"Hallelujah, son! Praise God! Who else will follow this man's lead, and the call of our blessed Savior?"

***

The show is over now, and we have followed the loop of the yellow line, past the backside of the water park with kids and families howling and splashing, past the rides and rollercoasters, past the fancy high rise hotels: all off-limits.

Too early for lunch or naptime—and hoping for something to do—we go off track and into an open field dotted with small cabins. My brother and I are picking daisies when I hear my father exclaim a greeting.

I look up. We are inches from the blue line, now, and strolling casually along its path is the Bakker family.

"Pastor Jim, Pastor Jim! Hello! It's me, Victor, the man of God who pledged the first investment in the Kingdom today!"

Tammy Faye reaches for her two children, older by a few years than Jack and I, and shuffles them off in the other direction. Pastor Jim's arm shoots out, palm facing my father, elbow locked rigidly.

"Looks like you folks are a little lost; I don't see any wristbands. Your section of the park is back the other way."

My father halts in his tracks, clutching the oversized *Gold Edition Bible* to his chest, mouth agape. "But, sir, you said God had a plan for me! I was hoping we could discuss furth—"

"Do I need to call someone to help escort you back?"

My father's shoulders slump, and I can see wetness in his eyes again.

"Come on, Vic; come help me with the kids. We need to get them back to the campground for lunch, anyway."

CHAPTER FOUR

New Girl, Again

FIRST DAY OF THIRD grade. For me, anyway. New house, new town, new girl, again. I've got the drill down pat, now; never get too settled because as soon as I do, we are off into the night once more. I walk through the halls—filled with apprehension—in my second-hand, too small coat and scuffed boots, clutching my reused Pee-Chee folder and my Miss Piggy and Kermit the Frog lunchbox. The kids—especially Charlene—love to make fun of my lunchbox. We cannot afford another one, though, so I try unsuccessfully to hide the screen-printed image from hateful, laughing eyes and snickering faces.

Through my oversized glasses—which slip down no matter how many times I push them up—I warily inspect my new classmates, and it is glaringly apparent how much I stick out here in the tough inner-city of Detroit.

***

Recess. Our play area consists of a flat, empty blacktop painted in faded colors with a map of the United States and surrounded by a rusty cyclone fence. Jenny—the one friend I have made—and I circle the outskirts of the courtyard during playtime, telling stories and sharing the brown paper bag of free snacks most kids in our class receive.

Rounding the loop, Charlene and the rest of her clique are blocking our path, and a menacing smirk spreads across her face as we approach.

Charlene is a daunting figure of rage mixed with outbursts and fists; each day, she goads her troop of followers into terrorizing me: pushing me down, calling me names, stealing my shoes.

We come to a halt; Jenny is silent and slightly behind me. I look anywhere but at Charlene.

"Excuse us, please."

"Nah. Not today. Right, guys?"

The other kids nod and scoff, stirred to a frenzy by Charlene's tone. She glares in my direction, until flustered, I blush and face her.

Charlene narrows her eyes shrewdly. "Jenny, don't you want to be friends with *us* instead of *her*? You can be if you want to. You just have to stand with us."

Her tone is syrupy sweet, and I turn to Jenny for reassurance.

Jenny takes a step forward, pretending she doesn't see me, her voice a mixture of caution and optimism. "You mean, *we* could be friends, Charlene?"

I gasp, and whisper: "What are you *doing*, Jenny? Charlene's not nice at *all*. You don't want to be friends with *her*, do you?"

"Sure, she does; don't you, Jenny? Just come over here and stand by me."

Jenny looks from Charlene to me, shrugs, and gives me a half-hearted smile, then joins the horde of tormentors.

"That's right. See?" Charlene laughs caustically. "Now you don't have *any* friends, *new girl*. Nobody likes you, not even *this* loser."

They move as one—a flock of geese headed south for winter—split into a V-formation and encircle me, packed tight, arm-to-arm until there is no opening to escape.

"Yeah, nobody likes you."

"Four eyes."

"Freckleface."

"*New girl*."

A rock whizzes past, barely missing my shoulder. I don't see who throws it, and I shrink back, searching for a way out. "Please, you guys, stop! Please!"

Another rock flies, this one glances off my hip.

"Please, I'll do whatever you want!"

More rocks, now.

And, more.

As the rocks fly, they step forward one-by-one, lean in inches from my face, laugh while I cry, tell me they hate me.

Charlene holds out the biggest rock yet. "Okay, Jenny, your turn!"

"Please, no, Jenny! I thought we were friends!"

Jenny takes the palm-sized rock, straightens her shoulders, and launches it at me. Her aim is immaculate; the angular stone slams into my cheekbone. "Dumb new girl. We were never friends!"

I crumple in a heap on the blacktop, the taunts and jeers my only company as the world disappears.

CHAPTER FIVE

Parallax

SEVENTH GRADE: A SPEAKER at a school assembly leads a discussion on domestic violence. They say it is not okay to deal with anger through violence.

My mind is spinning.

I listen, captivated, to the description of a dysfunctional family—my family—I thought *all* families doled out discipline in this manner.

An ember of hope ignites in my heart.

Maybe Daddy doesn't know *there is another way! Nobody told* me *before, so it only makes sense he hasn't heard either, right? He must not* know *hitting is abuse.*

I will tell him! He will be so relieved! We will laugh together, and he will put his arm around me, and everything will change! I can see it now!

I smile as my plan to save my family takes shape. As I walk home from school, there is a skip in my step instead of my usual foot-dragging.

Daddy will be so proud of me for bringing home this life-altering revelation.

***

The sound of the shattered pieces of my fragile innocence skittering over the edge of a precipice—the beginning of an earthshaking landslide—shakes me from my naïve worldview.

Or maybe it is the sound of my bones grinding in their sockets as I land in a snarled heap in the bathtub, slammed backward by a fist square to the jaw.

Seems Daddy has heard the news after all.

CHAPTER SIX

Vegetation Fragmentation

THE UNPREDICTABLE NOMADIC life of moving, moving, moving concludes abruptly the summer I turn 14. My mother finally puts her foot down: tells my father she will not drag us kids to another state, another town, another school. That if he wants to move again, he will be flying solo.

The damage is done, though. I don't know anyone, haven't formed any long-term connections, or developed any social skills.

High school is no different than any of the eleven other schools I have attended—taunts about my glasses, my too-short pants, the books I carry everywhere—are abundant.

At home, anything deemed a secular activity—non-Christian reading materials, TV or movies with any sort of fantasy element, popular music—is forbidden.

The occasional friendship I manage to cultivate withers quickly: Inviting friends into the house is frowned upon. Church is the lone environment where social interaction is permitted, but even there, I am ostracized.

By sophomore year, the battle of wills between my father and me has skyrocketed. There is an activity bus for students who participate in intramural programs, so I fabricate reasons to stay after school each day.

Sometimes, I watch the teams practice whichever sport is in season; sometimes, I hang out in the student lab; other times, I sit alone in the cafeteria: anything to avoid going home.

***

I am sitting in the commons when football practice ends, and the team trails out from the showers. They are laughing and joking, and so absorbed in their roughhousing they don't notice me reading alone on the stairs until they nearly stumble over me.

I tense, expecting their teasing to turn my direction. One of the team—a clean-cut Junior with neatly combed black hair and brilliant jade-speckled eyes—kiboshes their carousing when he sees me.

"Chill, guys."

He steps in front of me, and as our eyes meet, he smiles. I grow warm with embarrassment and look away. He tilts his head to reestablish eye contact. "Hey there! My name's Justin."

I hold my breath for a moment and scramble for a response. "I know. I mean, everyone knows who you are."

He straightens and smiles wider. "Well, you have me at a disadvantage. I haven't had the pleasure of meeting you." He tips my book toward him so he can read the title. "*Little House in the Big Woods,* huh? Why don't you stop hiding behind that book so that we can meet properly?"

I search his face bracing for the cruel punchline, but none comes.

Could he be serious? One of the most popular boys in the school—a football *player—wants to know who* I *am?*

I shuffle on the stairs and adjust my skirt, trying to cover my knees. "Well…I–I'm Rachel. Rachel Carter."

"Nice to meet you, Rachel." He holds out his hand in greeting. "See? Now we are friends."

My tension begins to drain, and I take his extended hand; it is warm and engulfs mine fully. He squeezes and holds for a long moment before letting go.

"What's a pretty girl like you doing sitting all alone, anyway?"

I blush fiercely and attempt to articulate an answer. "I'm…I'm waiting for the activity bus."

His teammates snort and elbow one another. Never breaking eye contact, he casually puts them in their place. "Enough guys. Leave my new friend alone."

A couple of them shrug, and they migrate down the hall as if they share a hive mind—a murmuring of large, sweaty swallows—their interest in our interaction waning.

For all intents and purposes, we are alone.

Still smiling, Justin leans in, keeping his voice low. "The bus won't be here for another half hour. It's no fun sitting here by yourself, is it?"

I push up my glasses and shake my head.

His face brightens, and he leans in closer still. "I've got an idea! How about we go for a walk and get acquainted. You can tell me all about the book you are reading!"

I hold my book close, arms across my chest. "A walk? To where? I really can't miss the bus; I would get in a lot of trouble."

"Oh, we wouldn't go far. There's that patch of woods out front." He gestures in the direction of the main doors and the parking lot beyond. "I bet it's real pretty this time of day; wouldn't it be fun to explore together?"

I search his face one last time but see only his smile and emerald eyes. I set down my book and stand, still a little shy, but pleased now. "All right, let's go for a walk."

***

We set off across the parking lot, and as we approach the area where the pavement trails off, and the tangle of ground cover and evergreens begins, he holds out his hand.

I look up, surprised at the chivalrous gesture, and allow him to take my elbow; a tiny smile touches my lips, and I relax.

The deeper into the forest we walk, the more at ease I become. I am thrilled to find someone who shares my affinity for the deep, rich quiet of nature. It is my safe place. Jack and I often escape to the woods and act out the fantasy sagas I create to distract from the insanity at home.

Stories of these adventures spill out, haltingly at first, then bubbling out gaily as I find my stride.

Justin's grip on my arm tightens as we navigate a long-dead branch jutting from an old-growth tree. I laugh, so caught up in my tale, I barely see it in time.

I offer a sheepish thanks, but my words are cut off by an intense, burning pain: rough tree bark scraping my suddenly naked back; my borrowed, hyper-color sweatshirt riding up and baring my midsection.

How did this tree get behind *me?*

"Justin? What–?"

Searing pain sweeps red and full across my vision. The tree branch is now slicing my thigh, and the broken hilt of another presses agonizing fire into my ribs. As I struggle to regain my balance, bewilderment solidifies into understanding.

Hands that were guiding now roughly pin me in place. Eager, forceful fingers dig, scrape, penetrate with no thought or care of anything but their prize.

In shock, I struggle—cry out—but to no avail. Hands in places yet untouched, mouth brutally covering my desperate cries to please, please stop.

When he is satiated, he steps away, readjusts himself, and smirks. "You should clean yourself up. We can't go back with you looking like that."

Scraped and bleeding, my denim skirt around my waist, my face raw from his unwanted kisses, my flesh poison fire where his hands touched, I push myself off the tree and—determined not to let him see me cry—straighten my skirt as best as I can, then bolt toward the school.

He catches up with me easily—no generous offer of a hand now—and says in a low, gravelly voice: "If you tell anyone what happened here, I'll kill you. You understand?"

I wrap my arms around my midsection, and say nothing.

"They would never believe you, anyway. I'm on the football team, and you: Who are you, again?" He laughs cruelly. "Half the team saw you jump at the chance to sneak into the woods with me."

My mind empties of coherent thought, and my body goes cold and numb. I nod slowly, silently.

He is right. Who am I anyway?

CHAPTER SEVEN

Blackberry Snowstorm

I STOP RIDING THE ACTIVITY bus after school and fall into a pattern: homework, chores, and retreat to my room. One night though, I am too sick to follow the routine. My skin drenched in sickly-sweet sweat, my throat burning with strep, I watch the snow falling outside the window from my bed until I hear my father come in from work and turn on the living room TV.

Maybe, if I'm extra quiet, he'll forget about me and the chores tonight.

I try to stay out-of-sight and out-of-mind, but the fire in my throat will not be ignored.

I'm so thirsty!

I reach for my drink and realize my cat has knocked over my glass leaving nothing but a damp spot on the carpet.

I attempt a hoarse cry to my mother, hoping she will hear me from the bedroom she shares with my father, right next to mine.

"Mom, I need a drink," I croak.

No luck. Between the cranked-up volume on the television and my weakened state, no one hears. Feebly, I throw off the covers and plod toward the kitchen in a sweat-soaked t-shirt and panties. I inch my way to the sink and fill a glass with water.

My father bellows over the TV: "Put some clothes on, Daughter! And, get your ass in gear and finish those damn dishes!"

I turn off the faucet with a shaky hand and take three long gulps. "I can't, Daddy, I am so sick!"

"I don't give a damn *how* sick you are; you do those dishes, or there will be Hell to pay." He pushes himself out of his easy-chair and makes his way to the opening between the dining room and kitchen, blocking my way out.

Shaking in sickness and disbelief, I lean against the counter, gripping the edge of the sink with one hand, and swallow hard. "I really can't tonight, Daddy. I'll do them tomorrow, okay?" I set my glass in the sink and shuffle in the direction of my room.

As I step into the dining room, the full force of my father's fist connects with my temple. Before I grasp what is happening, I am airborne: flying up, up, over the dining room table, and slammed backward into the sliding glass door. It holds for a moment, then ripples and shatters under my weight. I fall to the concrete patio in a rush of cold air, tinkling shards of glass, and my mother's screams.

"Victor John, what have you *done*!?"

I stare in confusion at the night sky—directly above me now—watch as snowflakes the size of fifty-cent pieces course lazy trails down, down and land in my open eyes. I feel my arms, my legs, my torso for the blood I am sure is pooling everywhere, but miraculously, I am intact.

My mother hurries to my side. "Oh my God, Rachel, are you all right? Vic, how could you do this!?" Her voice is as shrill as an old rotary dial phone from a black-and-white film.

My father creates an imposing outline in the now splintered door frame. He remains silent and impassive as I brush myself off. With my mother's help, I stand on Bambi-like legs and start back toward the yawing opening to the house.

We hobble through the snow, braced like two children tied together for a three-legged race, her carrying the bulk of my weight. As we broach the doorway, my father lunges at me again. My mother falls to the ground amidst the fray, and—catching a second wind of adrenaline and self-preservation—I tear past him.

Steps from the safety of my bedroom, he grabs me by the scruff of my neck. His meaty fingers dig into my soft flesh, and jagged ribbons of pain shoot down my back. He spins me around like a windup toy and punches me in the face, launching me up and over his recliner and into the wall, knocking my glasses to the ground.

My head rings like a cartoon character knocked unsuspectingly with an anvil, and I bolt: past my formidable father, past my crying mother, past the wreckage of the warmth and normalcy of our suburban living room. I bolt out the cavernous sliding glass door frame, into the night, into the snow.

***

I blindly make my way through the woods on the side of the house, climbing through brambles and thorns, tripping over branches and roots, and finally collapsing under a fallen tree. The snow melts as it lands on my bare thighs, and I shudder in fear, my thoughts free-floating madness.

In the distance, I hear my mother calling, her voice hoarse and broken from crying. My father roars, huffing and puffing like a bull whose hide is full of punctures from an overzealous matador; my existence, the red cape coloring his vision with wrath. I struggle to swallow my sobs; certain he will hear me, find me, hit me again.

Time suspends: both mere moments and epochs pass before I realize the yelling has stopped. A brief reprieve of silence—both around and inside me—and then, sirens. Sirens and lights, heading down our street, stopping in front of our house.

My dazed and overwrought mind manages one unleashed thought: *I am saved!*

Heavy footsteps through the undergrowth. Unfamiliar voices calling my name. Flashlight beams crisscross through the velvet night, alighting on snow-covered branches, blackberry bushes, my face.

Foreign hands reach out, encircle my quivering arms, pull me upright. I stand tenuously, then am dragged half-walking, half-leaning against the coarse polyester uniform of a police officer, my bare legs and feet scraped and scratched against the overgrown vegetation. Hiccupping to control my tears, and nearly delirious with fever—fever and cold—I allow myself to be led away from my crude hiding place.

***

I'm seated, the warmth of the blasting heater a stark relief to the snowy hovel left behind. The leather seat sticks to the back of my legs, and my gooseflesh multiplies at the contrast. Thoughts arise distant and disconnected in my bleary mind.

I'm rescued.

Hope, at last.

The officer climbs into the driver's seat of the cruiser and shuts the door on the whirling snowstorm. "Young lady, do you know how much trouble you could be in right now?"

"Wh-what?" I shake involuntarily, and he passes me a plaid blanket from the back seat. I wrap it awkwardly around my knees, my body still clumsy from the cold. "I d-don't understand."

His tone is thick with an air of warning and superiority. "If your father weren't such a generous man, you would be on your way to Juvenile Detention as we speak."

"B-but…he hit *m-me*!" I blurt.

"That is beside the point. Your father has the right to discipline you as he sees fit. Let this be a lesson to you; next time, we won't be so lenient, your father's magnanimity aside. Time to learn a little respect and follow the rules your parents put forth."

I stare at him, my jaw hanging down in disbelief. Through the haze of shock and fever, I realize: *There is no salvation here.*

I nod, indicating my acquiescence without saying a word.

The officer responds with a curt nod of his own, steps out of the vehicle into the winter wonderland outside, and makes his way around the patrol car to let me out.

I view it all unfold like a bad off-Broadway play: floating somewhere up above, watching as I walk—shivering and defeated—back inside.

CHAPTER EIGHT

Exit Stage Left

COMMENCE THE FRENZIED where-is-Rachel-staying-this-week shuffle: couches and basements and shared bedrooms of church members I hardly know whip by so fast, I barely remember which bus to take after school.

None of them work for long. I cry too much, miss home, won't talk at the dinner table. So, eventually, the tide spits me back onto the graying wooden planks of my parent's front porch.

'Just be quiet. Just be good. Keep your head down. Don't bait your father.'

Back home, the days, weeks, months go by in a blur. Home, school, church: nothing changing, nothing changing.

Inside, though, I am besieged by arguing voices:

Just try harder; just be better.

Maybe run away?

And, then, another voice enters the din.

I could end it all if I only had the courage.

At first, I ignore the thought, horrified at the implication. But the voice grows in the darkness, more defined and robust than the others. The night arrives when I settle into the idea like an infant settles into the crook of her mother's arm; the impact of its blaring alarm worn smooth like the patina of a century-old stair rail.

With darkness comes relief.

I search through the house, considering options.

A knife? A razor?

Too scary.

The car running in the garage?

Someone will hear the engine.

And then, rustling through the contents of the medicine cabinet, I happen upon a bottle of Extra-Strength Tylenol.

Yes. Perfect.

This should do the trick—hopefully quickly and quietly—before anyone can intervene.

As I clasp the family-sized bottle in my sweaty, shaking hands, a sense of calm washes over me for the first time in months.

Here is the answer I am seeking.

Here is my escape.

I wash down handful after handful of pills with the room temperature, watered down TANG on my bedside table.

The voices go silent, akin to a configuration of doctors in an antiquated operating theater at the most pivotal point of a procedure. I stretch across my bed and stare—unseeing—at its frilly lavender canopy, wondering what will happen next.

How long will this take?

Will it hurt?

I wonder who will find me? How will they react?

As the questions tumble through my mind, the reality of what I have done sets in.

I can't do this! I will go to Hell!

Suddenly the agony of life seems far more tolerable than eternal damnation. I lean forward and grip the bedpost, my mind a kaleidoscope of jumbled thoughts, searching for something—anything—some way to undo my actions.

And then, an epiphany.

Mom! Mom will know what to do!

I propel out of bed and down the hall, collapsing into the doorframe of my parent's room, out of breath. "Mom! I need you; I need help! I'm going to die, and I don't know what to do!"

My mother looks up from her crocheting, her face as blank as a freshly washed whiteboard after science class. "What are you talking about, Rachel Kay?"

"I'm dying, Mom. I took all the pills! Please, help!"

She stands, taking time to arrange her hook and yarn into a neat pile, crosses the room, and leans down to search my eyes. "What pills?"

"The—the ones in the ba-a-athroom," I say, beginning to cry.

She glances over my shoulder and down the hall toward the living room, then replies in a strained stage whisper, her voice tight with tension. "Show me. Show me right now."

I lurch back to my room, retrieve the now empty bottle, and show her the remnants of my decision. "I made a mistake; I'm so sorry! I don't want to die!!"

She looks down at the contents of my outstretched hands and turns the bottle, so the label is upright. "Oh, Rachel! You had me so scared! These are just Tylenol. You'll be fine."

I stare at her, fearful and shaky, adrenaline crashing through my system like waves in a Category 5 storm. "Are—are you *sure*? Shouldn't I go to the hospital?"

"No, just go lay down, and if your tummy feels upset, try to throw up." She looks over my shoulder again, then directs me toward my room. "But be quiet about it. We don't want to make a big deal out of this and upset your father."

CRESCENDO

CHAPTER NINE

Enter the Giant

AND THEN, AMID THE SPRAWLING, craterous, IED-laden desert of Junior year, SHE appears.

Naomi. Electric, captivating, charismatic: Naomi.

When she first shows up at the church Youth Group, it is impossible to look away. She exudes confidence and poise, both qualities I cannot conceive of possessing. She is exquisite—waist-length, dark blonde hair with one face-framing tendril kept loose; doe-like eyes; full, wine-colored lips; and a slightly crooked Meryl Streep-like nose—but none of that matters. It is the way she carries herself; the way the whole room stops and takes notice when she enters. All eyes are on her, but she is utterly indifferent to the attention.

When she chooses to sit next to me and strike up a conversation, I am quietly awed, but I know once the other kids fill her in on the social pecking order, our friendship will be short-lived, at best.

When I realize we attend the same school, my heart sinks even further. Not only will Naomi learn of my social awkwardness at church, but my pariah status at school is sure to be a deathblow to any burgeoning camaraderie.

I give a half-hearted, watery smile when she says she will look for me during lunch. I do my level best to avoid the inevitable, but after days of skulking in the halls, it happens: We run into each other.

She is with her friends, the clique everyone longs to join; may as well be movie stars. I cringe as our eyes meet, knowing what is coming next: the glazed over eyes, the merciless insults—or worse—the cold dismissal.

She steps toward me, her face beaming. "Rachel! I've been looking for you all over!"

I brace myself, expecting the taunts to come, but see only her cheerful, welcoming smile, and it hits me: *She is serious! She wants to be friends.*

Naomi James wants to be my *friend.*

At this moment, I am hers. That saying: 'If your friends jumped off a bridge, would you follow?'

The answer is a resounding *yes*, and with bells on.

***

Tuesday—Youth Group night at church—Naomi comes in moments before service begins, races over and grabs my hands in a fashion suggestive of the children's game Ring-Around-the-Rosy, oblivious to the other teens and youth leaders milling about.

"Rachel! You'll never guess what I'm doing right now! I'm *tripping*!"

I search her face in confusion, trying to decipher her meaning. "You're…what?"

"Tripping! LSD! I took it earlier, and oh my God! Everything is so beautiful! There are colors everywhere, and it's just: I wish you could see!"

My mouth falls open, and, panicked, I glance around the room to ensure no one is listening. "You mean, like, *drugs*?"

"Yeah, but, Rachel, it's nothing like they say! It's so *perfect*; I can feel everything, *everyone*. I can feel *you*! There's a secret world they've hidden from us—more than you can imagine—it's all real! I wish you could share it with me. It's like magic."

***

Keyboarding class the next day, waiting for the lesson to begin. I can't focus. I can't stop thinking about Naomi and her description from the night before. I want that. I want to experience a world that resonates with my solitary imaginings, a world where I can be understood.

I tap my fingers on the table, jittery and distracted.

If I can find some way to enter the world Naomi talked about, it would bond us permanently. We would share something sacred then, something no one could ever take away.

A voice from behind me breaks my frenetic daydream. “Hey, what lesson are we on today?”

I look up in surprise, having forgotten I was at school. Louis, a classmate with a sweet disposition, long hair, and a revolving wardrobe of various band t-shirts and ripped jeans, is looking at me expectantly.

“Uh…lesson? I’m not sure. I—I wasn’t really paying attention.”

He laughs. “That doesn’t sound much like you. You are usually several steps ahead of the teacher.”

I smile brazenly and shrug. “I guess things change. Hey, Louis? Do you know where to get any acid?”

Stunned, he scrutinizes me, pausing a moment before responding. “Are you for real?”

“Yeah. I am.”

He smiles, and this time it is his turn to shrug. “I guess things do change, huh?”

***

The next day at the beginning of class, Louis hands me a white square of paper no bigger than a pencil eraser, wrapped in aluminum foil, and imprinted with a cartoon ant.

He laughs nervously. "Ant acid. Get it?”

I look down at the tiny ant stamped on the paper, then back at Louis. “What do I do with it?"

His chair makes a sharp squeak as he drags it across the floor, and catches the attention of the girl sitting next to him. He reddens and answers out of the corner of his mouth. "You put it under your tongue."

I open my mouth, lift my tongue, and pop it inside.

"You can't take that in class!" He grabs my arm trying to stop me, and several more students look our way.

Too late.

By the time class is over forty-five minutes later, everything has a surreal, disengaged quality. Louis, in a state of near-panic, asks if he should get someone for me.

"Go get Naomi. I need Naomi."

He leaves me standing in the hallway in front of the lockers, as he races to find Naomi. When they return, I am sitting on the floor, staring at my hand in amazement, heedless of my surroundings.

Naomi's eyes are huge. "What *happened*?"

"Man, she like, totally dropped acid in the middle of class!"

"Oh, wow, we have to get her out of here!" She helps me stand and walks with me to the payphones at the front of the school. "Come on, Rachel. We're gonna go on a little field trip."

***

Naomi runs interference with the attendance office when, a short time later, Willard—an older fellow who lives with her family and caters to Naomi's every whim—arrives to pick us up.

"Take us to Mario's, Willard," Naomi says, in her restrained yet direct way.

He waits patiently for Naomi to secure my seatbelt. "Sure thing."

Mario's is a smoke shop and pool hall in Olympia, Washington, populated by train hoppers, punks, and others in the '90s alternative scene. The shop owner is a kind man who makes it his mission to help street kids without judgment by providing a safe place to hang out, Naomi explains as Willard drives us away from school in his newer-model Cadillac.

She points to a business situated in the middle of a city block in the heart of a bustling downtown core. The floor-to-ceiling glass storefront glints and glows in the midday sun like iridescent jewels—resonant of the fabled Pearly Gates—an opening to a new world, a world where I will find my tribe, fit in, be accepted.

Drawn inexplicably to the blithely self-assured kids congregated on the sidewalk like clusters of exotic birds with skateboards and neon mohawks, I can wait no longer. I throw the car door open and barrel into the street, determined to join them.

Naomi jumps out of the car and jerks me out of the stream of oncoming traffic. "What are you *doing*? You can't just get out in the middle of the road!"

Words won't come: All I manage is a distracted shrug. I am on another plane: swimming through a world of fantasy, marveling at the sounds and colors and lights.

Naomi—amused—takes my hand and guides me inside, sitting me at a table across from a boy with long bangs, a shy smile, and high-topped converse.

“Man, is your friend all right? She doesn’t look very with it.”

Naomi giggles. “She dropped acid for the first time today. Alone. In keyboarding class.”

“Whoa. That’s metal, man.”

Their conversation fades into the background as I examine our surroundings, enthralled by the clacking pool cues, casual discourse, and sweet smell of tobacco. My attention settles on a booth across the room, and I cannot tear my eyes away.

"Who is that?" I interrupt, pointing.

They chuckle at my outburst and turn in their seats toward a woman with a shaved head, draped in scarves, and gesturing wildly. She is engrossed in conversation, except there is no one near her; she is alone.

"Oh, her? That's Penny. She used to be a cheerleader way back in the ‘70s. They say she took way too much acid and got, like, perma-fried. She talks to Jim Morrison. You know, like, from The Doors?”

As they explain, Penny continues her animated discussion with the companion only she can see. I watch—spellbound—until it is time for Naomi to take me home.

***

Back home that night at the ancient single-wide trailer my father bought on the outskirts of town, I fake a headache and go straight to my room. When everyone is asleep, I sneak into the kitchen and find an emergency candle at the bottom of a drawer.

I turn off the lights in my room, light the candle, and play The Doors debut album—borrowed from Naomi after our downtown escapade—on repeat until the sun creeps over the horizon and casts its light through the yellow, moldering blinds.

CHAPTER TEN

The Pact

SLUMBER PARTY: NAOMI AND I are staying with one of her cheerleader friends, Simone. Despite her well-cultivated goody-two-shoes routine, Simone is as entrenched in the drug culture as Naomi and I have become over the last few months.

After Simone's parents go to bed, the three of us drop acid and spend the evening dancing to The Doors in her candlelit bedroom. Our cavorting increases in momentum as the drug peaks in intensity.

At the height of our trip, a movement in the corner of the room catches my attention. I shush them and grab their hands as I watch in fascination.

"Do you see that?" I ask, nodding toward the ceiling, my voice full of wonder.

They follow my gaze, stare intently, then slowly shake their heads.

"I don't quite *see* anything, but I can *feel* something," Naomi says, her face the picture of veneration and worship.

"You can *see* it, Rachel?" Simone asks, her voice throaty with awe. "What *is* it?"

I squeeze their hands tighter and try to make sense of what I am seeing. It is more of a disturbance of angles and shadows than an actual shape; the way it moves and writhes is eerie and uncanny. Suddenly, there is the sound of rushing wind, and the curtains whip violently as if in a tropical storm, although the windows are firmly shut. Everything becomes dizzy and blurry, and I see the three of us from above, from the vantage point of the disturbance. Then, falling, falling, the air whooshing around me, distorting the texture of things, and—a jolt—as whatever was in the corner, lodges itself firmly into me.

Inside, warmth. A feeling of stretching like a black cat waking from a nap in a patch of afternoon sunlight. I can detect the boundaries and edges of a presence entirely other.

"It's Jim. Jim Morrison. He wants to communicate with us!"

Astonishment blossoms across their faces and they lean in closer.

"What does he *say*, Rachel? What does he want us to do?"

"He wants…*us*. He sees us. He's chosen us."

That's right. Tell them. Tell them I've chosen you. You are the sacred ones. You are my little flock. Let us lead them into the dark, to the other side.

"Whoa, Rachel, this is so rad!"

"Holy shit; he chose us!? He chose *you*?"

I look at them gravely and continue. "Yes! He has! But he says it must be a secret. Creating such a bond could never be for the masses. It isn't for public consumption. He says—he says we must pledge our allegiance."

"Oh, we would *never* tell! Would we, Simone?"

Simone shakes her head vehemently, her dark hair whipping across her round, freckled face. "No, we would never!"

I tighten my grip on their hands, tilt my head, and listen for the thread of his message.

Tell them. Tell them they must sign their oath this day. Must swear fealty. Must promise never to utter a word of this to anyone.

"He says—he says we have to sign a pact."

Naomi sweeps her hair to one side and jumps up and down like a whack-a-mole game at a carnival. "Yes, a pact! Like, a secret club!"

"In blood. On fear of death."

They both fall silent then, a deathly pall washing away their enthusiasm.

"I—in *blood*?" Simone pulls her hand back and fidgets with the strap on her two-piece satin pajamas.

"Yes," I continue. "There is nothing to fear, though; nothing at all. We are the chosen ones, selected to be Jim's acolytes. He will care for us, lead us. We need only trust. The blood will bind us; it'll be like becoming blood sisters."

Nodding and smiles, then.

"Blood sisters, yeah! That makes sense. Here, let me get a piece of paper from my diary." Simone races across the room and opens a drawer in the nightstand by her bed. She tears a sheet from her sparkly, flower-covered journal and brings it—along with a pen—to me.

"What should we write, Rach? What do we say?"

I take the pen and start scribbling, the words flowing through me and onto the page like water from an unkinked garden hose.

We wear black on the outside because black is how we feel on the inside.

And:

We swear never to reveal Jim's presence to anyone on threat of death.

I fill the page from top to bottom. "Now, we sign."

Naomi rifles through her overnight bag and pulls a pink razor out of her makeup kit. "Will this work?"

"Perfect." I break the plastic covering and extract the flimsy sliver of steel.

I go first, pressing its sharp edge into my hand, carving 'Naomi' and 'Simone' and, most importantly, 'JIM' into the fleshy part of my palm. The blood bubbles up and trickles onto the page.

I hold my dripping appendage out to Naomi, and she places her hand in mine. A swift slice, then it is Simone's turn. Simone trembles and cringes; I caress her face tenderly. "This will only hurt for a minute."

She steels herself, straightens her back, and gives me her hand.

We intermingle our life essence at the bottom of the contract, chant our promise to follow, be bonded and never tell, or suffer the consequence.

CHAPTER ELEVEN

Hubba Bubba & Rounding a Corner

WE FLOAT THROUGH THE NEXT few days in a spiritual haze. Life has a surreal quality; another more authentic version of existence lies just beneath the surface, and the veil lifts when we connect with Jim. The full depth of reality is within our grasp. During English class—the only class I attend semi-regularly—I drift into a trance listening for Jim's voice, and once latched on, write frantically, transcribing his whispers and directions in prose.

Vivienne sits next to me in English and notices my hectic scribblings. "What are you so engrossed in? You've been writing nonstop. Can I see?"

My reverie broken by the interruption, I look up into dark eyes set in a porcelain, ephemeral face. A cloud of wild, ebony hair reaches past her waist, and she is clothed head-to-toe in black save for the most epic Jim Morrison t-shirt I have ever seen.

Oh my God, she is perfection. *How have I never noticed her before?*

I cannot tear my eyes away. Enthralled, I turn the edge of the paper—filled with sonnets of Jim's murmurings—her direction.

She smiles and leans across the aisle to get a better view. "This is beautiful! Did you write this?"

"I mean, I *did*, but not really. It's a message."

She wrinkles her nose and tilts her head, perplexed, but the smile remains. "A message from who?"

I motion toward her shirt and shrug, a half-smile on my face.

She looks down, her voluminous waves briefly obscuring the silvery moon of her face. When she looks back up, her mouth hangs open.

"You don't mean *Jim*, do you? Like, you hear from him *directly*? Oh my God, I could just die! The Doors are my favorite music to trip to, like, *ever*!"

I grin and shrug again.

Rap! Rap! Rap!

We jump in response to the noise and see our teacher, yardstick in hand, eyebrow raised in annoyance. "Ladies. *Please*, excuse the interruption, but this is *not* the time for socializing. If you feel you must continue, you can spend the rest of class sitting in the hall."

Chastised, we face forward. After a few moments, though, I feel a tug on my sleeve. "Meet me after class in the smoking pit. I have to know more!"

***

We are instantly inseparable. Viv is the missing piece of our pact; she fits like a black glove on a white hand. Within weeks of meeting, she convinces her father to let me move in, playing on his sympathies with stories of the perpetual conflict between my father and me. A conversation with my mother quickly ensues, and just like that: we are sharing a room in her father's house.

Viv introduces me to a group of older guys who have their own place—apartment C-204—on the Westside of town. I am captivated by their freedom, their esoteric ideas, and philosophical discussions—and most importantly—their access to an endless supply of drugs.

Several times a week, Viv and I sneak out of school and go to the apartment to drop acid and wile away the hours listening to music under the black light.

***

Between classes one day, Viv is waiting by my locker instead of our normal meeting place out by the smoking pit: her hair a heavy curtain down her back; her milky-white face drawn and tight; and her dark, heavily-lined eyes filled with distress.

Eyes homed in on her, I cut through the crowd. "What is it? What's wrong?" I lift her chin and sweep her hair out of her flashing eyes.

She holds my gaze for a long moment. "Simone's talking," she says, her voice thick with emotion.

Rage courses through me: a rising tide of lividity tinged with crests and swells of betrayal and fear. "Tell me. Tell me *exactly* what happened."

"It's all over the school, Rachel. She told *everyone*. About the pact. About the messages. About *Jim*."

"That's against the rules, and she fucking *knows* it," I say in a flat monotone. "This can't be allowed to continue. She knows full well the consequences."

Viv smiles a shy, yet somehow calculating, smile. "I know someone. You guys should meet. He will know just what to do."

I fumble with my combination as she speaks, my fury and resolve compounding as I repeatedly get it wrong.

"Who?" I ask, distracted and unconvinced.

"Aleister," she replies, her smile anchoring in place as recognition dawns in my eyes.

***

Aleister. We had shared one small interaction. Rounding a corner coming into the school, we crashed head-on, the impact sent me reeling backward onto the cold cement floor. Rattled, I shook my drugstore-bottle-black curls out of my face and looked up. Our eyes locked through a cascade of falling textbooks, papers, and pens, and the air hummed with electricity that seemed to emanate from his mesmerizing, lurid half-smile. He was a force of nature with shoulder-length flaxen hair—evocative of Lestat prancing through the French Quarter in the

1700s—shrewd, penetrating eyes, and an upside-down pentagram emblazoned on his black-as-night shirt.

Yeah, I know who Aleister is.

The three of us meet during fourth period in front of the school. We sit together under the shade of the BigToy, our combat boots digging furrows in the dusty pebbles, the leather of our jackets squeaking as we shift our weight against the splintery exposed beams of the playground equipment.

Aleister turns his deep, impenetrable gaze in my direction, and says levelly: "Tell me about this pact."

In fits and starts, I attempt to express the gravity of the situation. Edgy and unsure, I circle the details—hesitantly at first—as if he were a shark, and I the prey. His intent eyes bore into me—never wavering, never wavering—as I relay the tale bit-by-bit. I gain momentum as the specifics come pouring out, and the words take on a life of their own: yearning to be heard, examined, consumed by this enigmatic, compelling being.

When I finish, I sit still—flushed and breathless—waiting. Viv, overcome with eagerness as I spilled our secret, is clutching Aleister's arm. Her chipped nail-polished fingertips dig into the creased sleeve of his jacket. Her dark mantle of hair spills over her shoulder and puddles in her lap as she leans in, velvety brown eyes sparkling: waiting. Both of us—waiting—tensed with bated breath, waiting for his response.

Aleister looks at us coolly. "Well, there's only one option here, isn't there, ladies?

"Simone has to die."

We listen, mesmerized, as he lays out the details of the plan, enraptured by the lure of Aleister's steadfast confidence and absolute adherence to the dark side.

"We will lure her out to the moon alone one night," he begins, referencing a plot of wooded land where everyone congregates after dark to party. No one's parents know anything about either the gatherings or their location.

"Okay, but once we get her there, what are we going to do? She isn't going to stick around if she sees Viv or me. And we can't fucking shoot her or something. Like, where would we even get a gun? I mean, even if we *did* find one, I'm not gonna *shoot* her."

Aleister ponders briefly, then that lecherous smile spreads across his face again.

"We can get ahold of some liquid nicotine and inject her with it, somehow. Pure nicotine will stop her heart, and since she smokes, no one will think twice about it," he muses with confidence.

"But she hates needles," Viv ventures, her face flushing. "She'd totally bolt if she saw you with one."

"What if we inject it into something she *will* take?" I lean forward, the idea gathering steam in my mind. "Like one of those pieces of gum she always chews with the liquid center. Hubba Bubba, right?"

Aleister's eyes narrow into a cunning twinkle, and my heart ricochets from my throat to my stomach and back again. I am caught in the rip-current of the profound, hypnotic darkness which radiates from him. His placid face transforms into a knowing grin, and I am frozen: In worship? In fear? Either way, I am sold. On the plan. On him. Body and soul.

He nods subtly, still grinning. "I will use myself as bait; she would jump at the chance to get me alone. Once out there, I will woo her to me, and we will smoke, and we will dance. And, before she goes back home, I will offer her a piece of gum—as a gentlemanly gesture—so her parents don't smell the Mary Jane on her breath.

"And that, as they say, will be that. Quick. Untraceable. Permanent."

CHAPTER TWELVE

Power Play

OVER THE NEXT FEW WEEKS, we exchange meaningful glances in the halls while we wait for the perfect opportunity to get Simone alone. We meet secretly as often as we can: skipping class and sneaking off to the woods past the school grounds to share a cigarette or smoke a bowl and continue to solidify the details of our strategy.

One such day, we drop acid and explore even farther into the woods coming out on the hillside of an old cemetery. Aleister and Viv lie down across the top of a grave and disrobe. After a moment's hesitation, I lie beside them, and Aleister's hand finds its way up my skirt.

After we finish, we stretch out together and watch the clouds amongst the piles of rumpled black clothing strewn across the dew-laden grass. A deep fog hugs the ground and weaves like a gray ribbon in and out of the gravestones. A dense, irreverent silence envelops us.

Aleister, still watching the sky, speaks firmly and directly. "We are going to have to do this soon. She can't continue to flaunt her saucy little cheerleader ass all over the school like she didn't commit a mortal sin."

I examine his profile outlined by the shadows of a nearby tree, his midnight eyes gleaming despite the overcast day. He is the picture of all things morbid and powerful; a sense of ancient wisdom exudes from him, and he holds me entirely in his sway.

Viv, delicate and soft, her head against his chest as he runs his fingers through her dark hair, shivers and does not tender a response. I nod solemnly in agreement for the both of us.

***

A few nights later, high on power and drunk on excitement, I share our intent with one of the fringe members of our little circle, a kind soul who would never harm anyone.

The next morning the cat is out of the bag; everyone at school is buzzing about our plan. As I make my way to Viv's locker, all eyes are on me.

Viv is close to collapse: eyes rimmed with red, breathing heavily, and gripping her locker door so tightly her knuckles are devoid of color.

"What are we going to *do*, Rachel! The whole school knows!" she says, her voice raspy from crying.

I frown and search for an answer—internally scrambling for the solution like a steerage passenger on the Titanic—anything to placate her and ease her mounting anxiety. Before I can offer so much as a platitude, though, Aleister appears next to us like a spirit materializing in an old B-rated flick. Viv whimpers and implores us wordlessly.

"We're not going to 'do' anything," Aleister purrs in a voice all cream and silk. "This could not have played out better if we planned it. Now, not only is Simone terrified with the lesson of disobedience well-taught, there is no risk involved for us. It's perfection."

I lock eyes with Aleister, and a slow smile settles across my face. "He's right, Viv. The cheerleader—and the rest of the school for that matter—now know who's boss."

My smile solidifies into a smirk, and I take Viv's hand and lead her away, sharing a saucy look with Aleister over my shoulder. "Come on, Viv. We're going to be late for class."

Down the hall is a tightknit gaggle of viciously whispering girls with Simone at its center. I parade straight through their midst with Viv trailing close behind; their escalating babble halts abruptly as if some unseen hand removed the batteries from a throng of Chatty Cathy dolls. Simone averts her gaze and cowers like a trapped animal. Viv clasps my hand tighter and quickens her pace to keep up with me.

Still smirking, and without missing a step, I turn and serenely say, "Hey, Simone; want a piece of gum?"

I glide the rest of the way to class towing Viv behind me as the sound of Aleister's laughter echoes down the hall.

CHAPTER THIRTEEN

Catalyst

ALEISTER'S GIRLFRIEND, TEMPEST, isn't very fond of Viv and me for obvious reasons. A plain, quiet girl not given to confrontation; it is several weeks before she addresses her suspicions about what is going on between the three of us.

In the smoking pit after class, she asks me directly if Aleister and I are having sex. Moved in a way I can't quite define, I find myself telling her the truth.

"You've gotta understand: That's not what it's about. He's, like, a *teacher* to Viv and me; a mentor, a prophet. It's on a whole other level, much bigger than some casual sex thing. I mean, sex is *part* of it, but Aleister says it's only to heighten our awareness, strengthen our power. He loves *you*, and we aren't interested in taking him away like that."

Her face crumples and darkens as I speak; she jerks as if I slapped her and staggers backward. "You slept with him. You *both* did?"

I hoped by explaining, the wrinkles forming between us would smooth out, but there is no illumination of understanding in her eyes.

"I mean, yeah, we did *once*, but I didn't really want to, and it won't happen again."

Her face completely closes off, and she gathers herself, and walks staunchly away. She recedes into the distance under a sun setting in an overcast sky, the day's last rays creating a bizarre, greenish filter over the landscape.

CHAPTER FOURTEEN

The Point of Palaver

THE SCHOOL YEAR ENDS, as it is wont to do, and the summer of 1992—the summer I turn 17—consists of endless stretches barricaded in meagerly furnished rooms with windows covered by blankets to keep out the accusing sun. I spend more and more time at apartment C-204—first with Viv, and then on my own—until I am basically living there.

The acid flows freely: Just open wide, and someone places a strip of little squares on your tongue. The lot of us only venture out at night—and then, only rarely—to race through the empty streets and explore the nearby woods in a hallucinogenic fog.

***

After days-on-end of dropping vast amounts of LSD, one-by-one, the boys succumb to sleep. Still riding so high I can't speak, I spend the night alone, wandering from room to room, cradling a rusty butcher knife I have taken to carrying, occasionally pausing to flip over the tinny copy of *Pretty Hate Machine* by NIN on the battered cassette player.

Knock. Knock. Knock.

One of the permanent fixtures at the apartment, Devin, is roused by the knocking. He rolls off the mattress on the living room floor, stumbles in my direction, then straightens, giving me—and my tightly gripped knife—a wide berth.

He opens the door to Merrick, our acid dealer, coming to make a delivery: nothing new or out of the ordinary. This time, though, instead of his usual solitary visit, there is someone with him. I peer around the corner—eyes dilated, butcher knife held close—to see who has accompanied the usually private and secretive Merrick.

It is Aleister.

Devin lets out a loud whoop, and he and Aleister exchange an enthusiastic bear hug. The rest of the guys wake and file to the door, expressing similar sentiment at his arrival. I stay hidden in the shadows.

Apparently, Aleister and my boys are acquainted.

I haven't seen Aleister since I spoke to Tempest; I have, in fact, done everything in my power to avoid him at all costs.

Aleister's voice cuts through the raucous laughter and greetings: "Where is she? Where's Rachel?"

Engulfed in uncertainty, I step around the corner and into view, my now clammy hand clenching the knife close to my chest. "Hi, Aleister," I say in a weak voice.

With a ferocious thump, I am pinned to the wall—immobilized—Aleister's sadistic smirk so close I can feel his hot breath. "Hi, indeed, Rachel. We need to palaver."

I nod almost infinitesimally as he continues in a voice so low only I can hear him.

"I hear you talked to Tempest," he says, with a tight chuckle. "You told her what happened. Why would you do that? She broke up with me."

"I'm s-sorry, Aleister! I was t-trying to *explain*; to m-make her understand. I n-never meant for that to hap—"

He strokes my cheek and looks me up and down, his eyes settling on my knife. Fear pounds through me like Niagara Falls on the rocks below, and my grip on the handle loosens.

He reaches down and takes the knife from my trembling hand. "Shhh, hush, little girl. I know. I know."

Behind him, I hear gasps and starts from the boys as he moves the knife between us and presses the cold steel against my exposed throat. He continues, unhindered by their cries; his sinister, icy gaze holds me motionless.

"Do you know what's going to happen now? Now, you are going to die. Oh, not by this silly little *knife*," he says, emphasizing each word by pressing the blade harder against the soft flesh of my neck. "Oh, no, nothing as simple and mundane as *that*.

"Your death is going to be slow and terrifying and without escape. I curse you, Rachel. And not just any curse: a death curse. You'll never know where it will come from or in what form it will be. No matter what you do, no matter who you turn to, you won't be able to escape. And, anyone you tell; anyone you turn to for help? They will be cursed, too."

He begins speaking another language then, in low guttural tones, and the world shimmers and churns around us. Dark shapes whiz through my peripheral vision, and my terror converges into a scathing point as sharp as the blade pressed into the hollow of my throat.

The boys' protestations heighten, and a red, raging sensation of alarm permeates the narrow hall. It seems to come from another world, though; Aleister and I are cloaked in a bubble they cannot penetrate.

Aleister laughs softly, caresses my face again, and I cower against the wall, shaken to my core. He drops the knife onto the stained carpet and steps back.

"Always a pleasure to see you, Rachel," he says with a casual, devious smile.

I sink to the floor in a heap, and Devin and Merrick rush to my side as Aleister steps over me and saunters into the living room.

CHAPTER FIFTEEN

Inception

A CAMPING TRIP TO THE BEACH is in the works hence the extra-large delivery of acid, but I am still crumpled in the hallway between Devin and Merrick. Devin appears two parts concerned and one part anxious to escape and join everyone else on the long-awaited trip. He gives me a distracted pat on the arm, and asks if I still want to go.

I look at each of them in turn, unable to formulate an answer, gripped with rolling waves of terror.

Merrick answers in my stead. "Dude, I don't really think she's up for a road trip just now."

Devin sighs and nods. "I suppose she can stay here. She probably shouldn't be alone, though," he finishes absently.

"Go on, man. I'll stay and take care of her," Merrick assures him.

Released from any obligation, Devin kisses me briefly on the forehead, rises, and heads down the hall to pack.

***

Merrick: long, luscious, cinnamon hair; leather jacket; fawn-colored eyes. He is a year older than me, a legal adult of 18. I've only seen him in passing—when he comes to make deliveries—he never stays long.

He holds my hand and speaks tender words of comfort: first on the carpet, then as I follow him into the living room to the ratty old couch.

We settle together on the sofa, and he wraps his arm around my shoulder. I am beginning to calm down when I realize Aleister is still here, across the room, grinning malevolently in my direction. I start shaking again and lean farther into Merrick's embrace.

"What's *wrong*, Rachel?" Aleister asks in feigned innocence.

"Knock it off, Aleister," Merrick replies evenly. "You made your point, don't you think? She's totally on a bad trip now; let it go."

I nestle closer to Merrick, and he tightens his arm protectively.

"All right, all right, Merrick." Aleister raises his hands in surrender, smirk still firmly in place. "No need to get testy; look, how about a peace offering, Rachel? I have just the thing."

My nerves are frayed live wires whipping and shooting sparks. I ignore Aleister and lock my eyes—and my hopes—on the compassion I see in Merrick's sympathetic gaze. I lean in closer still and let Merrick take the lead in responding to Aleister's flippant offering of peace.

Merrick smiles down at me and gently strokes my hair, answering Aleister without making eye contact.

"What exactly do you mean by 'peace offering,' man?"

Aleister laughs under his breath and reaches over to the end table next to the decrepit recliner where he is sitting, his boot-clad ankles crossed. He picks up a grimy hand mirror, balances it across his knees, and puts his hand in his jacket pocket.

"Have you guys ever tried crystal?" He pulls out a clear plastic baggie filled with white powder and holds it up. "It's like meeting God."

Merrick and I turn to inspect his offertory olive branch. Merrick looks down at me, and I shake my head: No, I have never tried it.

He pulls me closer, kisses my forehead, and whispers in my ear, "I've never done it either, but I've heard it can end a bad trip. If you wanna try, I'll do it with you, and be right here the whole time."

***

The room is spinning. Spinning and laughing. Is that possible? For a room to laugh? Seems unlikely, yet there it is. I am prone on the floor, and the room is spinning so fast, I can't hold down the edges; strapped to a gothic merry-go-round with demons at the helm of ravenous horses, laughing and ravenous horses. The faded, water-stained popcorn ceiling is a pixelated whirling tornado akin to the designs we scribbled, bored and innocent, on our Trapper Keepers eons ago in second-period math class. The laughing reaches a crescendo and breaks apart at the corners. Geometric shapes rain down: shards of realization that Aleister is not only the laugher but the demon as well.

Merrick grabs my hand and pulls me off the dirty carpet and into his embrace once more. I stumble like a newborn fawn into the heady smell of him, the smell of cracked leather and baby shampoo.

"Come on, Rachel," he says, scowling at Aleister, who is still perched on the broken recliner. "Let's get out of here."

***

The cool, damp air smacks me in the face, and my breath catches at the contrast to the dank, muggy interior we've left behind. An uncontrollable shiver courses through me, and I lean a bit more on Merrick, whose arm tightens around my thin shoulder as we make our hasty retreat.

The night is alight with stars, and the tangerine glow of the streetlights throws a glare on the dewy pavement of the parking lots and city streets laid out before us like an abandoned maze.

As we walk down the hill back toward town, I tighten my hold on his jacket. I'm sure something is following us. The air seems too heavy, and the shadows too opaque: thick with too much substance. My neck is hot and sticky. With sweat? With otherworldly breath? I do not know.

I cry out, shaken and unsteady on my feet. I stagger into Merrick; my boot laces—only loosely tied in my haste to escape—are a wet, tangled mess after trailing through the shallow puddles collected on the sidewalk from the recent rain.

"Where are we going?" I ask, looking up at him.

A light wind blows tendrils of long, chestnut hair off his shoulders, and I catch the sweet, sharp scent of baby shampoo again. For a split second, a sense of displaced melancholy overshadows my mounting terror and confusion.

"To my mom's," he replies, with an almost musical lilt. "She lives about half-way down the hill."

His voice is equally lackadaisical and urgent—a seemingly impossible dichotomy—yet somehow perfectly nuanced to fit the soulful tenderness of his visage: a walking contradiction in black leather and an Iron Maiden t-shirt.

I regain my balance enough to walk unimpeded, and stare at him quizzically, my upturned face scrunched in a paragon of uncertainty and dark humor. "You can't be serious. Your *mom's* house? I can't be meeting anyone's parents right now; I'm totally *not* okay!"

He laughs softly, and a few steps ahead of me on the sidewalk now, turns and walks backward so he can face me straight on.

"Dude, it's fine. I, like, *promise*," he insists in his off-handed, impertinent way. "She drinks like a fish and will be, like, totally dead to the world by now. As long as we don't turn on the TV downstairs, we are all good."

A clandestine rustle comes from the bushes. I flinch, my senses heightened and overstretched. Without exchanging a word, our eyes lock. Merrick turns and faces forward, and our pace redoubles as we—practically sprinting now—navigate the empty sidewalks, alternating steps through darkness and the artificial light from the lampposts. Our combined focus pinpointed on getting inside, out of the dark, away from the impending sense of doom which stalks and circles ever closer. As we run, the last of my hesitancy surrounding our destination dissipates.

Where else is there to go? I'm not *going back to apartment C-204, I'm high as* fuck, *and I think something is following us. Going to his mom's house isn't the* worst *idea in the world.*

CHAPTER SIXTEEN

Blood-Red Ribbon in the Dust

A NOT QUITE DECREPIT TWO-STORY house coalesces out of the fog. Covered in faded, cedar shingles—loose in some places, missing in others—the abode slumps sadly on a corner lot, tired and daunting at the same time.

We steal up the concrete steps to the side door. Through the single pane window—covered partially by a dingy, ruffled valance—is an unexceptional kitchen, illuminated by the muted glow of a lamp left burning in the next room.

Merrick jimmies the deadbolt easily, then turns, index finger pressed against his lips.

I follow closely, eyes down, and head buried in Merrick's upper back. My boots squeak on the cracked and peeling linoleum as I am jolted to a sudden stop. My chest tightens, and I start to sweat, sure we are caught.

Merrick is holding open the refrigerator door, the hills and valleys of his face brilliant in its interior light. "Do you want a glass of milk before we go upstairs?"

"Milk?"

"Yeah. I've heard it can help soak up the drugs. Lessen their effect, ya know?"

I stare, incredulous, for one beat…two. "Milk…yeah, okay. Let's have some milk."

***

After slurping down the slightly sour milk, we join hands and tiptoe across the scuffed floor, through the shadowy living room, and into an adjoining bath.

"What are we doing in your mom's *bathroom*?" I whisper. "Like, I'm not gonna sleep in her *tub*."

Merrick's mouth forms a slight smile, and he shakes his head. Letting go of my hand, he steps around the chipped clawfoot tub and reaches across the pedestal sink toward the broad shiplap wall, and opens a door I altogether missed.

"Nope. Not gonna sleep in the tub. Honestly, it's not super likely we'll be sleeping much at all."

I steal a look over his shoulder and see a dusty set of stairs leading up to an unfinished attic. My breath catches, and I forget the night's terror for a moment. "*Ohhh*! It's like a secret room!"

He grins wider. "Not really a secret. I mean, *I've* always known it was here."

He retakes my hand, and I feel a hint of a smile—the first all night. He raises an eyebrow quizzically with the unspoken question, either, 'Do you want to go up?' or 'Do you trust me?'

The answer to both is yes, so up we go.

***

At the top of the creaky, old stairs is a large, open room separated by a clothesline hung with several roadside-stand graphic blankets, a kind of homespun room divider.

To the left, behind the improvised wall, I catch a glimpse of an unkempt bed, an amp and guitar, a chair on wheels; to the right, a set of splintered, old-fashioned bunk beds and a small desk positioned under the only window. Light from the waning moon casts a watery trail on the gaping floorboards.

Merrick gestures vaguely to the right. "This is my room."

We walk toward the bunk beds, our thick soles making hollow thuds on the attic floor despite our best efforts at stealth.

Merrick swings his hair to one side, removes his jacket and boots, then turns to help me with mine. We stand facing one another in our socks in the moonlit room. He turns and sweeps back the covers, and with a nod of his head, indicates I should climb in.

I don't hesitate, and he follows suit. Peace and calm flow through me as his arms wrap around me. Warmth. Safety. I nestle in closer to his embrace. His sweet, yet musky, scent swaddles me, and the panic begins to abate.

***

A fractured, distorted loop of the night's events play on repeat in my mind. I drift a little, though. When I close my eyes, whole lifetimes play out on the backs of my eyelids. Other worlds, entire story arcs of people I've never met, places I've never been. Each time I get settled, my eyes pop open. I tense and look around in fright, attempting to anchor myself to this reality, to the here and now.

Merrick finds his way effortlessly into the comfort of slumber—a sacred reprieve—and snores lightly, his head on my shoulder, strands of his hair stuck to his cheek with sweat, arms still wrapped loosely around me.

Sometime later, I awake, having dropped into a restless, in-between space for a time. I lie still—silent and disconcerted—as my eyes adjust to the dark, trying not to move, not to wake him.

Holy fuck, I hafta pee!

As I slowly acclimate to my surroundings, I become aware of the sound of a muffled discussion from the other side of the room. The voices carry easily across the open expanse of the attic, despite the crude blanket barrier.

I stiffen and hold my breath.

Merrick didn't say anything about his brother being home tonight! Fuck! I am in no headspace to make polite introductions on my way down to the bathroom.

"Merrick, wake up!" I whisper urgently. "I gotta pee, and I don't wanna walk through the other side of the attic by myself when someone else is here!"

Merrick lifts his head, still half asleep. "Whu da ya mean? My brother's not home. He's at our dad's this week."

THUD.

The entire attic reverberates with the sudden clatter from the other side of the room; it shakes the bunk beds and sets loose a veil of dust from the rafters above.

Merrick's eyes fly open, and his embrace around me tightens. "The fuck was *that*!"

The need to empty my bladder vanishes from my mind. "If *you* don't fucking know, how the Hell am *I* supposed to??"

The voices across the room grow louder, yet somehow more indistinct.

Conversing, laughing, *growling*.

No fucking good, any of it.

Merrick hisses through his teeth: "What the fuck; what the fuck; what the *fuck*."

I cling to him like an octopus: all legs, arms, and the sickly smell of fear. He responds in kind.

Suddenly, his brother's office chair hurtles across the floor with such force it nearly topples over, then comes to an abrupt halt at nose level next to the bottom bunk.

On it? A Bible—splayed open—its blood-red ribbon fluttering in the breeze created by the chair's unnatural journey.

We shoot out of bed, pell-mell, reminiscent of the fabled cannonball acts in traveling circuses of yesteryear. Covers flying, office chair knocked over, Bible cast aside—red ribbon now lying still on the attic floor—blanket-laden clothesline churning in our wake. Out of bed, down the stairs, nearly detaching the rail in our haste.

We catapult halfway into the bathroom and collapse, still partially on the staircase: a jumbled web of body parts, high voltage nerves, and toiletries. As we work to disengage ourselves and regain some semblance of balance, I glance back up the stairwell. Daybreak is eking over the horizon, and from this vantage point, I can see inklings of the sunrise shining from the upstairs window.

In brilliant relief to the day's first light cast upon the landing wall is a dark silhouette. The unmistakable outline of a male figure in the easily identifiable Peter Pan pose: hands on hips, legs spread in a wide 'V.'

"Merrick," I breathe, weak with horror. "*Look*!"

Merrick pauses in his attempt to get us back on our feet and twists his head in the direction I am staring. He registers the shadowy figure on the wall, and open-mouthed, we turn in unison to look up the stairs.

Nothing to see but a cartoonish swirl of dust, as if someone—something—moved out of our line of sight in a big fucking hurry. Then, laughter. Maniacal laughter, and not from us.

***

Like a real-life record skip, we are in the living room: one second sprawled at the bottom of the stairs, the next entwined in a sobbing and quivering ball on the tattered and sagging iconic 1970s autumnal-colored velour sofa.

I disentangle myself enough to survey the living room, lit by both the lamp in the corner and the now mostly risen sun. Directly across from us is a door, the top third a cloudy glass transom covered by yet another faded valance; to the right, the bathroom, now firmly shut, an aluminum folding chair wedged under the doorknob.

Merrick's body is quaking and pressing into mine; we barely take up one cushion on the couch. I can feel the overstressed springs pressing through the threadbare upholstery and into the small of my back.

"H—how did we get in the living room?" I stammer, unsure I want a response. "Like, seriously…what just *happened*?"

Merrick flips his hair in his now-familiar, unconscious gesture and leans over to kiss me on the cheek. I can feel wetness there; his tears or mine, I do not know.

"Listen, let's just lay low here 'til my mom goes to work. If we pretend to be sleeping, she may talk some shit, but she won't kick us out or anything."

I look away and chew on my lower lip as I consider.

There must be another option.

What, though?

Go back upstairs? Strike one.

Back to the apartment, to Aleister? Strike two.

Call my mom at half-past o-dark-thirty high as fuck *with stories of—of fucking what exactly? Strike-fucking-three.*

"Well, all right. If you're sure, I guess—I guess this really couldn't get much worse," I finally concede. I sigh and sink back into the lumpy cushions, overcome and undone.

***

We stretch out and balance precariously on the narrow, slumped sofa for what seems like forever. Eventually, Merrick's mom comes out of her room and shuffles around muttering to herself about "damn kids" and "chairs under my got-damned door."

Throughout her self-righteous monologue, I keep still and small as a mouse, repeating the mantra in my head: *Please don't talk to us. Please don't talk to us.*

Finally, her morning routine complete—if not her vitriolic diatribe—she is gone: out the door and off into the world of mundanity and routine.

I look up at Merrick, and see his eyes are open, too. We breathe a collective sigh of relief.

I manage a feeble smile. "Well, *that* was fun. What do you have planned for the second act?"

Instead of responding, his eyes widen in panic.

A distinct, unmistakable white vapor forms in the air in front of my mouth with every word, every exhale.

My breath.

I can see my breath.

In the living room, in the middle of summer; I can see my breath.

The hair on my arms stands straight up, and an uncontrollable tremor races down the length of my spine.

The clouds of condensation are more pronounced now and come from both me and Merrick. The temperature inexplicably drops 20-degrees, 30-degrees.

"Why is it so fucking *cold*?" Merrick's clammy hand squeezes mine, and we shiver in the suddenly arctic room, grappling for some sort of rhyme or reason to what is happening.

An electric pop breaks the eerie stillness, and then comes the music. Low at first, but quickly rising to an almost ear-splitting level.

The radio.

The radio is on.

Nobody is anywhere near it, and now the radio is fucking on.

"Thieves and Liars" by Ministry is blaring, drowning out any hope of a discussion in a conversational tone.

My mouth is a desert; I hide my face in Merrick's chest, and his body thrums and vibrates as he pulls me closer.

The lamp behind us—the one in front of the bathroom door—begins to flicker, first slowly, then accelerating to a veritable strobe light effect.

Stomping above our head ensues, then travels behind us in the direction of the attic stairs. Down the stairs, into the bathroom. The bathroom door creaks slowly open.

The bathroom door! Oh, fuck.

In her rantings and ravings this morning, Merrick's mom moved the chair away from the fucking bathroom door!

Terror flows through me like a thick, black tar creating a sink-pit in my gut. The room is a frenzy: lamp flashing a luminary Morse Code, boombox blaring Ministry on repeat, our breath crystalline clouds hanging in the air between us, and now the fucking bathroom door.

I am gripped with the overwhelming sense of someone—something—standing behind us between the couch and the door. Standing and staring. Leering. Waiting.

"What the fuck is happening?" I wail piteously, barely audible above the piercing discord of industrial death metal. "Dear Jesus, make it *stop*!"

Heavy footsteps thump past us, through the kitchen, and out the side door, which slams and shakes in its frame. The music echoes for one protracted moment then stops mid-note. The lamp ceases its vacillating madness, and the temperature self-regulates back to its normal range.

I stay crouched and hidden in Merrick's embrace, breath held.

The tension in the air—in our bodies—begins to dissipate.

I lean back to meet Merrick's eyes. "I think I wanna go home now."

CHAPTER SEVENTEEN

Industrial-Sized Dreamwalker

BACK AT MY PARENT'S trailer, well-past midnight, huddled alone in the living room, curled up on the corner of the tired and drooping couch. Picked up and brought home by my distraught, sobbing mother—Merrick, left behind to his own devices—my mother adamantly refusing to bring him back with us.

After spending hours hiding out of sight on the back porch and later the laundry room—waiting until my father won his battle with insomnia for the night—I sit soundlessly in the dark, unwilling to risk the cold comfort provided by the TV, aghast at the thought of facing my father's wrath at seeing me there. His occasional snore travels down the hallway, along with the creaking of the tired bedsprings, as one of my parents changes position in their sleep.

Outside, a single lamppost—the only one on this desolate stretch of county highway—shines sallow, anemic light through the foggy, single-pane aluminum windows and onto the visible OSB subfloor.

The last 24-hours (Or is it 48? I seem to have lost access to my internal clock and am wholly untethered from reality) have taken quite a toll, and all I want is sleep.

I sink farther down and spread out carefully. As I begin to unwind, a shadow darts through the periphery of my vision, and I tense, bolting upright and snapping my head to the side.

There is nothing there.

Okay, okay, I must be a lot more stressed and tired than I thought. My imagination is just playing tricks on me. Whew. Okay. Just go to sleep, Rach.

I breathe deeply, shake my head to clear the cobwebs, and lie back. My muscles soften, and my eyes grow heavy and begin to flutter, despite my overworked nerves.

On the precipice of oblivion, the wan light and dusky shadows in the room shimmer and spin, and a figure appears.

My eyes fly open—all thoughts of sleep erased—and I stare in horror at a wavering, man-shaped disturbance hovering a few feet away.

My breath catches in my throat, and I claw at the thin patchwork afghan strewn across the back of the couch, grasping at a leftover impression from childhood: *The monsters can't get you if you are under the blankets*.

The not-quite-transparent figure moves closer, gliding across a floor peppered with remnants of disintegrating green shag sticking up from galvanized carpet staples. The air in the room takes on a ghastly pall, and the temperature abruptly plummets, my breath once again visible.

Unable to speak, to move, I watch as this being created from literal nothingness slinks across the room and mounts me. It's lack of substance contrary to the immense weight now pressing into my chest, pressing into my throat, cutting off all hope of a cry for help.

Ice-cold daggers shoot through my belly as invisible claws rip my legs apart, and a giant torpedo of frostbite and pain thrusts inside my most sensitive parts. I gurgle and wheeze, attempting to breathe in the frigid, distorted air as my insides are ramrodded over and over and over by some massive, subzero, unfathomable member.

My thoughts chase themselves in circles through my tortured mind, unable to grasp one concept for more than a split-second. Through the murky fog of terror, one sentiment finally converges, and as my hope and will begin to fade, I choke out, "Dear Jesus, please help!"

The air in the room shifts as if someone turned on an industrial-sized vacuum; the glimmering disturbance above me intensifies, then disperses with an unceremonious *whoosh*, and just like that, whatever forced itself into the room—into me—is gone.

CHAPTER EIGHTEEN

Just Listen

GLARING, MID-DAY SUNLIGHT violently casts a molten orange glow through the thin skin of my eyelids. The scent of discount fabric softener fills my nostrils, and the coarse threads of big-box-store-sheets rub against my arm—all pins and needles—the circulation cut off at some point during the night.

Where am I?

My brain is congealed, unflavored oatmeal; I roll away from the unforgiving sun and off my heavy, deadened limb.

I open one eye a sliver, and my senses are overcome by a deluge of purple: purple sheets, purple lamp shade, purple wall hangings. Only one person I know decorates with such garish, monochromatic finesse: my mother.

I sit up, confused and disconcerted, shaking my still numb arm. The Trinity Broadcasting Network is blasting on the television in the next room. The sound of running water and pots and pans banging together in the kitchen carries easily through the paper-thin trailer walls.

I swing my black-nylon-clad legs over the edge of the bed, adjust my clingy, black rib-knit top as best as possible with my one working arm, and shake my head; a tumble of tousled, jet-black briefly obstructs my vision. I look around my parent's room and see my worn military-surplus boots in a pile on the floor with my black leather jacket. I slide onto the splintered floor and make my way over to my things, still half asleep.

Boots on, jacket in hand—and both arms working at full capacity—I tread unobtrusively down the dark, paneled hall. I don't know how or when I got into my parent's bed, nor do I know what time—or day, for that matter—it is currently.

I step cautiously into the living room and endeavor to make eye contact with my father. He is sprawled across the shabby love seat positioned under the window by the front door; to the left, I see my mother, but only from waist to shoulders due to the configuration of the kitchen cabinets.

Noting my entrance into the room, my father's focus on the television intensifies, he stiffens, and pointedly avoids my gaze.

"Daddy?" I begin softly. "Daddy, the *scariest* thing happened. It was, like, *really* bad, and—and I don't know what to do!"

My father redoubles his resolve, his entire countenance steely and unapproachable as he points the remote control at the TV, upping the volume to drown out my pitiful, desperate cries.

"Daddy," I throw out, louder now, tears streaming down my cheeks. "I need you! I'm so scared!"

His disgust and dismissal are palpable as he holds the button until the volume is all the way up. The running water in the kitchen stops, and my mother turns away from the sink and steps around the corner carefully. A caricature of hesitancy and indecisiveness, she stands in the threshold between rooms, wringing her wet, soapy hands and looking back-and-forth between the two of us.

I cast a desperate look—internally begging her to intervene—and find in her guarded eyes no hope of rescue, no hope of intercession.

"Rachel," she says in an unsteady voice, almost inaudible over the screeching television. "Maybe now is not the time to speak to your father…"

It dawns on me, then: I am alone.

My pleading turns and morphs and grows into anger, into absolve, into rage. Seething now, my eyes sweep the room and land on my black, plastic boombox—my prized possession—tucked in the corner between the couch and the pony wall separating the living room from the kitchen. I stride toward it with purpose, casting aside my jacket, and covering the distance in two-and-a-half steps. My mother reaches out to me half-heartedly—my father still willfully not seeing me—the deafening clamor of Pat Robertson on *The 700 Club* drowning out all other sound.

In one fell swoop, I lean over, grab the hefty radio-tape-deck combination, pivot on my uneven boot heel, and with all my strength, ram the stereo into my father's cherished television.

Once, twice, then: BOOM.

The TV explodes in a cascade of sparks and shards of glass, smoke tinging the air with the acrid smell of blown cathode ray tubes, my radio hanging neatly in the middle of the now shattered screen: a virtual bullseye.

"Now, you'll hear me, Daddy, whether you want to or not."

In a blur of soap suds, flying remote pieces, and black nail polish, the three of us converge into a violent, twirling, cataclysmic vortex.

My father's meaty fists fly, land squarely on my shoulder, my jaw, the soft expanse of my belly. The blow to my midsection takes my breath away, and I double over as my mother weakly attempts to insert herself—too late—to fend him off. I stagger, hands on knees, and spot my jacket on the floor. I cautiously reach out and grab it, my father's attention momentarily homed in on my mother.

Jacket in hand and still hunched over in agony, I make a break for the door, vault off the front porch in one giant leap, and race out to the empty road in front of the property.

I pause—out of breath, head down—and attempt to straighten into a standing position despite the excruciating pain in my stomach. Before I can collect myself, my arms are ripped backward and held roughly in place at the elbows, rendering me virtually immobile.

I whip my head from side-to-side, struggling in vain, not fully registering what is happening until my father's slipper-clad feet appear.

I look up and see his vicious expression and realize it's my mother holding me in an attempt to quell the chaos; in hopes of bringing me back into the trailer.

"Come inside, Rachel," my mother manages, dazed and out of breath herself. "That's enough for one night. Let's just—"

Her words flutter around my head like adolescent birds—like bats who have lost their radar—they fall to the ground unregistered, unheard as my father and I lock eyes at last. His eyes narrow into a malicious glint, and his lips curl into a cruel smile. I gasp in astonishment as I realize with paralyzing incredulity what he means to do next.

"Daddy, *no—"* I cry helplessly, but I am cut off by a sucker punch straight to my already brutally insulted abdomen.

My legs curl up to my chest as my tenderized muscles contract in protest, and my mother staggers backward and nearly topples over, my full weight throwing her off balance.

After an endless uncertain moment, she regains her equilibrium as I recover mine. My body unfurls, and my boots connect with the two-lane, blacktop road. I look through streaming tears and a veil of unruly hair into my father's sneering face.

"Serves you right, Daughter. That'll teach you to disrespect your father."

I inhale jaggedly, brace myself, and swing my right foot back through the open-legged stance my mother assumed to anchor us in place, and—with every ounce of energy I can muster—kick my father directly between his legs with my steel-toed boots.

Everything dissolves, then: my mother's grip on me, my father's ability to remain upright, my tenuous grasp on reality. I am floating above the scene, looking down on the three of us—on me—unconnected, unconcerned, unable to do anything but watch as the me below runs and runs and runs.

CHAPTER NINETEEN

It's Kismet

BIANCA. A GOTH CHICK of mythic status. All glossy blue-black hair just brushing her dainty chin; plump, pouty lips filled precisely with the obligatory Wet & Wild #508; generous, Rubenesque figure of epic proportions nearly bursting out of her dangerously short black skirts and lace-patterned stockings.

Yes, Bianca.

Having lived a full two decades, as well as having her very own townhouse, she seems incalculably wise and sophisticated.

I sit in the passenger seat of her old, musty smelling vehicle holding on for dear life as she takes corners with a nonchalant indifference, the car briefly balancing on two-wheels, tape deck blaring Sisters of Mercy.

She bats her eyes coyly. "Do you know what my last name is?" she asks, categorically unaffected by my growing discomfort at her driving skills.

"Ummm…no. I don't think I do."

"It's 'Kismet' as in, like, fate. Isn't that rad?" Her kohl-rimmed eyes twinkle as she exhales a cloud of smoke and flicks her cigarette out the open window.

I nod, fingernails digging into the patched vinyl seats—my own smoldering cigarette, forgotten—as I push back against the headrest, willing my body to stay put and not fly through the windshield on the next curve in the road.

"Yeah. 'Kismet.' Kinda like you and me, huh? I'm so glad you called me to come get you. I'll keep you all warm, safe, and toasty at my place; you can be my little pet and stay as long as you like!"

I went back to apartment C-204 after the fight with my father, but found no solace there. I needed to escape and find something different—something other than the frenzied delirium bleeding through the cracks in my foundation over the last few weeks—and Bianca was the first person who came to mind. We had crossed paths briefly at the apartment, and then only because she was sleeping with someone's boyfriend. She stood up for herself, though, when confronted. All talk of women's rights and bodies being vessels for pleasure and spirituality. Talk like that I had never heard, and it made an impression.

We take the last turn and come to an abrupt halt, somehow unscathed. I exhale a sigh of relief, untense my muscles, and slowly unclench my hands, the ash from my cigarette falling on the grimy floorboard. Past the dust-streaked windshield sits an impressive townhouse sprawled across a double lot.

"Is this it?" I ask, a little envy creeping into my voice. "Your place?"

"Sure is, lovely," she replies, her dazzling smile reaching her dancing blue eyes. "Well? Are you coming in, or aren't you?"

I inhale and let my breath out slowly.

Okay, Rachel. This girl has her own place, with no parents to worry about, and Aleister has never been here before. What could go wrong?

***

The main floor living room is modestly decorated: an off-white couch sits against the wall below the stairs; a cracked, tan Barcalounger—its recline function permanently stuck in the extend position—is wedged in the corner next to the front window. Between them is a wall unit bookshelf filled with half-melted candles—primarily black, with the odd red or purple mixed in—and various books and journals, most with fraying edges. The back of the bookcase is plastered with inserts from indie cassette tapes.

Bianca motions that I should sit where I like, so I curl up, catlike, on the recliner. She follows me but stops short at the weathered end table under the window and pulls out a crumpled pack of Basic Light 100s from her ample chest.

"Oo, can I have another one?" I ask, hopefully. "It's been a long few fucking days, and it would sure help calm my nerves."

She tips her head slightly to meet my eyes and clucks her tongue. "We are out of smokes, but I've got better than a cigarette for you, pretty baby. How 'bout a little pick-me-up?"

My face scrunches up in confusion until the crackling of the cigarette cellophane diverts my attention. Tucked behind the empty soft pack is a clear bag filled with white powder.

My mind erupts in a jumble of arguing voices.

Oh, shit.

Is that what I think it is?

It is.

Do I want to do this again?

What if I say no? What happens then*?*

And, if I do *say no, will she think I'm lame, too childish to hang out with her? To stay?*

What if she makes me leave*? Where will I go?*

Honestly, it felt pretty fucking great when I did it last time. If you ignore all the other stuff.

Maybe the bad parts were purely because of Aleister.

Maybe, this time it will be different.

"Yeah, that would be, like, totally awesome, Bianca," I reply, my voice an equal mix of manufactured composure and mounting enthusiasm. "Let's do some lines!"

Bianca's features transform into a smile, and she winks. With one hand, she opens the baggie, and with the other, grabs a circular mirror from the bottom shelf of the end table.

With professional aplomb, Bianca empties the contents of the package onto the mirror; arranges the snowy powder into finger-width lines using the edge of her driver's license, obtained from the vast reaches of her makeshift bosom carryall; and with a rolled-up dollar bill, succinctly inhales one of the rails of crystal.

She flings her head back, turns—arm outstretched—and offers me the improvised snorting implement.

"Your turn, pretty," she says expectantly, her pupils pinpointing as the meth takes effect.

Still second-guessing, I pause to deliberate. My heart rate accelerates and the overwhelming urge to evacuate my bowels grips me. As I take the dollar from Bianca's slightly shaking hand, I realize I've already decided.

I lean across the creaking chair, shove the sweaty dollar bill up one nostril while closing off my other with the tip of my finger, and snort the gargantuan line of crystal meth.

A fiery cavalcade of light, of color, of sound, crashes over me in waves, in virtual tsunamis. I fall back into the chair, the world swimming and spinning around me; inside, my breath is simultaneously an elusive phantom and a runaway train. The air shudders and shakes, vibrating and vague yet clear and concise, and I flounder for a hold on something, anything to keep me tethered to the here and now. I settle finally on Bianca—on her face, her eyes—gleaming and glittering in lush juxtaposition to the whirling dervish riptide I fear will sweep me away entirely.

"I sure could use that cigarette, now," I sputter, sinking into the heightened, alternate reality which encompasses us, and reaching for the cigarette pack to underscore my need.

Bianca shrugs and pats my arm. "Sorry, sweet girl. They are gone, remember? We'll have to make do without any."

I roll the empty pack absently in one hand as I hold her gaze. Something seems off, though; something feels different. I turn my full attention to the pack and look inside.

It is no longer empty; in fact, it is half full.

***

Cigarettes lit and smoldering, settled into the recliner awash with bliss and speed-talking through the events of the last few months, my tale is abruptly interrupted.

Bianca's lips—ripe and juicy like a split open peach on a summer's day—are pressed into mine. So different than the desperate, unskilled kisses from boys. I cannot breathe; I cannot think. A thousand glittery stars fly behind my closed eyes.

"I can make you feel *really* good if you just let me," she says, her voice low and thick with desire. Her warm hand is on my thigh, inching under my black-and-white miniskirt.

Oh my God, oh my God, oh my God*! This is homosexuality: an abomination. Daddy always said this was the* worst *sin. If I do this, I will go to Hell! This is wrong, evil,* unforgivable*!*

I jolt, my body stiffens, and my eyes fly open; I snatch her wrist away before she can reach her intended destination. "I—I am on my period. I can't."

She cries out in alarm and a little pain. "Oh. Well, that's a shame. You don't have to squeeze me so hard, though," she says, rubbing her wrist gingerly.

I force a smile and struggle to maintain my composure. "I'm sorry."

She shrugs again and moves to the floor, signaling me to join her. "It's fine. We can just do something else."

***

We sit face-to-face on the carpet chain-smoking the magically appearing cigarettes, talking furiously, our words falling over themselves like newborn puppies tumbling recklessly down a hill in springtime.

As if from another vantage point, I hear myself saying, "...and, I haven't heard much from Jim lately..."

Oh, fuck!

I just told her about Jim.

That is against the rules!

Fuck, fuck, FUCK!

I stare in silence, my heart thumping against my ribs like a howitzer, waiting for Jim to swoop in and strike me dead, or her to label me crazy and kick me out.

Neither happens.

She leans in close and grabs me by the shoulders. "This is so amazing, Rachel!! You've been chosen by an archetype; by a *deity*!! I know *exactly* how to reach Jim and find out what he wants. Have you ever used a Ouija board?"

My eyes widen, and I rearrange myself on the floor tucking my knees beneath me.

She believes *me? She wants to meet Jim; hear what he has to say?*

This must *be a sign I am on the right path.*

"I don't know, Bianca." I adjust the elastic band of my sagging stocking. "A Ouija board? Like, I know I'm not exactly following the rules of the evangelical church at this point, but I've always been told those are satanic, and call, like, the literal devil."

She scoffs and shakes her head. "Rachel, that's all religious nonsense; you have to know that. Didn't Joan of Arc hear voices? And, a bunch of other old-timey saints, too? You are *chosen*! We literally *have* to do this."

Before I can offer any further half-hearted protests, she is up and across the room, grabbing an old notebook and ballpoint pen from her bookcase. She eagerly rips out a page and sits on the plush cream-colored carpeting, next to me this time.

"Okay," I say, leaning into her, my enthusiasm growing as I discard caution at the thought of reaching Jim on my terms, on my timeline. "How do we do this? And, you're sure it will work if it's homemade?"

"It's easy. We just write out the alphabet in a kind of rainbow-shaped arc across the top of the page—see? Like this?" She gestures with the hand holding the pen. "And then we write 'YES' and 'NO' on either side at the bottom. It's a huge deal, though; it's, like, sacred to request an audience with such an illustrious being, even though you *are* the chosen one. So, it should totally be you who makes the board."

I nod, hanging on her every word. "You're probably right." I take the pen from her outstretched hand. "Where do I start the alphabet again?"

I concentrate, focusing on getting the board just right, the seriousness of what we are undertaking propelling my every move. While I follow Bianca's instructions for placement of the different elements, she tears another page from her notebook and fashions it into a roughshod planchette.

We finish simultaneously, and when Bianca looks down at my masterpiece, a smile bursts across her face.

"Oh, Rachel, it's *perfect*! There's no way Jim will not respond."

"Okay, then," I reply, emboldened and determined to assert some control over the when and how I receive the all-important messages from Jim. "Let's do this."

***

We move to opposite sides of the board, place our fingers lightly on the paper planchette, and wait.

I glance surreptitiously across the board at Bianca, making sure I am doing it right, and see she is entirely engrossed in the ritual; her attention is mine.

"What should we ask first?" I ask, nervous energy crackling through my synapses.

Bianca's forehead creases in concentration as she formulates a response. "I think…I think you should just demand Jim make himself known. He chose *you*, so *you* have a right to an audience with him whenever *you* want. Just assert control and make him show himself."

She's right; I am *the chosen vessel. This radio silence just won't cut it any longer.*

I brace myself, inhale, and focus all my energy on the tools we created. "Jim. JIM! Answer me! Show yourself!"

Nothing for a moment, and then—and then—the scrap of paper begins to move across the board, slowly at first, then whipping furiously from letter to letter, so fast I lose track of the order.

"Oh, my *gosh*, Bianca! Are you moving your hands? Something is happening! Something is actually *happening*!"

She whips her head back-and-forth. "No, it's not me!"

Suddenly, her cornflower blue eyes are pitch-fucking-black. The plains and soft curves of her face morph and sharpen until she is virtually unrecognizable. Her full lips twist into a depraved grin, and she launches—lightning fast—across the board. Before I can process what is transpiring, she is straddling me: hands around my neck, leering face a hair's breadth from my own.

An aberrant, snarling baritone full of sand and gravel rises from the depths of her throat, and her hands tighten with inhuman power. "YOUUU, do not call *me*, GIRRRL!!"

I choke, gasp, and fight with all the strength I can muster, but before I can land any blows, an unseen presence forcefully rips her off me and flings her against the far wall where she collapses into a whimpering, sobbing ball.

***

Upstairs, hiding under her covers. The transition from our divinatory forays to this moment—gone—the space between wiped clean like a chalkboard after class.

I peek my head over the edge of the blankets. "What happened down there? How did you make your voice *do* that? *Why*?? And how the fuck did you move so fast??"

Her eyes are focused on some unseen point in the distance. "I don't know what you're talking about, Rachel. All I know is what you said about Jim is *true*. He's incredible, and he's in *me*, now!"

He's in her *now? What is she talking about??* I *am the chosen one. Thief! Liar!*

I fling the covers back in disgust. "You tricked me! That's not what was supposed to happen at-fucking-all."

Her eyes still unfocused, Bianca turns and smiles at me dreamily. "It's okay, Rachel. There's enough Jim to go around. He loves us so *much*. He wants both of us! He says to tell you: Let go; come be with us. It's so beautiful here. Just let go…" She sighs in ecstasy as her words trail off.

What is she talking about? Nothing like this *has happened before; is she serious? And where exactly would we be going?*

"What do you mean 'come be with us'? You are right here, in bed with me!"

"Oh, but I'm not; don't you see? I'm in another world—Jim's world—and it's *so* beautiful. He wants us both here with him. To reign as queens alongside him in his universe! All you have to do is say yes, and step through the door."

Another world? That can't be true. But she looks so happy, *so at peace! Could it be? A place without pain, where* I'm *in charge, where there is no suffering? Somewhere safely tucked away from my father, from death curses, from Aleister?*

As I mull things over, movement under the doorjamb catches my eye; shadows, growing and receding as if someone were pacing on the landing just outside the room.

How could that be? I thought we were alone.

"Uh…Bianca? I think there's someone in your hallway. Is your roommate home, maybe?"

"Oh, don't worry about *that*," she replies nebulously. "Just let go of all this and come be with Jim and me forever!"

A crash and then muttering, inarticulate voices begin speaking in time with the twisting shadows, shadows which cast hectic displays of light and dark on the bedroom rug.

The theatrics outside the room draw me in, but Bianca's magnetism is too much to ignore: the angelic expression, the relaxed countenance, the inky-black eyes.

Okay, yeah, I think maybe. This is the out I've been searching for, the way to another world. And it's so close, *I can* feel *it! Let go, Rachel; how hard can it be? Just let go!*

I shut my eyes and inhale deeply, and—ignoring the clamor outside the room—search for the door inside myself. As I exhale, a hysterical Bianca screeches in my ear: "Rachel! *No*. Don't do it!! It's a trap, a lie!"

My eyes shoot open, seconds from releasing control. Inches away is Bianca: eyes periwinkle blue again, face a contorted mixture of agony and dread.

"A trap? What are you talking about? What is going on??"

"It's a trap, Rachel! I can't get out! The grass: the grass is purple shards of glass; to even stand still cuts you to the bone! And the screaming: Oh God, the screaming!! Don't listen—"

Her voice cuts out as if someone grabbed her by the windpipe, and her eyes are a momentary swirl of blue-on-black, then midnight prevails.

Like antique French silk, a new voice radiates from her: "Don't listen to this silliness, dear. Come, be a queen with me. Let us rule the astral plane together."

The commotion outside the door intensifies, and I struggle to break free of the hypnotic spell cast by her eyes, her voice. The room is glacial, an icy cloud forms with each exhalation. Despite my best intentions, my eyes grow heavy, and I begin to slip.

As the last thread of my will dissipates, the bedroom door swings open with such force, the knob sticks tight in the drywall.

My eyes fly open and behold Merrick standing in the doorway. A howl from Bianca underscores the interruption, and the Pied Piper spell over my psyche is broken.

I launch out of bed and through the wedged open door like a land-based cruise missile through The Pentagon wall. Propel into Merrick's waiting arms, nearly knocking him over in my eagerness to get out, get away, solidify a retreat anywhere other than the tottering edge of lunacy to which I nearly succumbed.

"Rachel, I've been looking for you everywhere, and calling here for hours! I was about to call the police." He gives the room a perfunctory glance as he helps steady my footing, his disposition turning cold when his eyes land on Bianca.

"Come on," he drawls, his voice lyrical even when irate. "Let's blow this popsicle stand."

He enfolds my hand in his firm, tender grasp, and in a mad dash, we race down the stairs and out the front door, not even pausing to grab my boots. Bianca's enraged shrieks follow us through the parking lot and out to the road.

CHAPTER TWENTY

Jake Brakes & The Sign of the Cross

WE HALF-WALK, HALF-RUN through the sweltering August heat, my feet singed and burning through my stockings on the scorching hot pavement, the Jim Morrison t-shirt I borrowed from Viv sticking to my sweaty midsection.

Merrick throws me a sheepish look as we run. "Don't freak out, but I called your dad before I got here. Like I said, when no one could reach you or find you anywhere, I was sure you were dead or worse: Aleister found you."

Before I can internalize his words, the deafening gunshot bang of Jake brakes, and the rumbling of a diesel engine fills the muggy air: My father is here.

My heart speeds up at the sound, and I scan the area for a place to hide. There is nowhere to go, though, so I shrug in defeat. My father seems way less a threat than the splintered landscape of insanity we left behind at Bianca's.

***

We ride in strained silence—a pensive look on my father's face—Merrick, in the passenger seat of the big rig, me, sitting on his lap. I desperately attempt to maintain a modicum of decency as my father laboriously shifts gears through the two-lane roads of suburbia. It's no use, though; my candy-striped nylons keep sliding down; my checkered miniskirt keeps riding up.

Some immeasurable amount of time later, we turn into the driveway of my parent's trailer. Several cars are parked in the overgrown, gravel area out front.

"Who's here, Daddy?" I ask, my tone edgy and abrupt. "I'm not in the mood for entertaining guests."

"Just go in, Daughter," he replies sternly. "You, too, son," he says, motioning to Merrick with an unexpected touch of kindness.

Overwhelmed and exhausted, I fumble with the door's cumbersome latch. The mechanism finally catches, and before slipping off Merrick's lap and outside, I pause and say meekly, "I love you, Daddy."

"Go on. Get on out," my father replies gruffly, his voice tight with repressed emotion. "I have to get back to work; you two just go on in."

***

We step through the door, Merrick and I, taking a moment for our eyes to adjust from the sunlight outside. As my senses acclimate to the dimly lit living room, I see my mother perched like a frightened owl—all oversized eyes and talons—on the armchair under the kitchen pony wall. On the other side of the room, two men flank the couch with an unmistakable air of authority.

Pastors from my church.

Two pastors from my church are standing in my parent's living room.

"Uhhh, what the fuck? I did *not* sign up for this!" I bolt for the door—shoes or no shoes—I am getting out of here.

Merrick's firm hold on my arm stops me short. "Come on, Rach," he offers in his deceivingly tranquil tone, tossing his long locks over his shoulder. "Like, what do we have to lose? There's bad, evil shit going on, and we *sure* haven't been able to make it stop on our own."

I look from him to my disconsolate mother, to the out-of-place preachers, and sigh in resignation.

Wordlessly, Pastor Andrew—the clergyman on the left—indicates Merrick and I should sit on the couch.

Deep breath. Okay.

I cross the rough floor noiselessly in my stockinged feet, and Merrick follows. We sit as close as humanly possible on the couch. The pastors take seats as well: one pulling up the battered ottoman and positioning it next to me, the other balancing unsteadily on the armrest next to Merrick. Across the room, my mother rocks back-and-forth almost imperceptibly in her roost, and between us sits a coffee table scattered with Christian magazines—and conspicuously on top—the revered, 24k-gold-leaf-edged, *PTL Parallel Gold Edition Bible.*

Without so much as a 'How do you do?' Pastor Andrew—the fair-haired 30-something in loose-fitting Wranglers and a sweater vest—places one slightly trembling hand on my forehead and raises his other in biblical adoration toward the mildewed ceiling tiles.

I cringe at his unprompted touch and burrow backward into the couch and closer to Merrick, trying to make myself small; to disappear. There is nowhere to escape, though. Pastor Randy takes a similar stance, one hand on the crown of Merrick's head, the other picking up the *PTL Bible*—and for all intents and purposes, we are trapped.

"Lord Jesus, save these children!" Pastor Andrew begins fervently, his eyes tightly shut and a sheen of perspiration forming across his intense, focused features. "Cast the demons out; release them from bondage. Break this curse!!"

"Yes, Lord! Yes, Jesus!!" Pastor Randy echoes, beginning to rock back-and-forth, as well, his voice rising each time he repeats the refrain.

My mother observes from the tatty, orange-and-brown armchair—a chiseled marble effigy—sporadically parroting back an unsteady 'Yes, Jesus' or 'Yes, Lord' under her breath.

The energy compounds and spirals up, up, up as they throw out prayer and supplication—demanding the demons be released and cast away—feeding off the mounting zeal, their words changing now into a chaotic string of sounds and syllables with no discernible meaning.

Unable to turn my head under the weight of the preacher's sweaty hand, I cast a furtive sidelong glance at Merrick, and we huddle closer together as the provincial Passion Play takes on a life of its own.

Pastor Andrew—eyes still closed—reaches into his shirt pocket and pulls out a small vial of liquid. He nimbly cracks the seal with one hand; across my brow, the weight of his other multiplies exponentially with each raspy, foreign utterance he directs toward the heavens. His pitch rises, a chaotic waterfall of noise with no rhythm or rhyme. He tips the vial, captures a drop of the clear contents on his index finger, and draws the shape of a cross on my forehead.

"Dear, sweet Jesus," he yells, in English, now. "Cast out the demons who inhabit this girl against your will! I claim the Blood of Jesus over her! Get thee behind me, Satan."

In my head, a whirlwind, a cacophony. I am floating again: up, up, and out of my body; I watch it all unfold below. Merrick's russet hair knotted and damp under the pastor's weighty hand. My head down, half-hidden behind his shoulder, my dark mane occluding my eyes and sticking to the oily cross painted on my forehead. The preachers and my mother, grounded in their respective stances as if death will befall them should they abandon their posts: a deconstructed Last Supper scene.

In the distance, there is a faint, '*No, I will not go!*' then even that is gone, and I am insubstantial, untethered, undone as a murky cloud encompasses me.

A breath, two, and then: With a roller-coaster-drop force, I am in the bathroom, looking in the mirror, searching my own eyes for myself. Gone are the thigh-high tights, the miniskirt, the Jim Morrison shirt; instead, I am enrobed in a loose t-shirt and long, flowy skirt: both snowy white.

I walk barefoot down the constricted hall, back to the living room. Everyone is distracted, enthusiastically congratulating themselves on a successful exorcism. My mother is crying—with happiness this time—and Merrick, still in his leather jacket and boots, stands expectantly at the door.

Turmoil enfolds me, and the world seems distant and surreal. As I survey the room, my mother flings her arms around me. Rivulets of her relieved tears wet my hair and cheeks. "Praise, Jesus! God is *so* good! My girl is delivered, and everything will be fine now!"

Over her shoulder, I see shadows merging and growing in the corner, and a disembodied laugh—nearly inaudible over the hubbub—reaches my ears.

I lock eyes with Merrick.

"Are you ready to go?" he says, hand firmly on the doorknob.

Tired, defeated, and on the verge of collapse, I shake my head.

"I don't know. I don't know *anything*," I say, my voice stifled by my mother's embrace. "I just can't anymore, Merrick. It's not safe anywhere."

He ponders, conflicted, then nods and drops his hand to his side. "All right, what now?"

CHAPTER TWENTY-ONE

Kine La Dat

We try Merrick's dad's house to no avail; the remote ranch in Eastern Washington only makes me feel more trapped. The insanity does not stop—only escalates—and being so isolated, there is no means of escape, no way to outrun what I am sure is coming.

Hawaii, then, my mother insists. You'll go stay with your aunt—no two ways about it. And, no, Merrick will *not* be going. If this *is* a death curse, it will follow *you*, and he'll be safer if he's left behind.

So, Hawaii, it is: a beautiful reprieve. Sweet, lazy days of reconnecting with family—especially Rowan—who at just five months my senior, is more a sister than a distant cousin.

Rowan is the golden child of the family. Her parents fell in love young and hard and created the perfect family unit: the epitome of a healthy, supportive, Christian environment. Homeschooled most of her life and raised on the island, she can't comprehend the landscape from which I come. The vast majority of Rowan's social group consists of kids from the fundamentalist church where she and my uncle lead worship.

Rowan and I spend our days at the beach, subsisting on Dr. Pepper, Twinkies, and Marlboro Reds. Her parents don't know she smokes, of course. Nor that she drinks on weekends with some of her older brother's not-so-churchy friends, and I certainly am not going to tell them. Cigarettes and a few beers seem pretty vanilla, comparatively speaking.

***

Each day we are awoken by tropical birds, tree frogs, and the melody of cicadas wafting in through the levered windows above the queen-sized bed Rowan and I share. The bed takes up most of her room and is parallel to the floor-to-ceiling mirrored closet doors that cover the opposite wall.

While getting ready to go to the beach a few weeks after I arrive, Rowan begins digging, asking questions, looking for a solid explanation of why I came.

Conflicted, I hold my breath. It is too much to keep inside any longer, though, and the dam bursts. I pour my heart out, relaying the details in vivid strokes, relieved and terrified to have it all in the open.

"The shadows, though, Row. They are still everywhere," I finish in a shaky voice.

She watches me thoughtfully in the mirror, her head bobbing backward from the tension of the braid I am adding to the nape of her neck.

"So, like, he for real put a *death* curse on you?" she asks, eyes shining with a twisted curiosity. "And you think it followed you all the way here?"

I give a perfunctory nod as she continues.

"And shadows? What do you mean, Rach? Like, are you talking about...*demons*?"

"I don't know anything about *demons*, but I *do* know Aleister said it didn't matter where I went, or what I did, I'd never get away from his death curse, and I think he's right!! The shadows: They are still here. In the corners, when everyone else is asleep. I don't know what to do, or how much longer I can go on like this." I drop my hands in my lap, and her braid unravels.

Rowan breaks eye contact with me in the mirror, turns her body to face me fully, and clasps my knees with both hands. "*I* know what to do, Rach. We'll just tell my dad and the youth leaders at church tonight; they'll know exactly how to fix this!"

I sigh. "But, Row, we already tried that, remember? It didn't work. That's why I'm here..."

"Nope. No way." She shakes her head firmly. "There just wasn't enough faith in that room. No, we will do this right. We'll get the whole Youth Group to lay hands on you. The devil—and Aleister—won't have a chance when we're done with them!"

***

On Saturdays, the Youth Group gathers informally at a church member's home for songs, fellowship, and prayer. The night is warm and clear so, when we arrive, most of the kids are hanging around outside, waiting for the evening's activities to commence.

Rowan leaps out of the car and into the yard, all cheer and enthusiasm. "This is my cousin Rachel who I was telling you guys about!"

I trail behind her, head down, and face flushed. With her introduction, the idle chatter switches to proclamations of 'Aloha!' and 'Welcome!' and unsolicited hugs inundate me from every side.

Once Rowan has everyone's attention, she continues in a low, melodramatic tone. "Listen, guys, Rach is dealing with the mother of all spiritual attacks: a death curse!! We have to intercede; we have to come together and do God's work!"

Gasps and exclamations replace the group's cheery, lighthearted welcomes, and the youth leaders—overhearing Rowan—make a beeline for the interlocked circle of teens forming on the front lawn.

Equal parts trepidation and awkwardness, I stand silently, avoiding eye contact as the group converges and one-by-one reaches forward and lays an outstretched hand on me wherever they can find purchase.

The sun is setting, and in the quickly growing twilight, the shadows grow dense, sentient, almost material—they are everywhere—in the palm trees, on the roof, pacing the perimeter of the circle formed around me.

I tremble and begin to cry.

"It's okay, Rach; it's okay!" Rowan calls out, her voice a spiraling fervor. "We are going to release you from the bonds of Satan for *real* this time. Just have faith!!"

Echoed sentiments ripple around the assembly; shaking, I exhale and close my eyes, tears course down my cheeks, and they all start praying in earnest.

"Father God, save this child! We all come to you in agreeance; we rebuke this death curse and claim Rachel redeemed by the Blood of Jesus!!"

A warm wind blows in from the nearby ocean, carrying on it the scent of sand and salt. My long tresses lift briefly and tickle my neck as the prayers continue growing in both volume and intensity.

Although I cannot see the lurking shadows with my eyes squeezed shut, I feel an ominous, suffocating sense of something watching, something stalking.

"Yes, Jesus! Save this child. Break the bonds of Satan; overpower this curse!"

A zealous, nameless youth leader addresses me: "Rachel! You must claim it in Jesus' name! Let go of your fear and stand in faith. Claim freedom from this curse!!"

I shudder, covered in sweat and the hands of strangers, paralyzed with fear and indecision. At long last, I take a shaky breath and cry out, "I rebuke this curse in the name of Jesus; Aleister, you no longer have power over me!"

The wind picks up and howls through the palm fronds, and we all sway in unison at its force.

Then, silence.

Stillness.

And with that, the prayer circle ends.

CHAPTER TWENTY-TWO

Scratch on the Break

LATER THAT NIGHT, ROWAN and I sit together on the edge of her bed—once more facing the mirror—and in hushed tones, rehash the night's spiritual extravaganza.

"But what about now? How do you feel *now*? Is it different than when *your* pastors prayed for you and…Merrick? Was that his name?"

I mumble an affirmative—chagrined she can't remember his name after all I've told her—and contemplate her questions. A quick scan of my senses shows no raised blood pressure, no looming terror, no nerves on high alert. It seems the threat is gone; really *gone*.

"Yeah, no. There's, like, nothing anywhere. I feel alone; I feel *safe* for the first time in months!"

She breathes a big sigh of relief and satisfaction, her eyes glowing with self-righteous pride as she meets mine in the mirror.

"See? I told you all you needed to do was believe, and—what are you looking at?" She whips her head over her left shoulder to follow my horrified gaze.

Gliding unencumbered about six feet in the air is a colossal, translucent, dragon-like creature made up of heatwaves and shimmering lines.

Rowan's face pales, and her eyes glaze over in disbelief. We watch together—dumbstruck—as this unspeakable not-being slithers through the air between us and the mirrored closet doors, traversing gravity and probability, then disappears bit-by-bit into the wall opposite the door until there is nothing left in the room but us, and stunned silence.

***

Sleep does not come for me, and not for lack of trying. Neither Rowan nor I say much, laying still but separate on her rumpled bed and doing our level best to avoid looking in the mirror. I ruminate over the events of the past few months, especially the prior evening. Somewhere around daybreak, it occurs to me: despite whatever was in her room last night, everything *still* feels different—normal—this morning.

My breath catches at this realization, and I turn toward Rowan, who has at last drifted off to sleep, and shake her gently awake. She mutters and mumbles inarticulate protestations.

"Row, I think this is for real! I think it's really and truly over!"

Waking up fully now, Rowan sits up, her mahogany hair tumbling into her eyes. Pushing it aside distractedly, she shakes her head once and rolls her eyes.

"Of *course*, it worked, Rach. I told you: All you have to do is have a little faith."

"I know you did, but I just can't believe it!"

She gives me a dour look. "It more than worked, cousin. We both saw what floated through the room last night. That was the demonic grip losing its hold. God is so good!!"

I stare at her, stunned she is confirming the previous night's finale. Over the last few hours, I nearly convinced myself the wavering reptilian creature was a figment of my imagination, or that I dreamed the whole thing.

"You saw it, too? Like, for real?"

"I absolutely did, and you did, too. Don't try to downplay God's handiwork. Last night was a miracle, and that was absolute proof."

I fall back onto the pillow in relief. "I still can't believe it's all over. Like, I thought I would *die* before I saw the end of—oh!!" I sit up straight again, interrupting my own thought. "I have to check on Merrick; I need to call him and make sure *he's* okay!"

"Welllll," she says after a long pause. "Long-distance back to the mainland is expensive, but if you're quick, you could probably get away with one call."

I nod excitedly and stand, preparing to quietly navigate the distance between Rowan's room and the phone hanging at the end of the short hall. I poke my head out of the bedroom door and register the sounds of subdued conversation coming from the living room. It sounds like my aunt and uncle have guests.

"Someone is in the living room with your parents, Row. Who's here so early?" I whisper, concerned.

She climbs out of bed and joins me at the door, listening. "Ohhh, that's right. The church leaders usually meet for prayer and planning before church. It must be scheduled at our house this week."

I look at her, nervous and unsure, but still determined to call Merrick.

"I think you'll be okay. You can't see the phone from the living room. Just be quick!"

***

I edge down the hall, staying close to the wall, and pick up the receiver carefully, twirling its corkscrew cord between my fingers as I dial Merrick's number.

Ring…ring…ring…

No answer.

I push the off-hook button gently, so as not to bring attention to myself, and chew on my lower lip.

What now? I can't just leave it; I need to make sure Merrick is all right, too.

Oh! I can call the apartment! He's more likely there than at his mom's, anyway.

Relieved, I smile and release the telephone switch, then dial the familiar digits to apartment C-204.

Ring…rin—

An unsteady voice, definitely not Merrick's: "H-hello?"

I sneak a quick look around the corner to make sure no one has noticed me. "Hi, who's this?" I reply, keeping my tone low.

The voice is shakier, now, and hitching with repressed sobs. "Th-this is Devin. Wh-who is this?"

"It's me: Rachel. Are you okay, Devin? What's going on? Is Merrick there?"

"No, no. I don't know where Merrick is. Maybe he's here? It's—I can't say for sure. And, no, Rach, no. Nothing is okay! It's a good thing you got out of here when you did."

"What do you mean? What is going on?" A sense of dread washes over me, I forget my surroundings, and my voice climbs like a hiker cresting Mount Everest. "What happened??"

"It's Aleister," he says, in a clipped tone. "He was murdered last night. There's cops and blood everywhere!" He dissolves into incoherent sobs, and the line goes dead.

This time, *I* am the one floating midair, watching as my body slides down the paneled hallway wall—phone receiver still in hand—the air filling with piercing, agonizing screams.

It takes a long time to realize they are coming from me.

CHAPTER TWENTY-THREE

Doubting Thomases

MY FLIGHT HOME IS TOMORROW; although I am terrified at the thought of going back, everyone insists there is no reason to stay. My cousins arrange one last hurrah to break me out of my despondent musings about the unmapped landscape of my future, and my cyclical machinations of who

(me; it's me; it's me; everyone knows it's me)

is to blame for Aleister's death.

***

The back of my older cousin Jeremy's jeep. Pearl Jam *Ten* blaring through the 6x9 speakers. We whip through the gravel on some back road under palm trees and a sherbet-and-chocolate post-dusk sky.

Laughter, and the soapy taste of cheap, off-brand beer. My hair a windswept mess as we spin brodies in the moonlight. The hours of drinking accomplished the intended outcome: My state of ever-increasing panic and fear is a distant, hazy memory.

I need to pee.

The jeep skids to a stop, and I climb over the oh-shit handles in the back, and squat precariously, holding my warm beer in one hand; it spurts and foams over the bottle's edges, shaken to a frenzy by the centrifugal force of the vehicle.

The balancing act is too much for my inebriated system, and I fall backward onto the gravel, laughing.

***

House party, stumbling in the front door, beer bottle empty now. Rowan is sitting on the couch with a beer of her own, legs crossed like a proper lady-in-waiting in the high court of France, looking away in obvious distaste; away from me—all sloppy drunk—as I stagger between two sets of strong shoulders: still laughing, still unable to stand upright on my own.

"I thin kiy nee to sidown," I slur, between hiccups and giggles.

The strong shoulders are attached to stronger hands, and I am guided smoothly by my self-appointed centurions—also laughing—through a living room full of lingering smoke and half-drunk people: through the living room, down a hall, into a dark room.

"Wayyt—wurr we goin'? I wanna si wif my couzin…"

Laughter, louder now, and harsher. Hands that were leading, protecting, now pushing. I am on the bed, and something—someone—is on top of me. Someone else holds me down, my face grinds into the pillow in time with the rhythm of whoever is grinding me from behind.

I call out: *please, no, stop*, but then my mouth is full—along with other parts of me—and I can barely breathe, much less protest. Powerful, sinewy hands shred and pull and tear: my throat, my breasts, my everything.

Skirt up around my waist; panties violently ripped off. And laughter: laughter changing into moans. The pain is unspeakable: hot and ragged as they split through me mentally, physically, entirely.

It is dark, but I see all three of them; their outlines highlighted in the black room by the stuttering motion sensor light outside the window.

They laugh and moan and high five one another; I am a mewling and squirming conquest beneath them.

***

The rough seams of the too-big corduroy pants—borrowed from my older, and much larger, male cousin—rub painfully against the delicate skin of my most feminine parts. I wiggle and twist in the window seat of the Boeing 737, attempting unsuccessfully to find a comfortable position on my way back home.

A kind stewardess catches my eye and asks if she can get me anything. The tears start, then, and I am not sure they will ever stop. Great, wet, choking sobs consume me, and the eyes of the other passengers zero in on me like a flock of frightened starlings.

The flustered, but still well-meaning, air hostess reaches over the thankfully empty seat beside me and walks me to the cramped latrine at the end of the aisle.

"Here, sweetie, here. Take a breath. Let's get you cleaned up," she says, opening the bifold door and gesturing helplessly. "Take a moment, and wash your face, then you'll feel as good as new."

I step in, still sobbing, and the door screeches angrily on its track behind me. As it clicks closed, I am illuminated by harsh fluorescent light.

Snippets of this morning's conversation play on repeat in my mind: '*You must have given him some sort of sign, Rachel'* and *'There's no way a nice boy like Sam would do something like that'* and *'Well, you know how Rachel likes to tell tales. Remember the time...'*

I turn carefully in the small space, grabbing hold of the counter for balance. I lift the molded plastic toilet lid, unbutton the torturous pants, and sit down gingerly, my quivering legs finding momentary stability on the cold, metal seat. I see fingerprint bruises and welts, toothmarks on my bare, white thighs. I take a shaky breath and focus my muscles, willing my body to relieve itself: The pain is quick, sharp, and without borders. I cry out in fresh agony as a splash of something landing in the water soaks my undercarriage. I look down and see blood: blood and a matte gray condom floating in the previously empty bowl.

DIMINUENDO

CHAPTER TWENTY-FOUR

Furvus Shepherdess

BACK IN OLYMPIA, I am floating, displaced.

Many of my circle of friends—Aleister's friends—want nothing to do with me.

My father demolished my bedroom wall—to create a bigger master suite, he says—effectively absolving me of both my place at home and as part of the family.

A categorical blackballing.

And, so, I roam.

Hop from place-to-place, couch-to-couch, night-to-night.

My singular focus, above even finding a safe spot to sleep, is convincing older kids—and the occasional parent—to buy me alcohol.

Alcohol blurs the harsh lines of reality. Creates blank spots, if there is enough of it.

I roam, and float, and drink and drink and drink some more.

Somehow, my mother always tracks me down, though, and—despite my father's commands—often brings food and other necessities.

***

I wake one Saturday morning around my 18th birthday—about 6 months after returning from Hawaii—and call my mother from the landline at a flophouse in town.

"Hey, Mom…ummm…so, like, when is the last time you bought me tampons?"

A pause; a long one. "I don't know, Rachel. I think it's been about six weeks."

More silence, this time on my end. "Um, okay…maybe you could meet me at our usual spot later this week?"

"I could do that. Tuesday? After work? Around six o'clock?"

"Yeah, okay. See you then."

I place the receiver on its cradle and sit down hard on one of the metal folding chairs in the dining room.

Well, fuck. I guess I better make an appointment at the Crisis Clinic before Tuesday.

***

First thing Monday morning, I am at the clinic door. The two blue lines on the test are vibrant, impossible to miss.

The next day, I trudge slowly to my mother's car—parked in an empty lot near where I am staying—and climb in the backseat, head down.

I sigh deeply and look up to see both my parents in the front of the vehicle. "Oh, shit, Daddy. You didn't say Daddy was going to be here, too, Mom."

My father turns in his seat to face me, no anger or malice in his expression for the first time in as long as I can remember. "It's fine, Daughter. Your mother said you might have something to tell us."

I redden and hang my head again.

"Go on, Rachel. Give us the verdict."

I tuck my hair behind my ear, and say softly, "I'm pregnant."

My father smiles tightly and takes my hand. "Well, there's only one option, then isn't there? I guess it's about time you came home."

So, come home, I do.

I cut off contact with most everyone—stop drinking entirely—and focus on the soon-to-be baby. My pregnancy is difficult. Most of it is spent bedridden or in the hospital, and Audrey's first appearance into the world is a hard and violent one.

Despite my health issues, I throw myself into church activities, rededicate my life to The Lord, and pledge to be good, to live in God's will, to raise my child the right way.

***

The day of Audrey's Dedication to Christ is brilliant and sunny. I save up and buy her a fancy white satin gown, and a smart skirt and blazer for myself.

I am nervous about standing in front of the entire congregation, but my mother insists it will be straightforward—the pastor will do most of the talking—straightforward and beautiful.

Another baby is being dedicated, too. I wasn't the only girl in the Youth Group who fell pregnant in 1993. The other baby's mother and the father were married in church about five months into the pregnancy.

I stand to the side of the pulpit—just Audrey and I—as the pastor performs the other family's dedication ceremony, the three of them a picture-perfect postcard. The audience cheers uproariously as they return to their seats, and then it is my turn.

I step forward, holding Audrey out to the pastor, mimicking what I saw earlier.

He turns brusquely away and grabs the microphone off its stand. "Folks, today, we have a young woman who has broken one of God's holy laws. She has created a child out of wedlock."

Gasps and murmurs ripple through the crowd.

I stand, frozen, Audrey held in my outstretched arms.

"She has come today to ask your forgiveness. To admit out loud, her treacherous sin. To show our young folk, the way of darkness only brings death."

"*Yes*, Jesus!"

"Praise *God*!"

"Redemption is nigh!"

"Church, will you hear her apology? Will you consider her request to become one of God's chosen again?"

"Hallelujah!"

"Yes, Pastor, yes!"

The pastor spins to face us, whips the microphone past Audrey—barely missing her satin-capped head—and holds it to my mouth.

"Say your piece, child! Confess your sins; repent!"

I gape at the sea of faces and pull Audrey close to my chest. She squirms and cries, and I try to comfort her—but I don't know how—so she cries all the louder. My eyes flit from the crowd to the pastor like uncaged birds, but everyone just stares and waits.

"I—I'm sorry. I didn't mean to? Please forgive me."

The microphone is gone, and I am left to wrestle my plum-colored, howling infant alone as the pastor continues.

"Church! Do you accept? Will we consecrate this baby to our Lord and Savior; accept this lost sheep back into the Body of Christ? Hold her accountable to God in raising this child?"

One hand, two, a dozen shoots up. A smattering of applause, and it is decided.

The pastor's hand then—thick and meaty—on Audrey's pursed, alabaster brow. Prayers are sent up. Her place is confirmed. My job to lead her given with a promise the church will intercede should I stray again.

***

As I step off the stage with my newly dedicated, inconsolable daughter, a stooped, diminutive, crone of a woman reaches one gnarled hand into the aisle and seizes my shoulder. Her wizened, enigmatic gaze roots me in place, and she speaks with an air of reverence and mystery.

"I have a word for you from The Lord: You are the chosen one who will break the generational curse on your family." Her irises are like wildfire encased in marbles: I cannot tear my eyes away. At last, she nods and releases her grip and turns back toward the pulpit as if she'd said nothing at all.

CHAPTER TWENTY-FIVE

Cheddar Biscuits & The Lord's Name

AUDREY IS 2 MONTHS OLD and will not stop crying, crying, crying. No matter what I do, she cries. I am so tired, and my efforts at mothering seem to be a failure, failure, failure. Maybe she hates me. *I* sure hate me. How can parenting be so hard? Why won't she listen?

"Shut that kid *up*," my father shouts from the living room.

It's been hours, days, weeks, and I cannot make her stop.

"Fucking seriously, I'm *trying*, Daddy. I don't know what you want from me! *Jesus*!"

There is irritation, frustration, anger in my voice. I am on the edge; over it, maybe.

The sound from the updated, large-screen TV cuts out, and the resulting silence carries a deadly weight.

"Did you just take the Lord's name in vain in my house!?"

A shadow looms. He has crossed the distance from the couch to the dining room in record speed. I feel him before I see him. Fists fly, I turn, trying to protect Audrey's sweet little head, but am too late. His ham-hock fist glances off her tiny skull.

Her sobs stop. Everything stops. I can't think, and the world stands still.

At last, her breath catches, and she bellows louder than should be possible for her fragile little lungs.

"You hit my *baby*!!! How could you! Get *out*; get the fuck away from us both, right now!" I scream—and for once—he is chastised. For once, there is penance in his stance, remorse in his eyes.

He slinks away, away, out the door and gone, but I don't see. All I see is my baby girl, and the so familiar red welt blooming across her skin this time, instead of mine.

***

Lunchtime at Red Lobster: It is slow on a weekday and virtually private at a back-corner table, far from the oversized tanks filled with crawling and climbing crustaceans, claws bound in thick black rubber bands, blissfully unaware of their impending fiery, red deaths.

My father sits across from me, fiddling with the condensation on his glass of Diet Pepsi, ignoring the cheddar biscuit on the small plate in front of him. His military haircut is combed and greased—every hair in place—and his faded denim-blue eyes are stormy and serious. He smells of Listerine, Brylcreem, and his signature scent, Paul Sebastian cologne.

We are alone; baby Audrey is home with my mother. It's been weeks since we last spoke, giving each other ample leeway as we float through the house engulfed in our respective day-to-day activities: icebergs broke free in the rising temperate waters of Antarctica.

I am only here for the satisfaction of telling him once and for all to fuck off.

Strained silence doubles, magnified by my tightly crossed arms and unwavering gaze. The tension is unmistakable as I formulate my response to his imminent dismissive excuse: the twisted blame which always, always comes. I reach for a drink of water as I map out the conversation in my head.

His arms fly across the table; he seizes my pale, thin hand between his burly, calloused ones. "Daughter, forgive me. Your father has been a terrible man. I never meant to hurt you, and then, that precious baby…" He chokes the words out between sobs and tears stream down his ruggedly handsome face.

I am awestruck, speechless. I have *never* seen my father cry, *never* heard him apologize. Not once.

"Every time I ever hurt you, I was wrong. I know that now. I can't take any of it back, but I promise you: I will never lay a hand on you—on either of you—*ever* again." He dissolves into tears, still gripping my hand as if it were a life raft, and the whole world nothing but deep, dark, churning water.

And, it is, isn't it? Tears like this, I have never seen.

"I love you, Daughter. Can you ever forgive me for hurting you all these years? For hurting your sweet baby?"

I lean back in my chair, eyes wide. "Y—you're sorry, Daddy? You mean it?"

There is uninhibited sincerity—and anguish—in his eyes. "I've never meant anything more in my life."

I lean forward, squeeze his hand, and start to cry. "I forgive you, Daddy. This is all I ever wanted from you. I love you so much."

Time is held in abeyance as he collects himself, then a radiant smile breaks across his face like the sun crowning the Olympic Mountains.

"Well, we better go pick us one of them sea creatures for lunch, then, hadn't we?'

***

My father keeps his word and dotes on Audrey as if she is a priceless porcelain doll. He dotes on me, too, becomes my champion, in fact. Anything I need, want—even mention in passing—is mine. The volatile, treacherous side of him is retired, buried in the metaphorical graveyard of promises actually kept.

Despite the healed relationship, space at home is tight, so he buys a travel trailer for Audrey and me, and we move to a sweet little spot on a lake. I am in heaven, picking out decorations for our first real home. My father tears out the camper's old floor and lays new carpeting, and my mother has a friend from church make new curtains for all the windows.

The day comes when the decorating is done, and my parents drive away and leave us to begin our life together. As they turn the corner out of sight, I spin around with Audrey in my arms, full of hope for our future.

"Now we will be our very own family, Audrey! Just wait and see."

After a few months of living alone, though, the solitude starts to get to me. I haven't maintained relationships with my friends since getting pregnant. Most are still drinking or doing drugs, and I don't have time for that with a baby. Occasionally, someone stops by, but it isn't the same; we have nothing in common anymore.

I must *have had friends before all this, right?*

After dismissing the first few faces that trail through my mind, a cascade of fond memories comes back, and my heart warms at the thought of rekindling one specific friendship.

Jonathan.

Yes, Jonathan. Dear, sweet, constant Jonathan. Quick to accept, sure to listen, never to judge. Too long have I let our friendship gather dust in the shadow of my poor choices.

Yes, I should call Jonathan.

CHAPTER TWENTY-SIX

Batman & Art Class

ART CLASS. FRESHMAN YEAR. I take the second to last table in the back of the room, only because the back table is already occupied. I'm the new girl, as per usual, and this is the only class on my schedule that does not fill me with apprehension. Art I can do; excel at, really. And, most students here are likely to be either the artsy type or looking for an easy "A." Not the popular kids who can be so cruel.

The bell rings, and kids trail in; the teacher shuffles papers preparing for class to begin.

"Hey, what's your name?" I hear from the table behind me.

I turn and see a blond Charlie Sheen lookalike wearing a black and yellow Batman t-shirt and a big sunny grin.

"I'm Jonathan!"

I smile slightly. "Oh…um…hi, Jonathan. I'm Rachel."

He taps his pencil on the cover of his sketch pad. "Do you like art?"

I lean over and wipe an imaginary mark off my white, knockoff Keds. "Yeah."

He blushes a little. "I do, too, but I also figured this class would be a great escape from the preps and jocks who can make the day Hell for us normal people."

My unease falls away, and my hesitant smile becomes genuine.

"I know *just* what you mean."

Maybe this place won't be so bad after all.

Throughout high school, Jonathan and I become fast friends. When things are chaotic at home, he offers moral support. When I start using drugs, he listens without judgment. Any time of day or night, I can call him, and he is there. Always.

***

Audrey is a few months old when I reconnect with Jonathan. Home for the summer after basic training, there is plenty of time to rekindle our friendship. He visits our little trailer often, and Audrey takes quite a shine to him.

By the time he receives his assignment to Camp Lejeune and is shipped off to North Carolina, our friendship has grown into something easy and comfortable. Talk of marriage seems the natural progression in our strong, solid camaraderie.

Phone calls and letters are a daily occurrence after he leaves. Jonathan's parents own a business in town and give me a part-time job, even allow me to bring Audrey to work. Both our families are thrilled with our levelheaded plans and talk happily about our future together.

With the drugs behind me and a child to care for, it is time to settle down. And, who better to settle down with than such a close, understanding long-time friend?

About four months after Jonathan leaves, Audrey and I fly out to join him. The night we arrive, we drive to his barracks, and after brief introductions, Jonathan nervously asks one of his buddies to watch Audrey so he can speak to me alone. We step out onto the balcony, and Jonathan slips a diamond ring on my finger.

Just the way I always dreamed, and exactly why I came. So why am I not happy? Why isn't my breath taken away?

It's probably just nerves—that or jetlag. Jonathan is great *and* precisely *what Audrey and I need. I just need time to process. He is a* great *guy.*

So, I say yes, and smile as we embrace. We go back inside, and Jonathan whoops and hollers as he tells his friends. I give a weak smile and pick up Audrey.

"I'm tired, Jonathan. Can we please go check into a motel for the night?"

"Uh, yeah...sure," he replies, his exuberance faltering just the slightest bit. "Of course, you both must be exhausted!"

He apologizes on repeat on the way to the motel. Feeling guilty for taking away his steam on such a significant night, I try to smooth over his anxiety with platitudes and empty reassurance.

He is such a good guy, Rachel. Get it together!

Jonathan and I have never been intimate, and when we get to the motel, I insist on a room with two beds claiming I want to do things right and wait until we are married. He is respectful, if not entirely on board with my requests.

As I lay alone in bed, I mull over my unexpected reaction to his proposal. Marriage has been our primary topic of conversation for months, so his proclamations of undying love didn't come as a surprise. Starting a new life with him is the intent; why else would I have traveled across the country with my baby daughter?

After a mostly sleepless night, I decide to push aside these unanticipated feelings and dive feet first into the life we planned.

Over the next several weeks, Jonathan is the picture of a doting fiancé. He moves us into his mobile home off-base, fully furnishes it to my every specification, buys me a new car, and provides for all our needs. With each act of kindness, though, I grow more distant and withdrawn as I struggle to overcome—or successfully conceal—the growing certainty I am making a mistake.

Finally, I can take it no longer. One evening while telling me about his day, I abruptly interrupt him.

"I need to go home. I can't do this."

He stops his story short and is quiet for several moments. "Why, Rachel? Is it the house? I know it's not the nicest place, but I will get a raise soon and find us something better."

I take his hand in mine. "No, it's not the house. The house is great. Everything you do is great. *You're* great."

He pulls his hand back and rakes it through his hair and begins pacing the floor in front of me. "Then what is it? Whatever is wrong, we can fix it."

I sigh miserably. "You can't fix it, Jonathan. I don't love you, and I need to go home."

He takes a step backward, and his shoulders fall in defeat. Red-hot pokers of shame and regret slice through me as I realize he already knows. He knows it is over.

The drive to the airport is the longest of my life. He tries and tries to change my mind, and my heart breaks more with each attempt.

Can't he see? It isn't my mind that won't cooperate. It's my heart.

CHAPTER TWENTY-SEVEN

House of Horrors

BACK IN O-TOWN once again. I get a minuscule one-bedroom apartment for Audrey and me using my meager welfare benefits. Struggling with breaking Jonathan's heart and my resulting failure at creating a complete family unit for Audrey, I slip back into drinking: drinking a lot.

My place quickly becomes a party house—only one strict rule: no drugs allowed. I've seen what drugs can do. But, drinking? Drinking is *fine*...it wouldn't be legal if it caused any *serious* problems. And, I am practically 20 years old—*almost* the legal drinking age—close enough for government work, anyway.

Amidst my drunken stupors, I enroll in college, but when my first financial aid check comes, I blow every dime on liquor: for me, for my newfound friends. As my partying increases, my ability to care for Audrey—now toddling around unsupervised in the mornings after the continual raging parties—plummets. Her stays with my parents become longer and more frequent, and in quick succession, they gain legal custody of her, and I am evicted.

Fashioning myself as possessing a sort of anti-Midas touch, I dive deeper into the bottle. In one of my near-blackout states, I meet Nate. A friend of my brother—a gutter-punk with a quasi-impossible leopard-print-Mohawk, shifty eyes, and dog-chains around his neck—he is the bass player in a local band and inherently allergic to all that is healthy and mainstream.

We quickly become an item, and with nowhere steady to live, I find myself staying with Nate at Ace's house: the central hangout for the punk rockers in town. Ace's pad is a character study in filth and dementedness. Most of the crew are addicted to heroin, and they claim the back room as their shooting gallery. A parade of underage girls comes and goes through the house, and their carousing can easily be heard through the thin walls.

Nate refuses to let me go in the back room, which is fine by me. I am terrified of needles and sickened by the crudity of how the other guys brag about their conquests.

I am thankful Nate keeps me separated from what is going on. I feel protected; I feel like he genuinely cares.

When he expresses his concern about how much I am drinking, I stop.

When he mentions how I dress causes other guys to want me, I change.

When he says my friends are taking away from our time together, I cut them out.

The two of us don't leave Ace's house much. We stay holed up in our room away from everyone else, only making occasional trips to the store for soda and smokes.

One night, though, we get word one of my favorite bands, Fugazi, is playing at the theater downtown. I am thrilled at the prospect of seeing them live, and the whole house makes the journey to watch the show.

***

The crowd is big and rowdy, and I quickly lose track of Nate, so when I see Ace and some of the other guys from the house, I am relieved.

"Have any of you guys seen Nate?" I bellow over the near pandemonium of the crowd.

"Yeah, we just left him," Ace yells back. He grabs my hand and pulls me toward a side door to the alley. "Follow me!"

Ace and two of his friends guide me through the writhing, sweating swarm of fans and out into the bleak frostiness of the fall night.

"Thanks, guys. I don't think I could have made it through the crowd alone," I shout, my voice muffled in my head, my ears still ringing from the concert. "Where did you say Nate was?"

"He was right over here," one of them replies. "But don't you want to have a drink with us first?"

"Umm, I don't think so...Nate doesn't really like it when I drink."

They all laugh and sneer.

"What is he, your *daddy*?" Ace taunts. "Come on. Have a drink with us."

"Yeah, come on."

"Just one drink."

"Well...all right," I reply, my resolve wavering. "I guess just one wouldn't hurt."

One of them passes me an open beer, and I gulp it down quickly.

"Ok, *now*, can you show me where Nate is?" I repeat, trying to catch my breath after chugging the drink.

"Yeah, sure," Ace says, his face a full-on smirk now. "I think he is over in the van waiting for you."

I follow Ace, the other two flanking my sides as they herd me away from the crowd and to the van. Ace slides the side door open and sticks his head inside.

"Nate?" he calls into the dark interior. "I found Rachel."

A push from behind and I am sprawled face-first on the broken back seat; my mouth and nose shoved into a pile of oily rags, arms pinned to my sides, cold fingers gouge the skin of my belly as my pants are ripped open and pulled down. I try to scream, but laughter drowns out my cries. I try to fight, but they are three, and I am only one. I cannot think, breathe, anything.

As the last one finishes, the van door is ripped down its tracks, and cold biting air cuts through my pain.

"What the fuck, Rachel?? What the Hell is going on?!"

It's Nate. Ace, still buttoning his pants, jumps out of the van, followed close behind by his friends. I am left in a crying, disheveled heap with my jeans around my ankles.

I hear them clearly. "What the Hell is going on, Ace?" Nate demands.

"Dude, I'm sorry," Ace replies. "She had a lot to drink and wouldn't stop begging us to do her. I know we are friends and all, but she was begging for it, man. You understand, right?"

I hold my breath—waiting—knowing I am avenged, I am saved.

"That stupid *slut*," Nate seethes.

I inhale sharply, ignoring my tears, and try to hitch up my pants. Before I can pull them over my hips, Nate yanks me out of the van and throws me onto the blacktop.

"You stupid whore! I leave for one minute, and you fuck my friends?!"

I cower in the fetal position against the alley wall, and it hits me: They planned it. The drink before; they *knew* Nate would smell it on my breath and blame me.

"I'm sorry, Nate," I sob. "I didn't—"

Furious, he storms away, leaving me half-dressed on the ground.

I scramble to my feet, button my pants, and—still sobbing—chase after him; the music drifting out from an open stage door fading in the distance as I run.

***

I finally find Nate and spend hours tearfully attempting to explain. He refuses to believe me; the alcohol on my breath lends credence to his friend's version of events.

Maybe I did *ask for it. Why did I follow Ace to the van? Why didn't I fight harder? Maybe I wanted it like Nate says. If it's so easy for him to believe his friends, then I* must *carry at least* some *of the blame.*

Finally, exhausted and undone, I offer a defeated, "I'm sorry, Nate."

He forgives me.

But, with forgiveness comes rules.

Not only am I to stay out of the back room, I am not to leave our bedroom.

At all.

Days turn into weeks with nothing to see but four walls and his glowering face.

When I need to relieve myself? Nate supplies an empty two-liter of soda for me to do my business. When I cannot force myself to urinate into the old bottle beneath his lording, glaring, accusatory stance? It is proof of the plan he imagines I have devised: to sneak out and fuck his friends again.

Punishment is mandatory for such betrayal, he explains after throwing me across the room.

I stay huddled in the corner until I am sure Nate is passed out for the night. When his breath evens into the familiar rhythm of sleep, I creep around the bed—a futon mattress propped off the floor on an arrangement of milk crates—around the TV stand, and out the bedroom door. My senses are taut and frayed; convinced a creaking floorboard will wake him, unleash my downfall in a hail of brimstone.

As I steal through the darkness

(no plan, no plan; just go, just go)

I become aware of a more significant issue. My lower back: It throbs and sears and rips with pain, as if I am enacting the Ten of Swords card in mime. I keen and weep and moan, and unable to stand, crawl inch-by-inch across the uncharted sea of the living room, sweating profusely, willing myself silent as I claw my way into the expanse of the dining room.

At last, I see my prize: attached high up the peeling grease-covered kitchen wall is an old rotary dial handset. I force myself to keep going, to keep silent, until—at last—I am positioned on the floor beneath the phone.

I brace my shoulder against the wall—my back too insulted to use as leverage—and scoot into a hunchback stance. I sway briefly as my vision darkens, then clears, and reach up in unfettered agony to bring the receiver to my ear.

I dial from memory, shaking from exertion, and hold my breath as I wait for the click indicating the call is connected.

"Daddy, Daddy, please…" I whisper. "I need help. I think I need to see a doctor."

No pause, no questions; just an immediate, "I'm on my way, Daughter."

I sink to the floor, relief flooding my overtaxed nerves. I take a breath, wipe away a tear—Of gratitude? Of pain?—and begin the torturous trek back to the bedroom to await my father's arrival. It won't do for Nate to catch me just before the cavalry arrives.

Just as I settle in next to Nate—oh so careful not to wake him—a battering ram pounding at the door jolts him awake. He springs out of bed to investigate, pausing briefly to address me.

"You *better* not come out of this room while I am gone, bitch," he says through clenched teeth, his voice venomous.

I strain to listen through the closed bedroom door, and when I hear my father's voice, gather all my nerve and crawl toward the sound. It is now or never.

I make it to the front door, but Nate's silhouette blocks my view. I can hear my father interrogating him, demanding answers. And, if I can hear him, he can hear me, too.

"Daddy!" I cry feebly.

"You let me see my daughter right now, son, or you are going to regret the day you laid eyes on either of us."

Nate tries to maintain his stance, but I rally my fading strength and push past him; we land on the front lawn locked in a vicious struggle.

My father's stern command cuts through the roiling brawl: "That's enough!!"

Nate and I freeze, and my father bends down, gathers me in his arms, and takes me to the hospital.

My bladder and kidneys are dangerously infected.

I go home with my father, crying the whole time, too ashamed to look him in the eyes.

***

While I recuperate, Nate calls nonstop, sends messages home with my brother, even sends roses. After a few days, my resolve begins to weaken.

He must *love me if he is trying* this *hard to win me back, right? Who am I to judge someone unworthy and cut them off? Haven't I proven—so many times—the only thing I am good at is hurting people?*

So, against the adamant protestations of my parents, I go back.

The entire dynamic changes. Our interactions are delicate and guarded, like two wounded animals circling in battle, attempting to ascertain if the threat still lingers.

Not long after returning, I realize I am significantly *late*.

A trip to the drugstore confirms my suspicion: I am pregnant. Nate is thrilled; this will be his first child. He talks of regaining custody of Audrey and raising both kids as a family. I am hesitantly optimistic; maybe the new baby will turn things around.

***

I'm two months pregnant now, and Nate is winding up, up, up, and I just want to leave.

"Get away from the door, Nate. Let me out. I don't want to do this anymore."

The room flies by in a blur of empty soda bottles and Sid and Nancy posters as I am slammed violently into the entertainment center. I fall flat on my back, and the massive television tumbles off its stand and onto my unprotected belly. I heft it off and onto the floor like the fabled mother whose child is trapped under a vehicle.

I spring into a sitting position and am met by Nate, his face inches away, his voice seething with rage and dripping with malevolence.

"You will *never* leave me. Never. No matter where you go, you will always belong to me. And just when you think you are free, I will find you; I will climb in your window, and I will kill Audrey in her sleep, and then I will cut that baby out of you and make you watch it die."

His dead-calm certainty is unmistakable, and something inside me snaps, races to the surface—past my fear, past my indecision—and takes on a life of its own.

"You will *never* touch *either* of my children!"

I am on my feet before the words are out of my mouth, and then *he* is flying across the room, smashed into the bookshelves lining the far wall. He folds in a heap on the garbage-strewn floor like a poorly made origami crane, the look of astonishment on his face is only rivaled by the fury and resolve on mine.

"We are *done*, Nate. You hear me? Done. You stay the *fuck* away from my children and me, or you will regret it for the rest of your puny, pathetic life."

He is still gawking when I walk out the door for the last time.

CHAPTER TWENTY-EIGHT

Knot the One

AND, JUST LIKE THAT: baby number two.

Nicholas is a chubby, content, cuddly child, and after seeing how well I do with him, my mother gives me back custody of Audrey. She purchases a new doublewide trailer a half-hour away from town with enough space for everyone. Life is simple: home, momma-time, church, repeat. Months turn into years, and I revel in the calm, quiet, predictability of it all.

***

When church leadership suggests I carpool to religious activities with Preston, I agree. An outlier, newly saved, and freshly off drugs with no vehicle of his own, he spends the trips to town facing the kids in their car seats singing made-up songs and creating silly games. It is music to my ears. They adore him, and with no father figure in their lives, they drink up the attention.

At first, I drive in silence, observing. But before long, I am won over by Preston's attention and interest. I begin to wonder again if maybe this is the way life is supposed to be: a man, a woman, and children. Maybe it is time to settle down; maybe this is God's plan.

By the time Preston proposes, the kids and I have moved out of my mother's house and live in a small duplex a few blocks from the church.

With the impending nuptials, the trips out of town to pick up Preston before church seem senseless, so he spends the night—on the couch—on Saturdays.

Eventually, the inevitable happens, and it isn't the couch he sleeps on.

I get pregnant the first night.

What am I going to do? What will the church leaders say? What will my parents *say?*

But we are engaged and both saved; so, everything will be fine, right?

With the pregnancy confirmed, Preston moves in. It is only a formality until we are official anyway. The church is reservedly supportive of us: glad we are engaged but pointedly avoiding the topic of the imminent arrival of my third baby formed out of wedlock by the age of 21.

***

If Nate's and my relationship was fire and ice, Preston and I are ice and fire. Preston is malleable and folds to my every whim. Having some semblance of control within a romantic relationship is foreign. I push and challenge him, and he quietly concedes again and again. I walk out on thinner and thinner ice, looking for his boundaries, searching for the scenario in which he will finally assert himself.

When I say his hair is too shaggy, he cuts it.

When I suggest contacts instead of glasses, he acquiesces.

When I tell him to choose one of his last names instead of keeping his longer, hyphenated version, he has it legally changed.

About three months pregnant with baby number three, the cracks in the ice give way.

***

Fresh out the bath and preparing for bedtime stories—Audrey, almost 4 years old, and Nicholas, around 18 months—are all snuggles and giggles as I kneel on the floor and suit them in zipper-front footie pajamas.

"Where are the smokes? All I found was an empty pack," Preston demands, storming into the bathroom.

"We are out, sorry. I figured I'd get some in the morning, on the way to work."

He shakes his head in defiance, tossing his grown out, shoulder-length dirty-blond hair away from his eyes. "No. That's not going to work. We'll just go now."

I stop combing Nick's hair and look up at Preston. "It's bedtime; the kids need to stay on a schedule. I'm not going to put them in their car seats and get them all riled up at this hour. Can't you just wait until tomorrow?"

Preston clenches his jaw and pushes the glasses he has reverted to wearing up his nose. "It's only a few blocks away; we can just leave them here. They will be fine."

"Are you *crazy*?" I set the plastic comb on the counter and stand. "They are just *babies*!"

"No, they are not. They will be fine," he snaps, his tone a shot of lightning through a pregnant, purple sky. He pushes past me and ushers the children out of the bathroom, down the hall, and into the bedroom they share, closing the door firmly behind him.

I follow him into the hallway, and he casts a haughty look over his shoulder.

"See? They won't even notice we are gone. Now let's *go*!"

Before he makes it more than two steps, the bedroom door opens, and Audrey shuffles out with Nicholas trailing right behind her.

"Where goin'?" Audrey asks, her inquisitive nutmeg eyes shining.

Preston jerks to a halt, his body rigid. He whips around and corrals them back into the bedroom, shutting the door harder this time while glowering at me. "You kids stay in there for a while and play, you hear me?"

The door opens again. Giant, crystalline tears wobble in the corners of Audrey's eyes, threatening to overflow, and Nick's breath hitches as he prepares for an all-out wail.

"Preston, stop! Let them out; this is a bad idea!" I shriek, a ribbon of icy panic constricting my thoughts.

Never breaking eye contact with me, he bends over and shoves Audrey with both hands, toppling her and Nicholas backward onto the floor, then slams the door shut once more. He straightens and strides deliberately down the hall toward the kitchen, shoving past me.

Both kids are howling now, and I race to comfort them. I get to the bedroom door just as Audrey opens it again, and gather them close.

Preston tears back down the hall and hisses at me: "*Don't* encourage them, Rachel. I *said* they are going to stay in their room, and they *are* going to listen!"

Audrey stares up at him, sobbing, "Why you be so mean at us, Pweston?"

He stares down at her hatefully, then turns and glares at me as he pours a cup of water he obtained in the kitchen over her head. She gasps at the unexpected onslaught of cold, her cries momentarily suspended.

Unable to register what blue madness has sprung up in my happy home, I look him up and down, searching for the man I chose to complete our family, sure he is tucked away somewhere in a corner of this beast in front of me. My eyes stop dead when I see what else he is holding.

A rope.

I watch—rooted to the floor, sure this must all be a dream—as Preston pushes my soaked, sputtering little girl back into the bedroom, knocking Nick onto the floor again in the process. He takes the rope and ties the bedroom doorknob to the knob of the hall closet, locking them in.

"What are you *doing*?!" I screech.

"Get. In. The. Car," he seethes as the children bawl in hysterics from behind the door.

I have seen this look before, and I know what comes next. I shrink under the weight of his anger and slink to the car, suppressing my sobs.

"Preston, why? Can't I just stay here? Please let me go to them!"

"You coddle them, and they never listen. They need to learn some discipline, and if you won't teach them, I will."

I stop talking; we both do. I can hear the babies' cries as we pull out of the driveway and down the street. The trip to the store takes less than ten minutes, but it feels like lifetimes. By the time we return, I fully grasp the harsh truth: My relentless pushing has created an insurmountable landslide, and the vision of our future together is nothing more than a disintegrating pipe dream wafting away in the breeze.

CHAPTER TWENTY-NINE

The Hardest Part

THE BREAKUP IS UGLY, but the reaction from the church is uglier still. I am chastised at every corner for 'not working things out and giving him another chance' and 'having another child out of wedlock.' Devastated by the rejection, I retreat and shutter myself away in isolation. I was so *sure* I made the right choice by breaking things off with Preston, but their judgment weighs heavily on me, and I fall into a deep depression.

How am I going to do this? Raise three little ones on my own? I can hardly afford to pay my electric bill. I barely have the mental and emotional bandwidth to keep up with two *babies.*

After tucking the kids into bed at night, I lie on the floor and cry into a pillow so they won't hear me.

How can I manage a third?

The more I think about it, the more it becomes clear: If I spread myself any thinner, *none* of them will get the life they deserve.

Not to mention Preston being a part of their lives forever.

I dance around and around the facts—looking, looking, looking for a solution—a way to make everyone happy, where everyone wins. The day finally comes when I can no longer avoid the harsh reality—and drained from the emotional battle of trying to find a sane, suitable answer—I open my eyes and mind to the truth: There is only one option.

Adoption.

With a decision made, day-to-day life becomes tolerable. I find an attorney who specializes in adoption and make an appointment to learn about the process. I feel small and unsure in the pristine, gleaming office; the attorney is kind as she lays out all the steps, but the information is difficult to process through the tidal wave crashes of my emotions.

At the end of the appointment, she brings out a massive binder full of potential parents, images of smiling faces punctuated with heartfelt pleas to make their family whole through the most precious of gifts.

There are so many of them. How can I ever pick the right ones?

Disheartened, I leave her office and drive to Vivienne's house.

I sit on Viv's secondhand couch, picking at the threads of the multicolored, homemade quilt thrown across its back, head down, defeated. Viv sits across from me, holding my hand in hers, compassion plain on her face.

"Like, I don't know what to do, Viv. I can't keep this baby. I just can't. But, how can I trust any family just from looking at a few pictures and reading a couple of paragraphs?"

She thinks for a moment before answering. "You know, my aunt has a friend who's struggled with several miscarriages, and when she finally *did* have a baby, he died a few months later."

I gasp and look up. "Oh my gosh! How awful! Her baby died? I can't even imagine."

She nods and scoots a bit closer on the couch. "I could call and see if adoption is something she and her husband have thought about."

"Really? That would be amazing! Like, someone who has been through all that would have so much *love* to give! What's she like? Where does she live?"

She leans across me and picks up the telephone sitting on the coffee table, bringing it to her lap. "As far as I remember, they are an older couple—in their 40s—and live a couple of hours away. Her husband is a CPA, and she's a teacher, I think. They are Catholic and have money. It might be just what you are looking for."

"Oh, wow, that *is* perfect!" I hug her hard. "The baby would have such a good life with that kind of family. Way more than I could ever provide."

***

Waiting. Waiting for the day to come, for the pain to end. I go through the motions of day-to-day life, but inside—a supernova—its luminous debris strewn in serrated chunks across my mind, my heart, my soul.

A month before my delivery date, new neighbors move in next door: a guy about my age, Lee, and a girl, Holly, who looks to be about eight months pregnant herself. Lee strikes up a conversation with me. He and Holly are not a couple, he says; he got her pregnant and is seeing it through to the end. They are giving their baby up for adoption, too.

Holly is young—only 17 or 18—and quiet, spending most of her time home alone. Lee comes over most days, and we talk about the imminent adoptions and our resulting emotions. It is good to have someone to talk with who understands.

Lee drinks a lot—to cope with the pain of the impending reality, I figure—but I say no each time he offers.

In due course, I see Holly get into a car, obviously in labor. I glance out the window often as I go about my routine. It's late evening when headlights shine in the drive next door, and with them, I hear only one car door closing.

The baby has come and gone, and so has Holly.

Lee's visits increase exponentially, as does his drinking. He is heartbroken, grieving. I push my own emotions down deep, as far out of reach as I can. Tears are not an option. I listen but am consumed by my own looming delivery and caring for my little ones.

Two short weeks later, it is my turn. The morning of my delivery comes brilliant and warm, mocking the black sheet of ice gripping my insides. When my mother arrives to take me to the hospital, most of the neighborhood is still sleeping.

As I make the endless trek to the car, I hear Lee call out from his window: "You can do it, Rachel. It will all be okay."

I start crying then, all my suppressed emotion bursting free.

The drive to the hospital is short and the labor quick. Contractions come and go until there is no space between them.

Suddenly, it is time to push.

My legs, though, they won't open. I can't make them.

My mother holds one leg up, and a nurse holds the other.

"Rachel," the nurse says firmly, her voice tinged with concern. "You have to open your legs and let him out."

"*No*!" I wail through my tears. "I don't want to let him go!"

More nurses, then, two on each side, pulling with all their might. The monitors screeching *the baby is in distress*, *the baby is in distress*, and still, I cannot.

I cry out, choking on my sobs until finally, I can fight no more, and he is born.

He is born, blue and silent, the cord wrapped around his neck.

They race him to the NICU. I turn my head to the side and weep, convinced I have killed him.

"It's okay, Rachel. He is going to be all right," my mother repeats as she strokes my forehead, her eyes welling with tears. "It's okay."

I am moved to a recovery room, and shortly thereafter, the hospital staff announces the baby *is* okay, just needs to be kept under observation. I can see him if I want.

I wheel myself to the NICU and look down at my son, so small and helpless.

"I'm so sorry; I didn't mean to hurt you," I whisper, my tears falling onto his pink cheeks. "Please forgive me."

Back to my room, depleted and drained.

My baby's new mother and father are here, but I don't want to see them.

My father is here, too, but he doesn't want to see me.

Every two hours, like clockwork, hospital staff asks, "Do you want to see your baby?"

Every time, I say no.

Then, they are asking for the last time. The last time before my little Caleb—the name I picked, but he will never be called—is to go home with his new parents, to his new life, the life I chose for him.

"Do you want to say goodbye?" a nurse asks, her voice reverberating through the empty room and catching on my raw emotions.

After a long pause, I nod slowly and whisper, "Maybe for a minute."

She is gone before I can rethink my decision. A moment later, a hospital bassinet is rolled in holding a tiny, swaddled bundle.

"Here he is," she sings in a low voice. "Do you want to hold him?"

"Um, sure; I guess," I reply, my voice shaking.

She gently picks him up and hands him to me. "I'll leave you two alone for a few minutes." She slips out of the room, closing the door behind her.

And here we are—mother and son—for the moment at least. I cradle my newborn child in my lap and drink in every detail of his frame. He holds my eyes intently as if he understands the magnitude of this moment as deeply as I do.

I take a deep breath and try to steady my voice. "Hi, Caleb; I am your mommy. You probably won't remember me later, but I want you to know I love you *so* much, and all I ever wanted was for you to have the best life possible, better than I could give you. I hope you understand someday; I hope you understand and can forgive me. I love you, and I am sorry I can't be your mommy all the time, but I promise: You will always be my son in my heart."

My words and tears gush like water from a fire hydrant burst in the inner-city in the summertime, and his eyes never leave mine. I hold him close and pray a prayer of a life of love and peace and abundance for him. I kiss him once and push the call button for the nurse.

"I'm ready for you to come and take him," I say when she appears in the doorway.

"Are you sure? You can have longer if you want."

I snap my head from side-to-side and hold him out to her. "No, if I don't let him go now, I won't be able to at all."

"All right," she replies, a fleeting shadow of disapproval crossing her face as she takes my son from my outstretched arms.

I watch, decimated—my heart a post-apocalyptic landscape—as she returns him to the bassinet, rolls him out of the room, and out of my life.

CHAPTER THIRTY

One Is Too Many

TIME TO GO HOME. The mood is somber and heavy with unspoken emotion.

Nick, nearly 2 years old, toddles around the hospital room in his tan, OshKosh B'gosh overalls, a Sesame Street binky planted firmly against his plump, rosy cheeks.

"Where baby at, Momma? Where baby?" he asks, his words indistinct behind the pacifier.

Audrey, her semi-sweet chocolate hair swept into matching prim ponytails and wearing her favorite apple blossom dress—saved for special occasions—attempts to explain in a voice which belies her tender 4 years.

"He was 'dopted, Nicky. We gave him 'way to his new momma." Her chin trembles as she reaches to console him, and her eyes fill with tears.

Nick looks up and seeing the expression on her face, begins to cry. "No give our baby 'way, Momma!! No!!"

I look to my mother in desperation as I scramble to hold myself together in front of the children, but it is useless: my insides are ravaged.

"Mom, please…" I choke.

My mother, barely holding back her own tears, gathers the babies to her. "Come on, guys. Let's get the car and bring Momma home. How's that sound?"

My mother heads to the parking lot with two little ones in varying states of meltdown clutching her hands. I follow behind, but wait on a bench outside the hospital to try and collect myself. A few minutes later, her car whips into the vestibule and screeches to a stop; the sounds of the children's sobs carry easily through the open windows.

I stand, but the pain of giving birth is too much; I sit down hard, dizzy with the effort. As my vision clears, I see there is a flat tire.

My mother leans across the passenger seat and throws the door open.

"Come on, Rachel. Let's go," she says, her voice clipped and tight.

"But Mom—"

"But nothing, Rachel. Let's *go!*" she interrupts, her voice rising over the mounting cries from the backseat.

"We can't, Mom," I reply weakly, pointing to the back of the car. "The tire is flat."

"Great. Just *great,*" she snaps, reaching her breaking point. "Well, help me at least!"

I try to get up and make my way over to the trunk, but it is too much, and I stop midway, bent over in pain.

She grimaces and waves me away. "Never mind. Just go sit down."

I collapse back onto the bench—bone-tired and too weary to comfort my children—and silently weep while my mother changes the tire.

***

The ride home is a live-action version of the famous Alice in Wonderland scene: the whole world washed away in tears. I stare out the window floundering for control, scrambling for stability before we arrive back home, and I must be momma again.

Back home, and there is no calm to be found. Goodbyes are short and curt, and then my mother is gone, and I am left alone to comfort my inconsolable children.

I collapse onto the couch; Audrey, still sniffling, curls up next to me.

I motion Nicholas to join us, but he stands staunchly in the middle of the living room, his little feet planted firmly on the floor.

"Why, Momma? Why not bwing baby home wif us?" he demands through tears.

I search for a suitable answer but find none. I reach for him, weakly. "Come here, Nicky, sweetie. Come see Momma."

"No!" he shrieks, stomping his foot. "Where baby at?"

I hear Lee, then, from the front porch: "Hey, how are you doing?"

Unable to answer, my throat choked tight with emotion, our eyes lock through the dirty screen door. I see understanding reflected there, and a depth of pain that mirrors mine.

He swings the door open and steps in, swooping Nicholas into his arms. "Hey, kiddo. Wanna come over and watch a movie?" he says in a cheery voice, his grave eyes holding mine.

I nod, thankful and relieved for the distraction, and chime in. "Yeah, Nick. Wouldn't that be fun? Let's go over to Lee's for a while."

Nick stiffens, then goes limp. "Tay, Wee. Watch movie."

Before we can put a movie on, the kids become engrossed in exploring Lee's collection of computer parts and video games, giving us the space to talk. Lee sits across from me as I relay the details of the day, and we both cry.

This time, when he offers me a beer, I don't say no.

As the afternoon progresses, I don't stop crying, and I don't stop drinking. Around suppertime, it becomes clear I am in no shape to take care of the kids, so I call my mother.

"Please, Mom, please. Can you take them? Just for the night? I'm so not okay; I need to pull myself together." I enunciate each word clearly, so she won't hear me slurring.

She pauses. "All right," she replies with an air of uncertainty. "But, just for the night."

CHAPTER THIRTY-ONE

Drink, Drank, Drunk

MONTHS GO BY IN A HAZE of drunken numbness. Audrey and Nick spend more and more time with my parents, and between the grief and the alcohol, I barely notice. My idea that by giving Caleb up for adoption I'd somehow be a better, more present mommy to them? Indisputable, absolute, resounding bullshit.

Despite this, I somehow manage to find a much nicer place for us to live and land a job as a preschool teacher at the school Audrey attends. From the outside, things seem to be looking up, but inside, I am an empty shell.

When Lee proposes, it seems the natural decision to say yes. Who else understands what I have been through—am still going through? We are secret partners in our shared tragedy.

***

Wedding day: I am in the passenger seat of my older model Chevy Cavalier, Lee is driving. My department store, ivory, two-piece suit is uncomfortable and a little too tight; it slips up from the vibration of the engine and catches on the nylons my mother lent me.

You can't have bare legs at your wedding, even if it is only a courthouse ceremony.

We drive through town. It's early, so few people are out. I watch the small, colorful shops pass by out the window.

"I know what you are planning, and I won't be made a fool!"

Startled, I sit up straight, sure the radio dial has inadvertently been turned to some live-action soap opera.

But no. The radio is off.

Lee is gripping the steering wheel and leaning forward: the veins on his arms taut, his eyes bloodshot, his face contorted.

"Lee? Are you okay?"

"I *know*, Rachel! You are going to leave me! I know it!"

My head flinches back slightly. "I'm going to *leave* you? I'm in a wedding dress on the way to marry you! Where is this coming from?"

He turns toward me, eyes wild. The car fishtails down the thoroughfare as he keeps his laser focus on me. "No, it's a trap. I know it! You are too good for me, and you are going to figure it out, and then where will I be?"

I grab the dashboard with both hands, trying to hold myself in place amid his erratic driving, and begin to cry.

"Stop it, Lee," I plead, trying to diffuse his sudden outburst. "Everything is okay. I'm not going to leave you, I promise. My mom and the kids are waiting at the courthouse. Let's just go meet them, all right?"

He floors the accelerator and weaves madly through traffic. "Shut up, Rachel! I'm not stupid; I know what you are planning!"

I dig my nails into the dash and will the car to find a clear path. He swerves sharply, drives the vehicle halfway onto the sidewalk, and comes to an abrupt halt.

"Get out," he says, glowering at me.

"Get out? What? Lee, can't we just talk about—"

"I said, get *out*!"

I stare, unbelieving: He is serious. I grope for the door handle and trip on the curb, snagging the borrowed nylons in the process. He backs up, sideswipes a parked car, and tears away, leaving me gaping after him on the sidewalk in my crumpled wedding dress.

What just happened? What did I do wrong to make him think something like that?

I lean against the nearest building, face in hands, gutted. Strangers keep asking if I am all right, but I cannot respond. Their kindness and concern only make me cry harder.

After an eternity—or twenty minutes, it's all the same, really—I hear the familiar clunking squeal of my car coming up the street. Lee pulls up to the curb he so recently drove over, rolls the window down, and mumbles, "Come on, let's go."

I hold his gaze and consider my options.

Stay on the side of the street, crying?

No.

Call off the ceremony with my family waiting? What will I tell them?

No.

He apologizes profusely on the way to the courthouse claiming a wave of insecurity struck him. Says I am too good for him, and he can't bear to be without me.

Everyone gets insecure. And I have been so withdrawn and hurting; maybe it came across like I was having second thoughts.

I push and shove and fight away my doubts—bury my intuitions—and marry him.

CHAPTER THIRTY-TWO

Dinner Theatre

OUR ONE MONTH WEDDING anniversary: We would go out to dinner to celebrate, but it's not in the budget with only one income. I am working late at the preschool, anyway, waiting for the stragglers to pick up their children.

The kids are tired, and so am I. As parents trickle in, I gather their child's things and share stories of the day's activities. Finally, the last one is gone leaving Audrey and me to do the final clean up before heading home. We are putting away puzzles when the door swings open, and a hysterical parent bursts back into the room.

"Somebody robbed me!" she shrieks, holding her purse open. "My money; it's all gone!!"

I look up, stunned, and ask her what she means.

"My money is gone!" she repeats shrilly, her words coming fast now. "I left my purse in the car when I came in to pick up my daughter, and when I went back outside, my wallet was open and empty.

She starts to cry. "I came here straight from the bank. I had $3,000 in my wallet; it was for my mortgage!"

"Oh my gosh! Come here, sit down. I'll call the police right away!" I get her seated and race to the front office to use the phone.

The police arrive quickly and start a report. During the commotion, Lee comes in carrying Nicholas on his hip.

"What's going on?" Lee says, hitching Nick up higher. "I saw the police cars and was worried."

The officer taking statements nods toward Lee and asks, "Who is this?"

"Oh, this is my husband, Lee. He's fine. He always picks us up at the end of the day."

He faces Lee and continues, "Is this the normal time for you to pick up your wife?"

Lee shakes his head and adjusts Nick again. "No, sir. She's off a little late today. When I saw she wasn't ready yet, I made a quick run to the store."

The second detective turns to me. "Miss, can I speak with you privately? In another room?"

"Certainly, officer, right this way." I lead him down the hall to an office.

The detective closes the door behind us, and in a stern voice, says, "I would highly suggest if you know anything, you tell me now."

I take a step back. "Know anything? What do you mean?"

He raises his eyebrow and scowls. "You don't find it a little odd your husband was waiting in the parking lot all evening and then conveniently 'ran to the store' at the exact time the incident occurred?"

"Well…I don't know," I falter, my pulse beginning to race. "You don't think Lee had anything to do with this, do you?"

"Ma'am, I am *positive* he had something to do with it. What I am attempting to ascertain is your involvement."

"M-my involvement?" I sit down hard on one of the chairs positioned in front of the desk. "You can't be serious!"

"I am *completely* serious. I would suggest you come clean about what you know, or you are going to spend a long time away from your children."

My mouth goes dry. "I-I don't know anything; I swear. Can I please talk to Lee?"

He pauses, then nods curtly and opens the door. "Go ahead and try. But if your husband doesn't admit to it, things are going to be a lot worse. For both of you."

I slip past his imposing frame and go back to the classroom where Lee is standing, still holding Nicholas in his arms. The victim and the other officer are nowhere in sight.

"Lee, what is going on!" I hiss through my teeth as I approach him. "The police say you had something to do with this; they are threatening to send *me* to jail!"

Lee's eyes meet mine, and he says in a measured tone, "I would never do something like this, Rachel. I love you."

I lean in farther, my brows drawn down low. "Do you promise me, Lee? You swear? This is so serious!"

He holds my gaze and repeats, "Rachel, I love you. I would *never*."

As Lee speaks, Nicholas keeps kicking his chubby little leg. "Momma, my foot hurts. It hurts."

I idly reach over to adjust Nick's laces, and his sneaker falls off in my hand. Tucked between the sole of his shoe and his foot is a roll of hundred-dollar bills.

Uncomprehending, I stare down at the tiny shoe and wad of money. As shock turns to bitter realization, I snap my head up and search Lee's face. "In my baby's *shoe*??"

Behind me, the door opens, and the detective comes striding back into the room; I turn toward the sound, still holding the evidence.

Lee steps in front of me. "She had nothing to do with it, officer! It was all me; I felt worthless not providing for my family, and..." his voice trails off, and his face reddens.

I stand there, inept, as the detective gathers the evidence from my outstretched palm and passes Nicholas off to me.

As Lee is led away in handcuffs, I call out, "How could you *do* this?"

He looks over his shoulder but does not reply.

CHAPTER THIRTY-THREE

Self-Committed

I OFFER MY RESIGNATION in the aftermath of Lee's actions. My supervisor refuses to accept, stating no one blames me other than myself. My drinking comes up during the conversation, and when she suggests treatment, I readily agree; the cracks in the fault lines of my foundation are cavernous, and I cannot keep my balance on the wildly unstable ground.

My mother consents to keep the children—they are practically living with her full-time, anyway—while I complete a two-month inpatient treatment program.

***

Treatment is gut-wrenching. The classes are geared toward uncovering the root of the problem—the core issues—not just the symptoms. The shame and insanity surrounding Aleister's death, the adoption and my resulting catastrophic failure at mothering Audrey and Nick, the impending divorce: It is too-fucking-much. I can't focus, can't find the strength to dig down deep to the genesis of things.

So, instead, I focus on Trent.

Trent, who is floating through treatment with a half-cocked smile and tales of adventure outside the facility walls; Trent—the perfect comrade—as enamored with my tendency toward flights of fancy as I am with his errant whims.

He is obsessed with Jim Morrison—of course, he is—and I take it as a sign, an echoey nod from the past to follow the mad white rabbit. When he suggests we escape treatment, promising to show me real adventure, I don't hesitate. I have effectively napalmed every aspect of my life thus far; what else is there to lose?

***

After a quick stop at the local watering hole for a beer or six, Trent asks, "How'd you like to have some *real* fun?"

I sway on the barstool, more than a little drunk, and nod.

We leave the bar on foot and stop at a phone booth.

"I busted outta treatment," he says when the call connects, his mischievous eyes meeting mine. "And I brought company with me: Okay, if we stop by?" His grin spreads, indicating an answer in the affirmative. "Cool, we'll be right over."

He hangs up the phone, and with a twinkle in his eye, says, "All right, dollface, ready to see what it's like in my world?"

The day is hot, and the walk to Trent's friend's place is long. By the time we climb the front porch steps, my feet are covered in blisters. Trent strides through the door with me clutching his hand and trailing behind. Inside, the house is crammed full of people, and smoke permeates the air. I avert my eyes from the stares and shadow Trent to a room tucked away in the back of the house.

"I'm back," Trent declares, dropping my hand and throwing up both his like Caesar commanding exaltation from the masses. "Bring on the party!"

A burly, towering effigy of a man steps forward, his steely gaze locked on me. "And who is this?" he asks, in a forbidding tone.

I shrink back farther, grabbing Trent's hand again, my apprehension crystallizing into dread.

"This is Rachel, my fellow escapee. She's the one I told you about on the phone. She's cool, man."

Situated between the bearded, scowling inquisitor and us are two girls around my age—early 20s—sprawled across a mattress on the floor. One of them jumps up and takes my free hand.

"Aww, leave her alone, Cookie. Come on, sweetie," she says, her eyes shining. "Come sit with us while the boys take care of business."

I look at Trent for reassurance, and he smiles and shrugs.

"Well, okay…" I say, letting her lead me away as Trent, Cookie, and a couple other guys cross the room and begin speaking in hushed tones.

Once situated on the bed, the two girls begin firing questions at me in quick succession.

"My name is Buffy; this is Sara. What was your name again?"

"You escaped?? For real? That is *so* awesome! I'd never be able to do that; I'd be too scared! Are you and Trent, like, together now? Where are you from?"

I smile at their exuberance and start to relax, nodding here and there, but I can barely keep up with who is asking what, much less answer any of their questions.

Then, one of them asks, "Do you do crystal?"

Suddenly the room is deathly silent, and all eyes are on me. The fear, which started to abate, sprouts back thicker as I look around at the unfamiliar faces.

I shift positions on the mattress, and bite my lip. "I used to, but it's been a while."

This seems to be the right answer. The tension is broken. Trent smiles brazenly and walks back to my side, holding something I can't quite make out.

"Mmhmm. That's right. And we're gonna show her how we do it in the big time, aren't we, girls?"

They smile and clap and bounce up and down with enthusiasm. Trent reaches for my hand, the object he is holding glinting in the light. "You trust me, right?"

I nod and slowly place my hand in his.

"Good girl. Now hold still. This will only hurt for a minute."

***

Days pass by in fits and starts. Before I know it, a month—or maybe two—are gone in a blur. Freeze frame images of needles, people I don't know, and strange places form a jumbled montage in my mind. The shadows are alive again, and that familiar sense of impending doom threatens to swallow me whole. The insidious evil I left behind years ago has lingered—and flourished—in the darkness.

Unhinged and freefalling into the abyss—the final push being the infamous blend of sleep deprivation and paranoia—I make my way to a payphone outside a bar, in an unfamiliar town, under a huntress moon. I call the only person my overburdened, addled mind can conjure up—my father—beg him to please, please come save me.

Lifetimes have passed since we last spoke. There has been zero contact since the adoption—over a year-and-a-half now—but he comes with no hesitation. Doesn't judge, just finds me, and brings me home.

***

I sleep straight through the next week, rousing long enough to swallow a few bites of food every couple of days, then I am out cold once again.

When I finally wake, it is to the sound of my mother urging me to get up and pull myself together, telling me I have a visitor. I stumble blearily out of bed, my body still working to rid itself of the weeks-long binge. I trudge into the living room, squinting at the sunshine coming in through the front window.

Who could be here to visit me? No one even knows where I am.

I scan the room, stopping short at the sight of a little boy, not yet 2 years old, clinging to the leg of a man I can't quite place.

"Mom—?" I ask, disconcerted, my voice still thick with sleep.

She steers me toward the guests stationed by the front door. "Look who's here to see you, honey! Aren't you going to say hello?"

I stare intently, racking my brain for the hook of recognition. My eyes keep returning to the shy little boy whose big eyes are peeking around his father's knee, and realization slowly steals over me.

My son. The baby I so gut-wrenchingly left behind in the hospital, let go to give him the life he deserved, the life I knew I never could—a living, breathing piece of my soul walking around outside of my body—standing right there in front of me.

I thought my heart was broken into as many pieces as possible.

I was so wrong.

FORTEPIANO

CHAPTER THIRTY-FOUR

Attempted Escape

ANOTHER SUB-PAR APARTMENT—solo, this time; no kids until I get my act together, my mother says—another waitressing gig. After work, I take residence at the local bar and drink until closing. Most mornings, I am still drunk when my shift starts, so I devise a solution: Between customers, I hit the bathroom and do a couple of lines off the back of the toilet. Just enough to get me through the day.

***

Gabriel Moore is the cook at the pancake house where I work, and he is magnetic. His muscular frame and coffee-with-cream eyes draw me in, but it is his aloofness that holds my attention. The strong silent type. When he speaks—which is rarely—his dialogue is weighty with meaning. It becomes my sole mission to get him to notice me.

And, notice me he does: Our romance blooms quick and bright. He is mysterious, intense, and beautiful, and I fall for him hard. He uses meth, too—was recently released from prison, in fact—and I am captivated by his tough yet gentle persona. Before long, we are inseparable, and there is no time for anything else—jobs, rent, kids—it is all about us; us and the meth.

Gabriel uses needles but refuses to help me use one, saying he won't be responsible for making such a monumental choice for me. I am frustrated; I feel left out. I want to participate fully in Gabe's lifestyle. Be a part of the ritual.

So, I ask Trish, one of Gabriel's closest friends, if she will help me shoot up. She and her boyfriend, Henry, are both also fresh out of prison and at Gabe's place as often as me.

"I don't know, sugah," Trish says in a deep Southern drawl, flipping her short, perfectly coiffed, highlighted hair off her tanned forehead. "Have you ever done it like this before?"

We stand together outside Gabriel's rented room under a mammoth oak tree, its branches swaying in the late-spring breeze. I intercepted her as soon as she arrived and before she could come inside; before Gabe could talk her out of my request.

"Oh, yeah! It's totally fine. I used to do it this way *all* the time. For, like, *years*," I lie. "I'm just not very good at it."

"You have? You promise? 'Cause Momma ain't in the business of getting sweet little things hooked on the needle."

I smile my most innocent smile. "I, like, *totally* promise."

"All right, sugah-pie. I'd rather help you than see you hurt yourself. Come on; let's go in the bathroom where we can have some privacy away from our cackling menfolk."

After nearly an hour of searching and poking and digging for a suitable vein, Trish is as agitated as I am anxious.

She sighs in frustration and drops her hands in her lap. "I don't know, Rachey, honey. I'm not sure we are going to find anything. Your veins are so *tiny*."

Crestfallen, I mumble, "Thanks for trying, anyway."

I follow her back into the main room to rejoin Gabriel and Henry. I flop onto the couch—coming down hard from the small line I snorted hours ago—and watch everyone else with envy. They are all high, high, high.

I fidget with my pen and journal, thinking maybe I'll write for a while, but I can't focus. I sigh and reach for a cigarette as the door opens, and the dealer, Mark, strolls in with a big bag of dope. With his arrival, the atmosphere in the room shifts; the chatter and energy surges.

I sit and watch, half-dejected, half-relieved, I can't join them.

Mark looks up from divvying out hits and catches my eye. "What's wrong, little miss?" he says, tilting his head to the side.

"Well…I don't know how to shoot up by myself, and Trish said my veins are too small…" I trail off, lowering my head.

He chuckles and sits up a little straighter. "Sweetheart, there is *no* vein too small for Uncle Mark to hit. Why don't you let me take a look?"

My palms grow damp at the prospect of success, and I turn toward Gabriel for input. Our eyes lock, and after a moment of silent pleading on my end, he nods.

"All right, man, but be careful with my girl."

Mark grins and stands, motioning to the couch where I am sitting. "Lie down, little miss, and let me show what it's *really* like to get high."

I lie back on the couch and bury my head in the cushions as Mark takes my arm. Before I can tense, there is a twinge. My breath catches, and on reflex, I turn to see the source of the sting.

Bullseye: The translucent, amber liquid in the barrel of the syringe blossoms with a flower of my blood; it churns languidly, then shrinks as Mark pushes in the plunger. The mixture slams through me like a locomotive—I cough before he hits the halfway point—my breath taken away in a deluge of adrenaline and ecstasy, and then the world goes black.

CHAPTER THIRTY-FIVE

Down the Rabbit Hole

WHEN I RESURFACE, it is into a world I never dreamed existed. Every detail stands out in poignant contrast, imbued with a depth of intensity and meaning even my most involved fantasies never concocted. I analyze the room and gasp in wonder. It is as if I vibrated to a higher plane of existence, and the answer to every question ever asked is encapsulated in this moment. A sense of rightness—oneness—with the most mundane of ideas permeates my entire being.

Literal, Heaven.

I drink in the phenomenon, glued to the couch as I marvel at each detail. When my eyes alight on Gabriel, a honied wave of fulfillment courses through me; a deep, abiding assurance my every desire is met in our connection.

I zero in on his smile; it ignites the room—the entire world—nothing matters but us.

He positions himself next to me, takes my hand, and breathes comfortingly in my ear. "See, Missy-girl? This is what it's *really* like; magic is all around. This is my world; our world now."

I nod slowly, overcome with awe as I revel in this new-found glory.

"I want to stay here forever," I murmur, huskily.

He smiles and leans in for a kiss. "You haven't even stepped through the door yet! Let's go for a walk."

We go outside and into another universe. I stand in awe of trees that seem to breathe to the beat of my heart and shadows that dance with secret life just outside my view. The air crackles with substance, and every nuance of movement holds meaning; the secrets of the galaxy are ripe for the plucking.

Each step is more fraught with mystery than the last; the slightest movement floods my senses with profound beauty. Gabriel—caught up in a rush himself—smiles, takes my hand, and leads me farther down the path.

No turning back now; I am all-fucking-in.

***

Time slips and stretches through the months which follow. When the high starts to fade, and bleak, blunt reality seeps through the edges of my awareness, my ticket back appears—thick and golden in the barrel of a syringe—its glistening tip carrying with it the promise of continued habitation in Neverland.

Throughout our sojourns into other realms, the necessity of keeping the dope supply plentiful needs to be addressed. There must be a way to stay high without technically breaking the law, Henry says. No one wants to go back to prison, and I certainly don't want to take up residence there myself.

***

"How's my girl?" my father asks during one of his weekly calls from his over-the-road trucking job.

A lightbulb goes off, and with it, the solution to all our woes rises in my mind.

"Good, Daddy," I reply, my voice saccharine sweet. "Things are looking up. Gabriel and I found a place we want to rent. We just need $2,000 to move in, and then everything will fall together! He also found a job but can't start 'til we move closer. If we can figure out how to make it happen, the kids could even come…" I trail off, silently willing him to latch on to my fabrication.

The long-distance connection snaps and hisses. "Well, Daughter, I don't have $2,000 right off-hand, but I *can* send you $500 a week if they'll hold the place for you—"

"Oh, Daddy, that would be great!" I interrupt, the words coming out in a rush. "That's just *perfect*. I'm *sure* they'll hold it for us while we save up!" Beaming with pride at my ingenuity, my eyes lock with Gabriel's in excitement. "I love you, Daddy. You're a lifesaver!"

CHAPTER THIRTY-SIX

The Fabulous Pancake Eating Dog

TIRED OF THE MONOTONY of doing our hits inside, Gabe and I wander through nearby neighborhoods—drugs tucked safely in his pocket—looking for a private spot to get high. Somewhere more sacred—more spiritual—than the bland, cramped space of his one-room apartment.

Tucked in the corner of a run-of-the-mill residential area a few blocks away, we stumble upon an unassuming little park, a secret borough surrounded by towering trees and lush shrubbery encircled by a short pathway.

We step into the park, and in so doing, cross a threshold into another reality. The instant our feet touch the grass, the air changes, the trees become more alive, the sounds sharper, the colors brighter. The occasional passing car sounds muffled and distant, although the road is mere yards away.

To the left is a short incline—just a few steps up—and at the top, a small plateau adorned with a weathered picnic table is situated under a massive, soaring oak.

I squeal and fling my arms around Gabriel, then race up the incline, and climb atop the table. Gabriel follows and shoos me off with an impetuous grin. I stand to the side as he takes off his short-sleeved, plaid shirt and spreads it across the aging gray wood in a gallant gesture to keep my bare legs from getting splinters.

I return his smile, hop back up into a cross-legged position—kicking off my shoes so as not to soil his shirt further—and look up at him expectantly.

He reaches over me to the calculator pocket of his shirt and retrieves the case we use to store our works. His tan, muscular arm grazes mine, and I breathe him in: an intoxicating musky aroma mixed with a hint of Zest soap. As he straightens, he kisses me full on the mouth. My muscles soften, and I am washed away in the touch, the taste, the texture of him.

***

Gabriel finds a vein in his arm with an uncanny smoothness and nonchalance; he coughs as the crystal floods his system, but does not waver in his stance. Rooted to the ground like a majestic pine, he tilts his head back and contemplates the canopy above us.

"Holy shit, Missy. You have to see this!" he says in amazement.

I glance up briefly, hands shaking. I am holding my rig—trying to find a vein without help—yearning to be on the same wavelength as him.

"Um…I want to! Wait for me. I'm trying! Can you maybe please help? I've been doing it this way for a while now, so it's not like you'd be making any decision for me at this point…" I stare at him in hopeful supplication.

At last, he rips his gaze away from the covering of greenery and—pupils pinpointed—smiles. He takes the syringe from my untrained hands and effortlessly finds my vein with the same lackadaisical professionalism he displayed finding his own. Heat rolls through me from the inside out, and the back of my throat tightens—along with my most womanly parts—I cough, fall back on the picnic table, and watch the branches above me twist and broaden in texture and depth as the drug takes hold. What I thought were birds, or maybe butterflies, come together with new meaning; leaves become iridescent wings, branches become pointy little noses. There are fairies in the trees. They are everywhere. And they can see us, too.

Wonderstruck by the transformation above and around us, I lay unmoving: my breath taken not only by the flood of methamphetamine but by the ethereal scene which ensconces us. My rapture increases as Gabriel's talented hands caress my smooth skin, and I respond instinctually—a deep primal well of arousal tapped to overflowing—when I feel his weight upon me, his presence inside me.

We move to a rhythm outside ourselves—in concert with the bend of the wind—the alert eyes of fairies glued to us as they jump and frolic from branch to branch, mirroring our dance of passion and desire.

A swell, a crescendo, and we are spent. The mass of him is a solid force above me, contrasted by the preternatural stares of the fey all around.

We disengage our bodies, and I sit up, straightening my hair and clothes as Gabriel lights us smokes. I reach out distractedly for the cigarette and take a deep drag, still spellbound by the foliage and its previously unseen inhabitants.

"Gabriel, what is even happening?? Like, am I going insane? You see the fairies, too, right?"

I see him nod calmly in my peripheral vision, and I tear my eyes away from the scene before us long enough to search his face for sincerity.

"Yes, I do. Are you surprised, though? I've told you and told you: There is magic all around us, all the time."

"I know, but...*this*! This is beyond anything I've ever *imagined*!!"

A sincere, self-assured smile lights up his Botticelli-like features, and he tucks a strand of my tousled hair behind my ear.

"Look. I will show you something. Do you trust me?"

I nod enthusiastically.

"All right. No matter what happens from this point forward, always remember this: Years from now, when you try to tell yourself this was all your imagination, or we were just high, remember what happens next. Remember, and *know* magic is real."

I adjust my legs slightly and bend forward for a kiss. Gabriel leans in and meets me halfway, placing his hands on either side of my hips to hold his weight. We kiss long and ardently, and then he pushes himself into a standing position, his back to the short path encircling the park.

"Tell me about your favorite pet growing up," he says, with a casual tone unmatched by the intensity in his liquid brown eyes.

"My favorite pet? Uh…we had a dog named Dinky. He was blond, and my mom used to toss him the extra pancakes she'd make on Sunday mornings. He loved pancakes. But why?"

"Just think of him. Picture him in your mind and keep your eyes on me. Let everything else fade away."

I look at him, dubious, then exhale and do as he asks. Dinky died years ago, but I easily call up his image in my mind.

"Okay, now what?"

Some undefinable emotion crosses Gabriel's face, and the air around us seems to bend and waver. Then, from behind me comes a sound like a cork expelled from a champagne bottle on New Year's Eve. The air pressure drops, causing my ears to pop, and Gabriel breaks eye contact to look over my shoulder.

"Like that? Is that what he looked like?"

I turn and see the impossible: a yellow-tan, medium-sized terrier standing underneath the giant tree and wagging his tail happily.

"How in the—Dinky? Is that you?"

The blond dog trots over to me—tongue lolling out in a carefree smile—and I reach down, thunderstruck, to pet his head. He pushes his snout against my hand, then gallops away—down the decline and out of sight—as if he were never there.

I stare after him, my mouth hanging open, my cigarette burnt down to a smoldering filter and cylinder of ash.

Gabriel takes the Marlboro Red from my unsteady hand and puts it out. "Okay, are you ready for what's next?"

"There's more?? How is there *more*? Was that my dog? How was my dog here?? He's dead! What just *happened*??" My voice rises in pitch with each question.

Gabriel smiles and turns my head gently back toward him. "Are you ready?"

I take a deep breath and nod. "Mhmm."

"In a minute, a man wearing gloves is going to come walking up behind me on the path."

I look over his shoulder and to the left. I can see the entire park, including the path.

"What? What do you mean? There's no one here but us. And why would someone be wearing gloves? It's the middle of July!"

"Just trust me, Missy-girl. And keep looking right at me."

The hypnotic weight of his gaze sweeps away all my doubts and questions, and I am engulfed in him, in the moment. The world shimmers briefly, and that muted 'pop' comes again. Out of nowhere, a man in faded blue coveralls and yellow work gloves steps off the path behind him—throwing us a confused, sidelong glance—and strides across the plateau and down the wooden steps.

"Holy fucking shit, dude," I whisper.

Gabriel just smiles all the more, leans over, and kisses me again.

CHAPTER THIRTY-SEVEN

Unbalanced Checks

THE MESSAGE WAITING LIGHT is blinking on the answering machine back at Gabriel's place. His brother is moving and needs some muscle. Henry and Trish are gone, leaving us to our own devices for the first time in a while.

"How much is left of the money your dad sent, Missy-girl?"

Still overwhelmed by the day's events, I sit dumbly on the floor, not comprehending the question for several moments. My body is numb and tingly, my once soaring euphoria is crashing down around me, and despair and insecurity are swallowing me whole.

Coming down is the fucking worst.

"Missy? Did you hear me? How much is left? We need to get some more shit before we go over to my brother's."

I finally register the question and manage to pull the neon-plastic, zippered wallet out of my purse and empty its contents on the beige carpeting. "Uh…looks like maybe $40 and some change?"

Gabriel's face darkens in a mixture of anxiety and concern. "Man, that's not nearly enough. We've got to figure something out."

Just then, the phone rings. Gabriel picks up the receiver and offers a gruff hello. After a brief pause, his face brightens. I can hear Henry's voice faintly.

"Yeah, man. Fuck. I'm so glad you called. We are running low on funds—only forty bucks left—and we need a plan."

My enthusiasm ticks up, despite the internal downward spiral as the drugs leave my system. Henry will know what to do; Henry always has a plan.

I watch Gabriel intently as the phone call progresses, catching a word and phrase here and there: "…have Rachel…" and "…her dad…" and "…be back soon…."

"Yeah, all right. I'll talk to her," Gabriel replies, smiling, as he hangs up the phone and sits on the couch facing my spot on the floor.

"Henry and Trish say you should hit your dad up for more funds, and we can get another quarter ounce. That should last us the next few days; for sure enough to get us through moving my brother."

I shake my head firmly, rejecting the idea.

"No way, Gabriel. Like, my dad has already sent over $2,000; I'm not going to get more out of him without him being suspicious!"

Outside the open window, a car door slams, then another. Henry and Trish are back.

Frustration sweeps across Gabriel's face, but he nods in agreement as the door opens, and the other two members of our quartet file in.

"That plan isn't going to work, Henry," Gabriel begins.

Henry looks at me thoughtfully, then sits on the couch. "Okay. All right. I understand. But we have to figure *something* out. Forty bucks just isn't going to cut it for all four of us."

"What's all this now?" Trish asks, with her take-charge aura, as she takes a seat next to Henry. "I thought it was all settled, and Rachey was going to talk to her daddy again."

I shake my head again, emphatically.

"No, that's not going to work this time," Gabriel repeats, ending that vein of conversation.

Henry looks from Trish to Gabriel, and back to Trish again, and lets out a heavy sigh.

"Looks like we are about out of options. We'll have to procure some checks, Trisha Jo."

"Checks?" I ask, perplexed. "What do you mean?"

Trish smiles, leans over, and pats my hand. "Don't you worry, sugah. Momma's got it handled. Ain't nothing you need to worry your pretty little head about."

The conversation between the three of them deepens, and I sit on the floor, fiddling with the change and meager dollar bill offerings I acquired from the depths of my purse. As the discussion continues, so does my miserable plunge from the heights of my last hit.

Depression intensifies in equal measure with despair, and at last, I can take it no longer.

I need another hit, and I need it now.

"You guys; *I* have an idea."

The room goes silent, and I lift my head to see all eyes on me.

"You need checks? Like, from a legit bank account, right? That's what you're saying?"

They look at each other, amused, and Trish again takes the lead. "Yes, sugah; that's right. You pick up on things pretty quick, don'tcha?"

I shrug and blush. "Maybe yes, maybe no, but either way: I *do* know where my mom keeps her checkbook."

CHAPTER THIRTY-EIGHT

Helping Hand

IT'S DARK. WAY PAST LATE o'clock actually, and sleep hasn't been on the agenda for so many days and nights I've stopped trying to keep track. We are in my father's dented and peeling, but still sturdy, '69 Ford F-150 pickup with the wide hips and stick shift on the column. Gabriel is driving, as per usual, and my head and shoulders are hanging out the passenger side window, my face turned toward the heavens, trying to catch the stars moving out of their assigned places. They do this if you stare kind of off-center—never look at them directly—kind of like I imagined my dolls and stuffed animals did when I left the room as a small child.

I'm somewhere in between a disconnected, etheric ecstasy and a gnawing, morbid desolation—we both are—awake for a seeming eternity, driving aimlessly in the borrowed, too long now, vehicle. Gabriel's rented room, unpaid and therefore no longer the ollie-ollie-oxen-free landing pad it once was. Henry and Trish MIA: off chasing a bag, or who knows, really. The reams of money we'd scored, mostly from my—at first—unsuspecting parents, also a distant memory.

"Let's find some woods, Gabriel." My words catch both on the roll-tide of my wildly vacillating emotions and the wind whipping around outside of the truck as it shimmies and shakes, gathering speed, down some dark county road. "Find some woods, park the truck, and mix up the last of what we've got. Just do all of it. Do a big fat hit and go to the other world where the fairies are!" I slide back into the truck and turn to face him.

"Two steps ahead of you, Missy-girl," he says, his voice thick with emotion. He takes his strong hand off the wheel long enough to reach across the torn bench seat, brush my hair to one side, and give me a longing look.

The truck creaks and groans as Gabriel turns off the poorly lit main road and onto a barely detectible pathway into a park. The entrance is wide open: the chain intended to keep vehicles out after hours, conspicuously missing from the eyehooks set in roughhewn posts on either side of the deserted blacktop road. A multitude of deciduous trees and other plant life—dark and lush in the silvery moonlight—surround us. The lampposts bordering the winding lane are off for the night; the carved wooden sign—visible in the soft, lunar glow—reads:

TOLMIE STATE PARK
WELCOME

And a few yards in:

PARK HOURS
8:00 AM – DUSK
VEHICLES PARKED
AFTER CLOSING
HOURS WILL BE
IMPOUNDED

Gabriel gives me that achingly gorgeous smile of his, and I mirror the sentiment.

"How's this for woods, girly?"

I light a cigarette and roll my window down as we meander slowly down the path, deeper into the park. Looking, looking, looking for a spot to pull off and get high, for anyone else who might have the same idea, for an overzealous security guard with something to prove.

The smell of saltwater and moonflowers is on the breeze, and I shiver in anticipation: This is it. This is the perfect spot. I can feel the magic all around, seeping through the edges and borders of things. Begging to break through—to be seen, felt, embraced—just waiting for us to do a hit big enough to tear the curtain between worlds.

I turn the volume up to its limit on the tape deck in the dash of the truck. Even more perfection: My favorite song—"Jimmy" by Tool— is playing; it's another sign.

After circling the entire park to ensure we are alone, Gabriel finds a discreet little turnoff to park between the upper and lower lots. Tucked away on this cul-de-sac to nowhere is one, still-working orange streetlight which directs just enough light into the cab of the truck to see.

I watch, eyes gleaming and mouth salivating, as Gabriel skillfully shakes the last of the translucent crystals into the cap of an old Diet Pepsi bottle fished off the floorboard of the truck. He takes our last needle—used only once or twice—from a hardback sunglasses case tucked in the visor, pulls the plunger out with his teeth, and uses the back end to crush the shards into a fine powder.

Reassembling the syringe, he draws the dregs of the warm, flat soda from the bottle and squirts it onto the small mountain of white. As it liquifies and bubbles, he takes my lit cigarette, tears off a piece of the cellulose fiber butt with his teeth, and spits it into the brew. Pressing the needle into the now soaked cigarette filter, he draws the mixture up, filling the rig to capacity.

With his usual unaffected coolness, he slams half into one of the pronounced veins on his outstretched arm, coughs, and hands the remainder to me.

I take the rig, my thoughts racing, my teeth clenching. I rearrange myself, my arm in between my crossed legs in a makeshift tourniquet to coerce my hiding, overstretched veins to visibility. I position myself as best as I can, so the feeble light hits my arm.

A faint, could-be vein catches my eye, and I poke; the needle, dull and jagged, takes more pressure than usual to break the skin.

I dig around, positive the vein is close: It *must* be.

I dig, and nothing.

Pull back, and nothing.

Push it in farther; still nothing.

Gabriel is fully engaged with the night outside the confines of the truck cab now; has, in fact, climbed out of the driver side window, and is walking around the front of the truck toward the woods, head back, gawking at the stars, the trees, the world I cannot yet see but want so desperately to join.

In frustration, I pull the needle out, and its fish-hooked end catches on my skin as it releases, sending a rivulet of blood trailing down my bruised arm. I scoot across the seat to the driver's side, where the lone light is positioned right outside the door, and stick my arm out the open window directly under its weak, but hopefully sufficient, beam.

One last try. I force the dulled point into the crook of my arm and pull back on the plunger. There it is: The elusive flower of blood blooms in the barrel of the syringe, and I shriek in victory.

I've got it!

Like the background of a cheap painted set in a high school play, the air underneath the streetlamp splits in two, and a hand reaches out from the void. A pale, slight woman's hand attached to someone or something on the other side of the veil reaches out, rips the rig out of my hand—out of my vein—and disappears back into oblivion. The seam in space-time zips itself up like a lavish designer dress, and I am left mouth agape, hands empty, arm dripping blood on the asphalt with no works, no high, no drugs, anywhere.

CHAPTER THIRTY-NINE

Market Research

WE PULL INTO THE MOTEL sometime after dusk, the truck carriage screeching and moaning as we come to a halt in front of its office. The 'Vacancy' sign casts a sputtering blue glow on the cracked concrete in the ashy, evening light. Gabriel jumps out, leaving the door open while he checks if they accept cash. When he reappears, I can tell by the look on his face, the answer is yes.

The motel—if you can call it that—is a conglomeration of colorless, cobbled together shacks halfway between nowhere and nowhere else. Our room—the last one on the left—abuts the street, and its stuck-open, mildewed, aluminum window looks out on a strip of woodsy overgrowth between the parking lot and the highway.

With arms full, we careen through the door, bowling over one another, attempting to stay out of view of any other overnight guests or management.

I pause once inside and survey the room. "This actually is really great, Gabriel. I could like, totally see us staying here. I could make it super cute and homey."

Gabriel throws me a sidelong glance and laughs despite the air of seriousness emanating from him. "That's quite an imagination you have there, Missy-girl, but remember: We are here for privacy while we set up business. Nothing else."

I glance from his ruggedly handsome face down to a small table where he is organizing our haul: a quarter ounce of dope—more than we've ever had all to ourselves—a triple beam scale, zip-lock baggies no larger than postage stamps.

He's right. It is no time for daydreams: We have work to do.

Raptly, I listen as he lays out the steps to accomplish our goal of independence and self-sufficiency.

"If we are gonna run our own hustle, we need to break this up into smaller chunks, so we can make more on resale. That way, no matter *what's* up with Henry and Trish, we can save enough for a fresh start somewhere else."

As he finishes, I step forward to inspect the cornucopia laid out before us. "But, like, we hafta test the merch first, right? We can't be selling shit to people if we haven't at least *tried* it..."

***

I'm in the woods again. Alone, this time. The needle found its target easily—my pulsing jugular—bypassing the circuitous route and showering my synapses with a firework show of dopamine, adrenaline, and multi-layered sensation.

The light here is green and otherworldly, and I can feel the life teeming around me, the myriad of unseen eyes following my every move. I call for Gabriel,

(*Gabriel, where are you?*)

but it's just me. I crawl and walk and climb over trees draped in breathing moss, through intertwined branches ending in fingers, toward the impossible clip-clop of hooves just out of sight. It's been days, years it seems, and the road never reappears. How is there so much flora and fauna to traverse in this sliver of land between the motel and the freeway? It keeps growing and expanding the deeper I go.

The moonlight shining through the trees creates strange, angular shadows and illuminates entire villages: a network of miniature houses, bridges, tiny flickering tiki lights. I stumble to a halt, ogling the scene.

A slight breeze moves clouds across the moon, and the vision dispels; I am surrounded again by dead, fallen limbs and hollow stumps. I shake my head, trying to regain a sense of equilibrium, and at last, hear Gabriel calling my name and see the outline of the ramshackle motel a few yards away.

CHAPTER FORTY

Bullshit Story

"THIS IS *BULLSHIT*. All the dope is gone—all of it! We need to collect from that punk dealer or get another goddamned front. We are never going to make it out of town if we have nothing to sell!" Gabriel paces the room as he talks, his face a chaotic display of emotion.

I stand swaying with a thousand-yard stare on my face: detached from the sane and rational reality of conversations and concepts, of trucks and motel rooms, of Gabriel and me. I spin higher and higher until I am floating—watching a pathetic cut-out copy of myself, scratched and bleeding from the underbrush, hair littered with twigs and brambles, glasses lost somewhere in the woods.

Yeah, that makes sense. Of course, we've gotta collect; what other option is there? The dope must *have been bad...there wasn't even enough to sell!*

We've done all the dope—one hit, and then two—and now we are left with my father's rickety old—likely reported stolen—truck, a passel of empty baggies, and a mounting sense of doom.

I straighten my spine and gather as much of my wits as I can muster.

"You're right; we didn't make a dime off this bunk-ass front; there was barely enough for us to get high! Let's get the dealer's address and take care of things. He needs to make this right. He needs to pay."

***

We sit together in tense silence as Gabriel navigates side streets and back roads. The sun is just peeking over the horizon, and there isn't another vehicle for miles. The dealer's address lies between us on the seat, scribbled on the back of a torn piece of junk mail—along with a full bottle of prescription meds—given to help me come down.

'Take one or two, Rach; no more. These are hella intense,' our information benefactor imparted with an air of warning.

The house isn't hard to find, and before long, Gabriel eases the old Ford into a secluded parking lot, backs into a spot facing the exit, and shuts off the engine. We look at one another gravely as the truck ticks and cools in the early morning fog. Gabriel takes off his overshirt; the fitted, white jersey underneath clings to his finely carved physique. I search the cab for something to make myself appear more menacing and squeal in delight when I spot a rusty, grease-covered crowbar tucked behind the seat.

"Keep it hidden up your sleeve, Missy. And don't show it unless you intend to fucking use it."

I nod, a small smile at the corners of my lips, the fine hairs on my skin raised.

I can't believe we are going to fucking do this!

A cursory knock and a well-placed kick from Gabriel handles the heavy lifting, and we are inside. Gabe assumes an all-business stance: legs wide, cracking his prodigious knuckles, and I take my place slightly behind and to the right of him, mirroring his energy, the heft of the crowbar tucked neatly up the arm of my long-sleeved denim shirt.

"Where's Frankie? We are here to collect," Gabriel demands.

The interior is dark; heavy, lined drapes cover the windows. The electric sizzle of anticipation pulsates in the air; in me. When my eyes fully acclimate to the low light, though, my breath catches, and I grab Gabriel's arm. A baby, just barely walking and clad only in a sagging diaper, is waddling across the room. Her mother is curled in the fetal position on the couch, trembling in fright. Her faded, pink terrycloth robe is open in the front and shows no clothing underneath. Through a doorway off to the right—passed out on a waterbed in only his tighty-whiteys—is the dealer who fronted us.

"Gabe, there's a baby here!" I whisper through my teeth, the nails of my free hand digging into his bare flesh. "I'm not going to do this in front of a baby!"

Gabriel nods and changes course without missing a beat. He juts his chin toward the open bedroom door. "Is that Frankie in there? Go find out where he got the shit, and we'll deal with them directly."

***

This time, there is no answer when we knock, and no need to kick anything in, either. The supplier's house is unlocked, and no one is home.

The inside is unremarkable: a small living room and kitchen beyond. I take the front room, throwing couch cushions on the floor and shuffling around magazines and tissue boxes. Gabriel barrels through the kitchen, ripping open cabinet doors and scouring through piles of mail: both of us, searching for the stash of dope which must be hidden somewhere. Finding nothing, I investigate the flat for another space to ransack, and my eyes land on a door at the end of a short hall, this one closed and padlocked: Bingo.

"Hey, Gabriel, come here! I think I might've found what we are looking for!"

I step over the pillows and lamps I threw on the floor and make it to the door first. I am attempting to wedge the crowbar into its frame when he joins me.

Gabriel leans over and kisses me on the neck, then takes over my ineffective efforts. He pries the lock effortlessly, and the door swings open. I step in first and pull out a nightstand drawer while Gabriel searches the stand on the other side of the bed.

I grab a molded plastic box hidden under some paperwork. "Oo!! There's a diamond *ring* in here!"

Gabriel swiftly crosses the bed and leans over my shoulder to examine my find. "Nah. That's not real; see how big the stone is? That's a knock off, for sure. Keep looking."

My fantasy of a proper engagement dashed, I set the box down, sigh deeply, and turn my attention toward the closet instead. It is slightly open, the door stuck on its tracks. I rifle dejectedly through the clothes, hoping to find something to take my mind off the ring.

"Missy, what are you doing over there? Going shopping? Look for the *dope*, girl, or at least something we can sell!"

I flip my hair and sigh. "*Fiiine*."

I reach up to the shelf above the clothes and take the lid off a shoebox. An unfamiliar, unexpected shape meets my searching fingertips: cold, angular, and metallic. From my awkward vantage point, I struggle to grip its foreign edges but finally catch hold and pull down my find for examination.

A gun.

It's a gun.

I am holding a gun, pointed squarely at Gabriel, with my finger naturally cradling the trigger.

"Um. Uh, Gabriel?"

Still consumed in his search, he glances up absently. Seeing what is in my shaking hands, he launches over the bed, grabs my wrist, and swings the barrel away.

"Holy fuck, girl. You did it; you fucking did it! This is even *better* than finding the stash; we've hit the motherload! All our problems are over."

***

Back in the truck, mid-day now. Gabe is going on-and-on about how we are set, how it's all coming together, how finding the gun fixes everything.

"We'll just use it as an intimidation factor; use it to get some quick funds, re-up another big bag of shit, and hit the road. We'll be home free in no time; you'll see, Missy-girl."

"I have a really bad feeling about all this, Gabe," I say, after a long pause. "Like, really, *really* bad."

Gabriel gives me a stern, sidelong glance and keeps driving, his teeth grinding in determination.

"Gabriel, like, seriously…I just—"

The engine revs, and he swings the steering wheel violently to the left, the opposite direction we are going. His stern expression turns to rage; I've never seen him like this before.

The pavement turns to dirt, turns to gravel, turns to nothing at all. We are in the middle of a valley, near the embankment of a river, entirely off-road. The truck comes to a shuddering halt, and Gabriel—still stone silent—slams the gearshift into park, leans over me, and pushes open the passenger door.

"You don't wanna do this? You wanna be a little girl, and not be taken seriously? You wanna be a joke to the shot callers? Get out, then. Get out and be done."

I look from him to the open door and back again, then throw myself at him, clutching his arm for dear life. "No, Gabe, no! I didn't mean it! I love you; I want to be with you! I just have a bad feeling, and—"

He shakes me off, callously, and continues. "No. That's it. I mean it. If you jinx us again by saying that shit, we are done here."

He turns away—ignoring my pleas and desperate apologies—and crosses his bronzed, muscular arms over his broad chest. As he stares out the driver's side window, his eyes flutter and his head jerks, and after a few tense moments, he nods out entirely.

What just happened? Did he break up with me? Did I just ruin everything with my stupid feelings?

Bereft, empty, and abandoned, I whimper quietly. My desires become tears—liquid and glistening—at the corners of my eyes. The sound of the breeze through the tall grass mingles harmoniously with his soft snores, and I am utterly alone.

It doesn't matter anymore; I've pushed it too far, and now he's mad. There's no coming back from this—nothing I can do to fix it. I may as well make it easy for him; take myself out of the equation for good. He'd be better off without me, anyway.

I cannot catch my breath. Tears cascade down my face as I pick up the orange bottle on the seat next to me. I read the label: Seroquel 200mg tablets. A full bottle, too.

One handful, two.

Gulp.

Then, wait.

I sit back and watch out the dirt-smeared windshield, waiting for something to happen, waiting for an end to this wretched, unbearable agony.

The trees begin to lose their definition, and the grass seems to reach and call for me. My thoughts become wobbly and incoherent, but somehow, I manage to lean over and close the still open passenger door so I won't fall out onto the ground.

The door slamming shut rouses Gabe, and he jolts awake, stretches, and shakes his head. "All right, Missy-girl. I guess a little nap was all I needed. Sorry about being such a dick earlier; we both just need to be on board with the plan—

"Missy? Hey, what the fuck?"

He shakes me, then, and my head rolls and lolls, my eyes unfocused and distant. I can feel drool on my chin, but try as I might, I cannot coordinate my arms to wipe it off.

"What did you *do*? What did you fucking *do*?!"

He clears the seat between us of the empty pill bottle and other paraphernalia and shoves two of his massive fingers down my throat. I gag and wretch and cry as a stream of bile and half-dissolved caplets splatter on my legs and the dirty floorboard.

He pushes his fingers farther down, ensuring it is all expelled; I sputter and dry heave, my face and limbs covered in vomit and tears.

"Why?? Why would you do that?? What the fuck am I supposed to do if you check out and leave me alone?"

"I'm s-s-sorry," I choke out between sobs. "I thought you d-didn't w-want me anymore!"

"Don't be dumb. Of course, I want you. I can't do any of this without you." He fishes a half cigarette from the ashtray, lights it, and hands it to me. "Here, take a drag and wipe off your face. We have work to do."

CHAPTER FORTY-ONE

Nine One One

DARK, NOW. A FEW DAYS LATER. The truck is a distant memory, left abandoned on the side of some road after our attempts at replacing the deteriorating timing belt with fishing line failed spectacularly. The car we 'borrowed' is much fancier; even has a built-in CD-player.

Not that we have any CDs to play, or dope, or even cigarettes for that matter. We've been bone dry on all forms of sustenance for ages despite the proclamations of the gun—the gun we quickly realized was only an airsoft pistol after all—being the answer to all our problems. The impending sense of doom has not lifted, only intensified, but I have curtailed my attempts to make myself heard on that subject.

Gas, too. Gas is a problem, as the swanky digital gauge on the dashboard is repeatedly underscoring with it's angry, red flashes.

"Gabriel, what're we gonna do? We hafta get gas somehow. We can't just keep driving forever on magic and the power of our own will."

He looks from the gas gauge—the readout tracking how many miles are left in the tank now showing only single digits—to me, pats my leg, and smiles.

"All right, girly. There's a 7-Eleven up ahead. You ready to do this?"

"Uh, do what, exactly? We don't have any cash, and gas-and-go is dangerous. There are cameras everywhere these days."

He doesn't respond; just coasts the car from the fast lane to the offramp and nods toward the center console: the console which holds the gun and not much else.

"Umm, like, what the fuck are you saying, Gabriel? You're gonna rob a store??"

He maneuvers smoothly into the 7-Eleven parking lot—and foregoing a designated parking space—positions the car parallel to its garishly lit, glass storefront and turns off the engine.

"No, *I'm* not going to rob anything. *You* are."

I search his face for the punchline. The ocean of dread I've been treading now threatens to drown me, its waves and swells shot through with torrents of crimson rage.

"Me?? What are you talking about?"

He turns to face me head on. "I just got out of the joint for a burg, so if *I* did it, I'd go back—probably for years—and you'd be all alone. You're a *preschool* teacher; even if you *did* get caught, you'd barely get a slap on the wrist."

I glower at him, my rage turning to fury, my fingernails digging into the faux leather of my shoulder bag. "Yeah, but if I get caught, *you're* in the car. You're driving. Wouldn't it be the same thing; you going away for years, except *I'd* be locked up, too?"

"Nope, all you'd have to do is tell them you were holding me against my will, and they'd have to let me go. Then, I could just bail you out, and it'd all be behind us." He pulls the pistol from its hiding place and continues enthusiastically. Behind him, his animated gesturing has garnered the clerk's attention. "Anyway, none of that's gonna happen. The gun's not even real, remember? It'll be easy as pie; no one's gonna get hurt. You'll be in and out, and we'll be long gone before anyone knows anything."

My fury is without borders, now. "Gimme the fuckin' gun and stop waving it around in front of the window like an idiot before someone sees what you are holding." I swipe the pistol from his hand, stuff it blindly into my purse, and jump out of the car before he can respond.

Easy as pie, huh? Nothing's gonna happen? I'm holding you against your will? Have you seen *the size of you compared to me? Don't fucking listen to me, then; I'll show you.*

I stomp through the double doors and into the glaring fluorescent light of the store, furious and indignant, barely glancing at the shelves full of candy bars, soda pop, and cigarettes. The only occupant is the clerk who is standing behind the register. I position myself directly in front of him, pull the gun out of my purse, and point it at his chest, keeping my eyes averted.

"Put the money in the bag, mister."

A moment, two, but no response.

"What the fuck, dude? Can you not hear?" I look up to determine the problem. The clerk is so enthralled by the sight of my tits pushing against my tight, knit top he hasn't realized there is a gun aimed at him.

Fuck this guy. Fuck all fucking guys. It's a good goddamned thing this gun isn't real.

I slam the barrel of the gun on the counter like a judge's gavel, trying to get his attention. "Hello?? This is a robbery, yo! Put the money in the fucking *bag*."

Finally, understanding comes, and with a gaping fish mouth and bulging eyes, he fills my bag with cash from the drawer. I run back to the car, jump in, and slam the passenger side door, gun still in hand.

Gabriel shakes his head and sighs. "Did you at least swipe a pack of smokes before you chickened out and ran?"

With my free hand, I pull wads of cash out of my purse and let it rain on my lap. "Chicken out? Does this look like chickening out to you? Drive the fucking car, Gabriel. Drive!"

***

Screeching tires fishtail on the freeway onramp, the road still wet from the typical PNW rain. The speedometer climbs—45, 60, 85MPH—and we zip past a black-and-white sedan with a light bar on its roof, a blur in midnight darkness.

"Was that a fucking, cop? Did we just pass a fucking *cop*!? Slow down!"

Gabriel pushes the gas pedal down farther; streams of water shoot out from under the tires as we merge onto the highway.

"It's fine; it's fine. Cops probably haven't even gotten the call yet. And, if they did, they're on their way to the store. They wouldn't know what car to be looking for. I can't believe you actually did it, Missy-girl! Holy shit!! You are way more badass than I thought. How much did we get?"

I drop the gun on the floorboard and pick up as many of the crumpled tens and twenties as I can see in the dark. "Uh, looks like around $264, I think."

"Woohoo! That's my girl! Did you get any smokes while you were in there?"

I look at him, deadpan and unamused. "No, Gabriel, it wasn't exactly at the top of my mind to ask for a pack of Marlboro Reds while clearing out the cash register at gunpoint."

Through the rear windshield, I see a car move over two lanes and get behind us. "Umm, I think that *was* a cop back there, and I'm pretty sure he is following us."

Gabriel looks in the rearview mirror and slows the vehicle down to a respectable 60MPH.

A loud 'whoop' cuts through the night, and flashing lights flood the interior of the car.

"Okay, okay, it's fine. We'll just take the next exit and lose them."

***

The next exit is a frontage road that paces the highway—a straight shot—all out in the open with no turns, no curves, no cover. Not that it matters. By the time we realize we are out of gas, we are surrounded: cops, cars, bullhorns, whirring helicopters.

I am on the ground, spread-eagled and soaked by the shallow, muddy puddles gathering in the potholes; face scraped from pressing it into the blacktop, guns—real ones—pointed at me.

I squint with one eye, my vision occluded by the steel-toed boot of the officer pressing the barrel of an AR-15 into my temple, and I start laughing and can't stop.

See? I fucking told *you this was a bad idea. Maybe next time you'll listen.*

CHAPTER FORTY-TWO

The Lady & The Tiger

STRIP SEARCH; CAN'T SEE MUCH through the battered pair of someone else's glasses I found in the glovebox of our ineffective getaway car: only shapes, and colors, and the blatant anger from the guard. Turn right, turn left, show your tattoos, camera flash. Women's pod. It's damp and gray and echoes. I climb into the only free bunk—a top one in the corner—and fall immediately asleep.

Days pass. I am woken at regular intervals by different girls to get my tray at mealtimes. I move like a zombie through the chow line, pass off my meal to the first outstretched hand, then back to bed, back to sleep.

Someone shakes me awake, again; this time asks why I'm there.

"I robbed a convenience store at gunpoint," I say, groggy and nowhere near awake.

"Oh, no, baby! You're gonna get 20 years!!"

I roll away, face the cold cement wall, and cry and cry and cry until—at last—I slip back into the blessed escape of slumber.

Day three, six, eighteen? The coma-esque sleep of detoxing behind me, I doze fitfully in and out of consciousness in the artificial daylight of the shared living space.

I hear the clunk of the exterior pod door opening: another new girl. Then, an unmistakable Southern drawl reaches my ears. Trish. Trish is here. I am no longer alone!

I launch out of my bunk, fly across the pod, and nearly knock her over in my enthusiasm.

"Momma!"

"What happened, baby girl? How'd you end up in here? And where is Gabriel in all this? I *told* him to take care of you!!"

I tell her—all of it—especially the part about me holding Gabe against his will. Trish says if I say that in court, they'll never let me out. I'm terrified of the repercussions if I don't.

Sentencing day. The prosecution has offered me a deal: Robbery 2 and 16 months with 50-percent off for good time. I'll likely be sent straight to work release from county jail, and back home with the kids in 6 months. All I must do is acknowledge Gabriel was aware of the crime. Not even that he was complicit, my attorney says. Just that he knew.

I ask my attorney if I can read a letter to the judge. A letter explaining it was all me, all my idea, no one else was culpable. She reviews it, shakes her head sadly, and says, "As your attorney, I strongly advise you *not* to read this, but I cannot stop you. It's your hearing, and you have the right to speak.

"On a completely separate note, you should have gone to school for law; I've never read anything quite so compelling."

The courtroom is daunting: all antique woodwork; high, coffered ceilings; and the judge in his full regalia. He stares down at me from his towering bench—stares at the creased paper on which the letter I've just read is written—bores holes in me with his penetrating gaze.

"Are you sure this is the story you want to stick with, young lady? You do realize you are admitting to a strikable offense, and it's within my rights to sentence you to 50 years?"

A wave of nausea washes over me; I swallow hard, sway on my knees—my vision goes black at the corners—and I stick to my story.

The gavel bangs down—the sound reverberates through both the courtroom and my entire being—and the judge unceremoniously sentences me to 31 months of incarceration on a Robbery 1 charge. Straight to prison—

until my 27th birthday—with the caveat that sentencing will be revisited if I choose to read my letter at Gabriel's hearing.

As the court bailiff escorts me away in shackles, I see my parents sitting a few rows back in the galley. My mother's head is down, and she is weeping softly; my father shakes his head and sighs. "Oh, Daughter; you've really done it this time."

Back in the women's pod, I am retelling the afternoon's events to Trish and the rest of the girls. I have their full attention; the unit is as still and silent as a chapel, paradoxically peppered through with the occasional 'holy shit.' The commiserating is interrupted by a garbled, crackling call over the loudspeaker.

"Carter to legal visiting."

I look around, perplexed. *What could it be now?*

I stand, wipe away my tears, and the girls converge on me with hugs.

A guard escorts me to a room marked 'Legal Visits Only.' I sit in the small, glass enclosure and pick up the telephone handset on the wall. A man I've never seen before is on the other side of the reinforced window. He picks up his receiver and introduces himself as Gabriel Moore's attorney. Mr. Moore's hearing is tomorrow at 2 p.m., he says. The attorney is holding a copy of the letter I read earlier; he'd like me to sign it and read it to Mr. Moore's judge.

"Do you—do you have the transcript from my court hearing? Like, do you—does *Gabe*—know everything that was said?" I ask, slowly and deliberately.

He nods brusquely and fastidiously taps his pile of papers to align their edges.

I don't say anything for a long moment. "I have a message for 'Mr. Moore;' can you give it to him for me, please?"

"I am sure that could be arranged," he replies, leaning in and sitting up straighter.

"Great. Thank you. The message is actually for both of you: Kindly go fuck yourselves."

CHAPTER FORTY-THREE

Property Of

ON AN ICY OCTOBER DAY—the sky gray, and a damp fog cloaking the tops of the criminal justice center buildings—Trish and I are escorted through back hallways, service elevators, and out sally port doors to a waiting van. We are shackled hand and foot: bound together with the other women joining us on this predawn sojourn.

All are dressed in matching jumpsuits with 'Property of D.O.C.'—Department of Corrections—emblazoned on the back of our thin shirts: no coats and no socks. The heat blowing from the dash vent does not reach us through the hard-plastic bars and plexiglass cage cordoning us off from the two officers and their weapons, and my teeth chatter involuntarily.

The mood is subdued as we back away from the county jail; I watch as the courthouse grows smaller and smaller until we turn onto the freeway where there is nothing but farmland and fields for miles.

I sit back and adjust myself as best as I can, trying to find a comfortable position for the trip ahead. The cold metal of the shackles on my bare ankles sends a shiver up my spine, and I scoot closer to Trish, leaning my head on her shoulder.

The officer in the passenger seat notices the movement. He turns abruptly in his chair, and bangs on the safety divider with his Billy-club.

"Inmate, disperse! There'll be none of that! *No touching!* You there, in the middle! Move over into your own space, pronto!"

I start at the unexpected aggression and sit up straight, creating a clear distance between Trish and me. She gives me a half-smile and shrugs.

"It's okay, sugah," she says in a hushed tone. "It's a whole new environment, and there's a lot to learn. But Momma's been to prison before, remember? You just stick with me and follow my lead. Don't make any ruckus with the guards; do whatever they say, no matter what it is. And, as for everyone else, I'll make sure they know I claim you—that you're Momma's girl—and you won't have a thing to worry about. Promise."

With that, she winks, turns her attention out the window, and we spend the rest of the journey appropriately spaced and in silence.

***

The receiving unit at the women's prison is a blur of khaki uniforms, steel toilets with no seats, and droning orientation after orientation. During my first few days, my unit is escorted to a small chapel the next building over. A nondenominational Chaplain passes out forms and dull golf pencils and begins to extol the virtues of following a spiritual path while incarcerated. The mimeographed sheet has space for our name, D.O.C. number, and religious affiliation. I read through the list, deliberating, my pencil hovering above the options, as the group leader drones on in the background.

The girl sitting next to me elbows me and whispers: "Aren't you the chick who's always interpreting everyone's dreams, or whatever? You should choose Wiccan as your religious preference. That one lets you go out to the yard to meditate and stuff when everybody else hasta stay inside. There's also, like, a whole catalog of neat stuff you can order from that no one else gets to have."

"Wiccan? You mean, like, witchcraft? They let you do that here?"

"Sure, they do! Freedom of religion is the one thing they can't take away from us, no matter how bad they want to."

"Holy shit. Thanks! Seriously, that is so cool!" I eagerly mark the small box next to 'Wiccan' and pass my completed form to the right to be collected.

This is great! Even if I don't *get assigned to the same unit as Trish, I'll be around people who think and feel like I do.*

Once the forms are collected, the Chaplain addresses the group. "All right, everyone, let's find out who else is in our community; can I get a show of hands of those who marked 'Christian' as their religion?"

Most of the girls in the room—sixty or so—raise their hands.

"Good, good, and 'Buddhist'?"

Another ten hands shoot up.

"And 'Muslim'?"

Twenty or so hands this time.

The Chaplain rifles through the stack of papers, and then with a quizzical look on her face, says, "Oh, I see we have some Wiccans here today? Could you raise your hand if you marked 'Wiccan' on your form?"

I shoot up my arm and inspect the room for the rest of my tribe. No other hand is raised—not even the girl beside me—and all eyes are on me.

The room breaks out in snickers and murmurings. A couple of girls throw glares my way and spit nasty curses under their breath.

"Now, now, ladies. Let's all turn to the front," the Chaplain says with a forced smile. Her eyes land on me briefly, then skip away. "And, I'm sure you'll find more of your kind once you get settled in your permanent housing unit," she manages, half-heartedly.

CHAPTER FORTY-FOUR

You are SO Licking My

THE PERMANENT HOUSING UNITS are like summer camp compared to receiving and county jail: private toilet stalls, keys to our rooms, our own clothes. Trish and I are assigned to the same unit, but I rarely see her as her old job takes her back immediately upon her return. We only cross paths on smoke breaks and the strict five minute movement periods designated for travel from one structured activity to the next. Without Trish to commiserate with, I spend much of my time forlornly awaiting my own job or school assignment, or for a kindred spirit to materialize from the ether.

***

After a lunch of indistinguishable meat products and other grayish-green slop disguised as a meal, I sit at one of the molded, six seat table and chair combos scattered throughout the pod, elbows on the chipped metal top, chin balanced on my palms, surveying the unit dejectedly.

A group of women come in gabbing and laughing playfully: the last wave of kitchen workers cleaning up after lunch. One of them—an older woman I've seen around—sees me sitting alone and drops down in the seat next to me.

"How are you adjusting, sweetheart? You seem a little lost."

I sigh deeply and shrug. "I don't know. Like, I thought there'd be more people my age to hang out with. Everybody here is so much older, and already has a group of friends."

She pats my hand stealthily, scanning the dayroom to ensure a guard isn't watching. "You're right; there aren't many youngsters in this unit. Most of us have a lot of time to do; some of us aren't ever leaving. Not many your age get assigned here."

I sigh again, my shoulders falling in disappointment.

"Hold on a minute before you give up hope! There may not be *many*, but that doesn't mean *none*."

I lift my head and look back at her, intrigued.

"See there across the pod? The one in the striped shirt going into her room? She's been here a hot minute, and still has a way to go on her sentence, I think. She's in your age range. You should go introduce yourself."

I follow her pointed finger and see a girl I somehow missed—short and pleasingly plump with long espresso ringlets—she flips her hair to one side as she leans over to unlock her door.

"Oh, thank you!" I say, jumping up and walking as quickly as I can without drawing the attention of the dayroom patrol. I need to catch her before she gets inside her room and off-limits.

"Hey! Hey, hi: What's your name?" I nervously call just as she is stepping through her doorway.

She jumps, startled by my unexpected introduction, turns to face me, and smiles a smile that reaches the bluest eyes I have ever seen.

"Oh, hey! You're the new girl, right? Carter, isn't it? I'm Davis. Elizabeth Davis, but you can call me Lizzie."

***

After dinner smoke break; it's already dark out this time of year. Everyone huddles together on the small, uncovered concrete slab trying in vain to shield ourselves from the sideways, sleeting rain. The few slated, wooden benches are empty; no one wants to sit in the puddles and soak themselves further.

I shudder and pull my oversized state-issue coat close to my slight frame; I still haven't fully regained the weight I lost when my daily regime consisted of meth and Diet Pepsi. I pull a yellow packet of Top Tobacco from my inside pocket, and with an ice-cold, trembling hand, grab one of the thin rolling papers glued to the outside of the pouch. It sticks to my fingers and is immediately soaked and useless. I sigh and shake it off. I search the group of freezing, chattering women for a friendly face, and my eyes lock with Lizzie's.

"Oh, hey! It's you again," she calls out boisterously as she pushes through the crowd and heads in my direction. "How goes it, girl?"

I sigh again, and flick another useless rolling paper to the ground. "Not great. I want a cigarette so fucking bad, but I have no idea how to make these damn things work. Regular packs are hella expensive on commissary."

"Yeah. No shit. No one here buys regular smokes. That's a luxury we just can't swing. Not if we want to afford to wash our asses." She lets out a braying laugh, throwing her head back, her whole body shaking with delight.

I smile faintly, not entirely taken by the dark humor of our reality. Her eyes are gleaming as she collects herself and reaches for my damp, meager pouch of tobacco.

"I can show you a trick if you want."

My smile turns genuine, and I hand her the pouch.

She pulls her arms out of her sleeves, keeping her hands inside her open coat to shield her movements from the rain. She takes a rolling paper, pinches a bit of the tobacco from inside the pouch, and places it into a valley she creates in the paper.

"The trick is to keep your thumbs still as you roll; see? Like, this." In one quick gesture, a perfectly formed cigarette appears. Lizzie holds it out and smiles.

"And voila! Now we smoke!" Another one of those whole-body laughs takes over, and this time, I laugh right along with her.

***

Yard time is scheduled after smoke break, and Lizzie and I stay outside. We don't even notice when everyone goes back in out of the hammering rain. Thoroughly drenched from head to toe, we talk and talk, eventually sitting cross-legged facing one another on the benches.

"How long have you been here? How much more time do you have? What do you miss most?" I shoot questions at her in a machine-gun staccato, wanting to know everything all at once, so grateful to have finally found a friend.

"Well, I've been here just over a year, and I still have almost eight to go. And what do I miss? Fucking. Dudes. Dick."

More laughter from both of us; the guard on duty glares, displeased by both our interaction and the weather.

"There are ways to handle things here, of course, but it's not the *saaame*."

"What do you mean? Like, *masturbate*?"

She grins. "I mean, you can get your pussy licked here anytime you want, and it's usually *way* better than any guy could do, but it doesn't compare to actual dick."

My jaw drops at her bluntness, and she throws her head back again with uninhibited glee.

"Your face!! It's too much!" She chokes out between snorts and giggles. "For real, though, girl; chicks do at least *that* part better. You know when you've got some dude between your legs, and you're dancing and moving your hips *trying* to direct him to your clit, and he is *still* nowhere near the Holy Grail?"

She hovers over the bench, demonstrating with body movements as she talks, gyrating and circling her hips while she straddles the wet wood.

I lean forward, palms on either side of my face, and laugh harder. "Oh my God, yesss!! That's the *worst*! Like, dude, you are *so* licking my thigh!"

We collapse into a sopping wet pile—both of us in hysterics, now—and the guard steps forward.

"Carter! Davis! That is enough; back inside! Yard time is over!"

We stand, but despite our valiant attempts at restraint, cannot control our laughter. The aggravated guard tersely orders us to our respective cells for the remainder of the night.

It doesn't bother me in the slightest.

CHAPTER FORTY-FIVE

Outside In

"CARTER TO VISITING. Carter to visiting."

The overhead speakers sputter and snap, but my name is clear enough.

"My kids are here!" I squeal to no one in particular, jumping up from my seat and clapping. I glance around the dayroom in excitement and receive several dour expressions for my trouble, with most of the women pointedly avoiding my gaze. Puzzled, I turn to Lizzie, who is sitting next to me, working on crafts.

"I'm glad you're happy, and even more glad you get to see your babies, but maybe tone it down a bit, girlfriend. Not very many people around here get visits, especially with their kids. No need to rub salt in their wounds."

"Oh," I reply, a bit more subdued. "I hadn't even thought of that. Yeah, that super sucks. I'll try to be more considerate."

I grab my coat off the seat and head to the podium in the middle of the unit, where the guard on duty keeps watch, to get a pass to the visiting area. I attempt to cloak my enthusiasm, but I am practically floating with joy, and I get a few more dirty looks as I leave.

The visiting area is on the other side of the prison complex, and running is prohibited. I speed-walk as fast as I dare, my long legs kicking up spray from the puddles on the cracked pavement. The murky water seeps in through the holes on the bottom of my used New Balance tennis shoes and waterlogs my dingy athletic socks, but I don't care; I am going to see my kids!

As I reach the locked metal door outside of visiting, I catch a glimpse of Nicholas's fair hair through the sweeping wall of windows encasing the family room. I hop up and down in elation as the guard unlocks the door and swings it open.

She holds her hand out impatiently for my pass, and I hand it over and flash my badge so she can verify my identity. "My kids are here; I haven't seen them in months!" I say, my words running together.

She looks from me to my badge with contempt, then ushers me to a frigid, windowless room to the left of the visiting area.

"Haven't seen them in months, huh? Aren't you 'Mother of the Year?' Now, strip, and be quick about it. I've got better things to do with my day."

Crestfallen, and trying to hold back tears, I take off my damp and muddy clothes, one article at a time. After roughly searching each item, the guard tosses my meager wardrobe into a pile on the floor, and I am left standing stark naked and shivering in the middle of the room.

"Arms out, let me see your hands. Okay, open your mouth and stick out your tongue. Flip your hair over, and show me behind your ears. Lift your breasts; both of them. Turn and show me the bottoms of your feet. Squat and cough; now bend over and spread your cheeks. Cough again. Get dressed, Inmate."

The door clanks shut behind me, and I gather my cast-off clothes from the floor—and cradling my items to my chest—cry, despite my best efforts at remaining in control.

After a moment, I shake my head, take a ragged breath, and wipe the angry tears from my cheeks.

I'll be damned if I waste another minute of visiting crying over her. My kids are here, and that's all that fucking matters.

***

Nicholas is a snuggly bug—all warm, chubby rolls; strawberry-blond hair; and pouty lips—glued to my lap from the moment the guard allows me into the room. Audrey is more reserved: limpid brown eyes wary and watchful, mouth pursed shut, only slightly nodding when I direct a question or comment her way. Aged 4 and 6, respectively, they have both experienced heartbreak and disappointment beyond measure.

"Why won't she talk to me? What have you been telling her?" I throw out spitefully at my mother, who sits across the wobbly laminate table, my face drawn up into a whiny pout.

My mother sighs in exhaustion and exasperation and opens her arms to Audrey. Audrey flings herself into her embrace, tears welling in the corners of her eyes, her chin quivering.

"Rachel Kay; don't you be mean to your daughter. I haven't been telling her *anything*. But what do you expect? She's not stupid, either."

Audrey buries her face in my mother's shoulder, her whole body shaking as she tries to stifle her sobs.

"Whatever," I reply harshly, tossing my head and adjusting Nick into a more comfortable position on my lap. "The least she could do is give me a hug and say hi."

Storm clouds rumble across my mother's face, and her thin lips disappear into a jagged line. She averts her eyes and pulls Audrey closer.

I roll my eyes and let out an annoyed sigh. "Fine, then. Nicholas, do you want to pick a book for Momma to read?"

Before he can respond, the visiting door opens, and Trish comes in. Thrilled, I straighten in my seat; Trish has never met my kids!

"Trish! Hi! I didn't know you were going to be in visiting today! These are my kids, Audrey and Nicholas!"

Trish's eyes flash in alarm, and she vehemently shakes her head. Before I can process her reaction, the guard has crossed the room and is leaning over the table inches from my face.

A lupine smile—all glistening teeth and sadistic humor—splits the expanse of her pasty, moon-shaped face, and with obvious relish, she spits out, "Consorting with other inmates is not permitted, Carter. There will be no socializing with *anyone* other than your approved guests, or your visit will be over."

Nicholas goes rigid, and his snuggle turns to a death grip. "No leave, Momma! No leave, Momma!"

"And control your child, or the visit will end, regardless."

I stare at her levelly, my heart pounding through my chest, sure my vision of knocking her sideways through the plate glass window is etched on my face.

She holds my icy gaze briefly, but her stony expression falters, and she straightens in manufactured control and crosses the room back to her post.

Both kids are inconsolable now, and Trish watches sadly from her table.

"It's okay, Nicky-bear. Hush, hush. Momma is still here. Momma is still here."

I reach out half-heartedly to Audrey and attempt to comfort her. She tenses, shrugs my hand off her shoulder, and burrows closer to my mother.

The children's cries are rising to hysterics, and nothing I try soothes them. I attempt to peel myself out of Nick's suction-cup-death-grip, but he only clings tighter. I look desperately for something to distract them—a way to get the visit back on track—and see the vending machines at the back of the room.

"Hey, guys, wanna go with Momma to get a snack? Maybe Grandma will even let you get a soda to share? Right, Grandma?"

My mother drills holes in me with her eyes. Pop and sweets are strictly forbidden. At the mention of a snack, though, the children's shrieks and sobs turn into hitching attempts at catching their breath.

"Nicky have pop, Gamma?" Nicholas says between hiccups, lifting his head off my chest to face her.

Audrey steps out of my mother's embrace, wipes her eyes, and sniffles. She turns her tear-streaked, swollen face toward her brother.

"Nick and I could share one; right, Nicky?" she says in a maternal voice, reaching out to stroke his hair.

Nick bobs his head in the affirmative—one final tear trailing down his fat, baby cheeks—and my mother acquiesces.

"I suppose so considering the circumstances. But only one. And, how do we use the damn things, anyway? Do you go? Do I?" she asks tightly, gesturing toward the row of machines.

Trish, easily overhearing our tense exchange, speaks loudly to her visitor. "I think I'll go on over to the vending machines and get me a Coke. You just give me some change, and wait here, sugah."

I sigh in profound relief at the unsolicited directions and offer a Rosary-esque thank you litany that I don't need to ask the guard for help.

My mother digs out a handful of change. I succeed in disentangling from Nick with the promise of an orange soda for him and Audrey to share, and make my way over to stand in line behind Trish.

"You're a lifesaver," I mouth discreetly.

She smiles and whispers, "Wait for me when visiting is over. Momma'll have something to cheer you right up, baby girl."

And with a wink and toss of her head, she makes her way back to her seat.

CHAPTER FORTY-SIX

Care Package & Color Crayons

WALKING BACK TO OUR UNIT after visiting, Trish passes me a small, cellophane-wrapped package. Instinctively, I look down and get a jab in the ribs.

"Don't look now, Rachey," she says, still staring forward and walking briskly. "Tuck it away in your bra 'til you get safely back to your room."

"But—but what is it? And won't they find it when they search me?"

She shakes her head briefly, a smile turning up at the corners of her mouth.

"They already strip-searched you twice today, didn't they? The most you'll get is a cursory pat goin' back inta the unit. You're good as gold. And don't you worry no-nevermind about what it is or what it isn't. Like Momma promised, I'll take care of my girl, and that's just what I'm doing."

I clasp my fist around the small, crinkly bundle, reach under my shirt as if to scratch an itch, then tuck it between the crease of my breasts and the worn-out band of my Department of Corrections sports bra.

"Good girl," Trish says, never breaking her stride. "Now be safe, and be smart, and Momma'll see you later."

***

Back in my room—alone now, my roommate is out socializing—I sit at the one-piece, metal desk-chair combo anchored to the cinderblock wall. Trish was right about the lack of attention I'd receive upon returning from visiting; the guard didn't so much as look up when I walked back into the pod.

The cell's overhead light is off, but the fading daylight—distilled through both the overcast sky and narrow triple pane window—illuminates the room enough for me to see the contents of the package I pulled from my sweaty cleavage. My breath is quick and shallow as I analyze the gift, willing it to be both real and unreal in equal measure.

It's crystal.

Meth.

There is a bag of meth sitting in front of me.

I stare at the wrinkled cellophane, my emotions fluctuating wildly between rapture and repugnancy, the familiar pungent aroma of ammonia fills my nostrils.

What do I do? What do I do? This is the shit that got me here in the first-fucking-place.

But I've followed the rules the whole time I've been here, and what good has that *done? I still get treated like shit.*

Fuck it. What does it matter if I do something to keep my mind off this shithole place and these shithole guards; something to take away the pain of being away from my kids. This is a blessing! *A* miracle, *even!*

And honestly, even if I did *get caught, what're they gonna do? Throw me in prison??*

My mind is made up before the thought is complete; I rip the baggie open; dump its contents on the surface of the desk; and form two fat, wobbly lines with the edge of my D.O.C. identification badge. I scan the room for something to take the place of a straw or dollar bill, and my eyes settle on a color crayon drawing from Nicholas. I roll it into a crude cylinder; lean over the white, powdery lines; and inhale them: one up each nostril.

I sit up and throw my head back as the familiar warmth courses through my brain and ripples down the rest of my body. I snort a couple of times—clearing my nose and ensuring everything is sufficiently consumed—then wipe the top of the desk and stick the empty plastic back into the band of my bra.

After flushing the evidence in the shared bathroom at the end of the corridor, I make my way to the table in the dayroom where Lizzie is still sitting.

"How was visiting? How was it seeing your babies?"

I only stare and sway in my seat, my head buzzing, my skin a roiling pyre of bliss.

When I don't respond, she glances up inquisitively, her expression growing grave as she registers my condition. She sighs and rubs her hand across her nostrils, indicating I should do the same.

Anxiety-ridden, my eyes shoot around the room—sure I am caught, and the goon squad is coming to take me down—as I roughly wipe my nose. No one is coming, though; the room and its inhabitants are business as usual.

"I'm sorry," I say, meekly, struggling to form the words.

"Maybe you should go to your room for the rest of the night instead of hanging out here in the open, you know?"

Unable to hold eye contact, I hang my head in shame.

As I stand to leave, she reaches across the table and takes my hand. "I love you all the time, no matter what."

CHAPTER FORTY-SEVEN

Teacher's Pet

DAYS TURN INTO WEEKS turn into months, with the same routine: Work, Lizzie, visiting, meth, repeat.

We have opposite schedules, though. Lizzie works graveyard as a janitor in the medical clinic; my job assignment is a plush one. Trish pulled some strings and got me an office position with business hours. After my shift is over, I wait on the drainage grate in the middle of the yard: the spot Lizzie and I have claimed as our own.

***

"Guess what?" Lizzie chirps as she comes bounding up behind me.

I look up, raise my hand to shield my eyes from the sun, then drop it as she steps in front of its glare. "Oh, hey! You slept in today. Where've you been? Did you work late or something?"

"Ooo, girlfriend, not only did I work late, it was sooo totally worth it! You'll never believe what I got last night!!"

"What do you mean? What did you get?"

She looks from side-to-side, plops down cross-legged opposite me, and leans in.

"I got my pussy licked!!!" she says, then howls with laughter.

I scowl and pull away. "You did? Who by?"

She clucks her tongue and raises an eyebrow. "Girl, you made it clear as fuck you were *not* interested in a romantic relationship with me, so there's no reason to give me that look."

Right. Yeah. I did *say that. Isn't the whole point of prison to get on the right path? Do things correctly? It* is *the Department of Corrections, after all. If I'm ever going to get the kids back and make good choices, I have to start somewhere.*

I huff and straighten my back. "Yeah, yeah. I know. Sorry. Please continue. I thought you worked alone in the clinic at night, though. How would that even work?"

She gives me a sideways smile, her eyes twinkling. "I'm the only *inmate* who works there overnight, girlfriend."

I gasp. "Ohhh, fuck. You mean?"

"I do indeed. Officer Wood. And giiirl, I'll tell you what; he worshipped me like the Goddess I am. I was squealing for *hours*."

"Oh, shit. I can't even with you!"

We both throw our heads back pealing with laughter, and several women walking the perimeter of the yard turn our direction.

"Shhh, before we have an audience, here, Rach," Lizzie says as she works to compose herself.

"I'm *trying*!! Oh my gosh, this is just too much!" I exclaim, holding my sides.

As we regulate ourselves down to the occasional snort and giggle, the gears in my head begin to tick.

"But, really though, listen, Lizzie: With Officer Wood's attention all wrapped up in the wonder that is your vagina, you'll be able to get away with just about *anything*. Including maybe, getting into the sharps container, and retrieving a needle for extracurricular activities?"

Lizzie's mirth fades, and her expression turns dubious. "I don't know, Rachel. That's a pretty big ask; I could get into a lot of trouble."

"I doubt it, girl. Even if you *did* get caught—which you won't 'cause you've got him by the literal balls at this point—he can't rightly say anything without getting himself in a bind. It's perfect, don't you see?"

I stare at her intently, willing her resolve to waver, and after a moment, it does.

"Yeah, all right. I'll see what I can do. I suppose if I'm finally going to do some shit with you, we may as well do it up all the way."

I sit up straighter—a half-smile turning up the corner of my mouth—my eyes twinkling. "Oh, goody! It's all settled, then. And it's about *time* you partook with me! I'll talk to Trish to make sure there's enough for all of us. She'll be *sure* to share with a rig in the picture."

***

During evening smoke break a few days later, Lizzie approaches Trish and me, and with a contrived casualness, shows us the contents of her pocket: a brand new 28-gauge syringe nestled in a wad of scratchy, recycled paper towels. Trish nods once and walks away.

"I think I'm going to get ready for bed," Trish says, in an overly loud, sing-song voice.

Lizzie and I lock eyes, and taking Trish's cue, make our way back into the unit. Most people are smoking their last cigarette of the day or getting settled in their rooms for the night. Trish, several yards in front of us, goes into the shared bathroom on the second floor, and we follow, each taking an adjacent stall and locking the doors behind us.

"Okay, Rachey," Trish whispers from my left. "Be a good girl, and pass Momma some toilet paper."

Down and to the right, Lizzie's hand pops under the divider holding the now-folded brown paper towel from her pocket. "Here you go, Rach. I have some extra."

With great care, I grip the contents of Lizzie's hand and pass it to Trish. I can hear the telltale sounds of cellophane crinkling as I await my turn.

After several moments I hear a cough and see Trish's hand under the divider again.

I take the bundle—careful not to let it drop onto the perpetually damp floor—and open the creased wrapping. Trish has filled the syringe with a dense, yellowish liquid to the 90cc mark.

"Make sure you share with your little friend, Rachey. Half for each of you."

I inhale, swallow hard, and wedge my arm between my crossed legs to coax my veins to the surface.

I can do this; I can do this. Just breathe, envision the vein, and poke.

I exhale and glide the needle into the crook of my arm, stunned as my blood swirls languorously in the tawny brew. I push the plunger to the 40cc mark, cough, and drop the rig on the ground, falling back against the damp cement wall.

"Rach?"

"Rachey? You okay?"

I hear them both but cannot do anything other than hold myself on the toilet seat.

Lizzie's hand shoots under the locked door, grabs the rig, and disappears. I hear Trish's footsteps heading down the stairs, and her admonition to Lizzie to make sure I get to bed all right. Then, Lizzie is under the door again—this time, her whole upper body—her pupils pinpoints, and her jaw locked. She slides in, reaches up to unlock my door, and then turns and seizes my shoulders.

"You're okay, girlfriend; you're okay. Breathe your breath and follow my lead. We are going to stand up, walk down the stairs, and you're going to your room for the night, got it?"

I bob my head and ask earnestly, "Did you get yours, though?"

"I did, but let's not worry about that now. Stick to the plan, all right? Follow me."

I rise like a fawn on newly created legs and mimic her steps, avoiding eye contact with everyone we pass—and somehow—make it to my room without incident.

At the door, I turn and grab her hand. "Thank you, Lizzie."

"You're welcome. We can talk about it later; just go to bed. Maybe keep yourself occupied by watching out the window for those fairies you told me about."

CHAPTER FORTY-EIGHT

Cease Movement

LIZZIE'S GUARD MAKES NO secret of their involvement; he seeks out our little coterie in the yard often to brag of their plans to run away together, regain custody of Lizzie's daughter, and raise her as a new little family. The fact his wife is the visiting room guard never seems to faze him nor tone down his boisterous proclamations.

That he is wrapped around Lizzie's little finger is putting it mildly. Anything we want, she only need ask, and it's ours: new Tarot decks for Lizzie, our friend Addison Brown, and me; cheeseburgers snuck in from McDonald's; fresh peaches—unheard of on our barebones kitchen menu, and all juicy deliciousness in the middle of the summer of love—whatever we desire, we get.

During the day, while Lizzie sleeps, Addison and I set up shop in the yard, trading tarot readings for Top Ramen noodles, coveted French vanilla coffee creamer, and Little Debbie Honey Buns, building a virtually guaranteed revenue stream from the contraband cards.

***

During an afternoon tarot session, the guard on duty, Officer Paul, steps between Addison and me, ordering the line of girls waiting for readings to disband.

"Carter, Brown; come with me."

I shoot Addison a rattled, side-eyed glance, sure someone has snitched about our cards. We stand, grab our respective decks, sweep the grass off our uniform-gray sweatpants, and follow him to a corner of the yard; to an area marked 'Out of Bounds.'

Officer Paul turns toward us and leers, a smirk on his face. "Inmate Davis was taken to Ad-Seg this morning; do you care to comment?"

Ad-Seg.

As in Administrative Segregation.

Otherwise known as The Hole.

No fucking good, man.

Addison and I look at one another, stunned and uneasy, then back at Officer Paul.

"Nooo," I reply, feigning innocence. "Why would *we* have anything to say about it? I didn't even know she was *in* The Hole!"

His features contort into a menacing grimace, and he seems to grow in size and presence, his antagonism unmistakable. "You know exactly *why*, don't you, Inmate? But do you also know Officer Wood and I are neighbors? That we are drinking buddies? That after he gets a couple of beers in him, he tends to spill his guts, so to speak?"

Oh, fuck; oh, fuck.

I look at Addison again; this time, the fear between us is impossible to hide.

"So?" Addison says, sarcastically. "Whatever he may or may not have said, it doesn't have a damn thing to do with us. We aren't the ones getting our pussies licked!!"

"Addison!"

"Well, it's true, Rach, and you know it. There's no reason for *everyone* to go down when we didn't even do anything."

Officer Paul's eyes narrow, and his brash smile cuts through the landscape of his pock-marked, weaselly face. "Is that right? And, if I were to pull your property list, would I find a legitimate receipt for those cards the two of you are waving around the yard like a pack of Gypsies? Having contraband will get you sent straight to Ad-Seg right alongside

Inmate Davis. Do you know what that means? No more cushy housing assignment, no more jobs, and no more visiting privileges."

He crosses his arms and simpers self-righteously. "When Investigator Barrett comes to question you about this so-called "situation" between Davis and Officer Wood, it would behoove you to make clear statements that absolutely nothing untoward occurred."

***

Back in the unit, trying to coordinate a plan, Lizzie's roommate speed walks across the pod and foists a full laundry bag into Addison's arms.

"This is all the stuff that guard gave Lizzie. I don't want it around when they come to toss the room; she's *your* friend, you deal with it."

Addison looks at me wildly, and I shrug helplessly. "I don't know, dude, but we can't just leave it in the dayroom!"

With an exasperated sigh, she gets up and stomps across the pod to her cell, bag in hand.

As soon as the door closes behind her, the loudspeaker crackles on.

"Cease movement! Cease movement!"

I snap my head over my shoulder and see the goon squad in full riot gear, with a sauntering, unaffected Investigator Barrett bringing up the rear.

***

Addison is gone for questioning most of the afternoon. I sit in my cell, nauseous, my thoughts whipping around like a plastic bag in the breeze, looking for a way out of this mess. Right before the dinner call, I catch a glimpse of someone outside the window panel in my cell door: it's Addison.

I jump up and join her as everyone is heading out of the unit for chow. We trail a bit behind, keeping our voices low.

"What happened? How are you back here? What did they say??"

"I told them I found the bag in the laundry room and was going to turn it in but didn't have time. Investigator Barrett didn't believe me for a second, but that's not what they wanted, anyway," Addison says. "They wanted me to write a statement swearing Lizzie made all this up. And they want you to do the same."

I take a step back. "Are you fucking kidding me?? What kind of bullshit is this?"

"I know, right? I told them I wouldn't do anything until you and I had a chance to talk. I couldn't make that call on my own."

I chew on my bottom lip. "Fuck, man. If we say she made it up, won't she get in *more* trouble? And, if we say it really happened, that puts *us* at risk with Officer Paul! I don't fucking know, dude. This is crap. No matter what we do, someone is fucked."

I look up and around. We are in front of the chow hall, now, the last two standing outside. To our right is the visiting room, and posted at the door, is the other Officer Wood: Lizzie's guard's wife.

I turn to Addison and tip my head in the direction of the female Officer Wood. "I mean, like, we could just tell *her* the truth. She deserves to know anyway, right? And maybe if we help her out, she can do something about them threatening us?"

Addison grabs my arm and smiles. "Yes! Perfect. That'll fix everything."

***

A week, two, a month, then another. Investigator Barrett visits daily in The Hole—the only visitor I am allowed any longer—each time with the same rehearsed rhetoric: "Falsely accusing staff is a severe matter, Inmate. Until you rescind this unfounded accusation, I can't let you out of here. If you continue to stick to this fantasy, you'll spend the rest of your time down in Administrative Segregation—your good time, too—and your visits will be permanently suspended. So, I ask you again…"

I become incredibly proficient at games of mental chess, returning icy glares, and foreboding nonverbal communication.

Finally, he calls stalemate, takes away sixty days of good time—thus moving my release date out two months—and assigns me to CCU: the maximum-security unit. Twenty-three hours a day on lockdown, office job a distant memory, and effectively separating me from my friends.

Although I eventually regain most of my privileges, I choose to spend the rest of my time quietly disengaged from anything other than thoughts of my children, of home. Each day, ticking off activities one-by-one: chow, smoke break, work detail, chow, bedtime. Counting down each night in my bunk—one-hundred-eighty-nine days, one-hundred-eighty-eight days, one-hundred-eighty-seven days—until, at last, there are no days left to count.

FORTISSIMO

CHAPTER FORTY-NINE

Out & Down

THE SKY OUTSIDE THE PRISON walls is massive; so vast and open, I am sure I will suffocate under the weight of its expanse.

On the way home, my mother stops to get snacks for the kids. The shelves inside the convenience store are filled to the brim with colorful, shiny wares all laid out in the open. I become a small, frightened child, hiding behind my mother, clutching my hands behind my back to ensure no one can accuse me of stealing.

Anyone could take anything!

My eyes jump from the clerk to the few customers pondering their selections.

Doesn't my mom remember I'm banned from 7-Eleven? Like, for life? *Does the clerk know? What if they have a picture of me behind the counter, like in a Post Office, or something? Can the customers tell I just got out of prison?*

I am convinced it is unmistakable, written all over my face. Any moment the truth will become evident, people will see my damage, scream and point and wave, throw me out into the street.

No one takes heed of me, though; not a single one.

***

Back home. The kids are thrilled and find any excuse to be close to me, to sit next to me, to tell me another story.

It is everything I dreamed, and so exhausting.

My brother is visiting in honor of my release. He sits on the couch, watching a Blockbuster rental. "Hey, Sis, the duplex on the other side of mine is for rent. I can put in a good word for you with the landlord if you want?"

My mother steps out of the kitchen, dishtowel in hand. "Jack, what a nice thing to do for your sister!" She turns toward me. "Being right next door to your brother would certainly ease the transition back into day-to-day life for you and the kids. What do you say, Rachel Kay?"

I look up from the DSHS paperwork I am attempting to fill out between sticky hugs and nonstop questions. "Yeah, I mean; that'd be great, I guess, Jack. Thanks."

My mother beams as she turns back to the kitchen to finish putting away the dishes.

My brother smiles. "Cool. All right. I'll let you know what they say."

I force a smile, and a strained thank you, then turn my attention back to the application.

This is all so damn complicated! Why do I have to spend a month going through this WorkFirst program? Why can't I just find a job on my own!

I sigh and drop my pen on the table. "Hey, Brother-dear. I need a cigarette; do you have one you can spare?"

Jack shrugs, hands in the air. "Nah, Sis, I quit ages ago; sorry!"

Fuck. I wish there was someone to talk to. I need a break; this is all so overwhelming; I can't breathe!

I push my chair away from the table and mull it over.

I know! Merrick! I should give him a call and see how he's doing.

***

The number to Merrick's mother's house hasn't changed, and I happen to catch him on one of his infrequent visits home. It is as if no time has passed; we immediately rekindle our romantic relationship.

Jack's landlord rents the other half of the duplex to me, and the kids and I move in a couple of weeks after my release. It comes together without a struggle. A program through the Department of Corrections pays a portion of my rent, and the kids' school is only a couple blocks away. The duplex is charming: a two-bedroom tucked away in a decent part of town. Merrick works within walking distance, and his overnight visits quickly become a permanent living arrangement.

***

The first day of the WorkFirst program is mainly a meet-and-greet. I am seated next to a girl who looks vaguely familiar, but I can't quite place her. I lean forward to see her nametag—Celeste, it reads—and a slew of memories rushes back.

"Oh, hey! You're Celeste Cook, aren't you? You used to hang out at apartment C-204, right? Back when Mario's was still open?"

She twists around in her seat to see my nametag. "Rachel…yeah, I remember you. You were all mixed up in Aleister's death, right?"

I tense and grit my teeth, but keep my poker face. "Well, I'm the only Rachel from back then, so…"

She cocks her head to the side and raises an eyebrow. "I don't care either way, honestly. Nor do I care about this class. You just got out, too, right? What're you doing for lunch? Do you smoke? Wanna smoke a bowl with me?"

I blanch and shake my head. "Like, pot? Blech. I've never liked that stuff. No, thanks."

She laughs scathingly. "No, not pot. Go fast. Like, crystal? I've got a dude right down the road. We'd be back before break is over, and then maybe this droning ass nonsense won't be so much to tolerate."

Smoke? Crystal? Oh, man. I don't know…although…it's not like I'd be shooting up or anything. I've never smoked *it before; it's probably way more chill. And, if I say no, she's going to think I'm a narc or something.*

I pick at the corner of my orientation folder for a minute, then reply, "Uh, sure. As long as it's not pot."

***

That night, I lie next to Merrick, pretending to sleep, mind flying, watching the shadows the evergreen tree outside our bedroom window creates on the ceiling. When the first rays of light blaze across the horizon, I shoot out of bed and cook a full breakfast for Merrick and the kids, shooing them off to school and work, and out of the house.

CHAPTER FIFTY

Hard Knox

I LAND THE FIRST JOB I apply for—waitressing graveyard shift—and Merrick works days, so our paths cross only briefly during the week. Every day around dawn, I call Merrick to say I am working a double shift, then spend the bulk of the day getting high at my buddy, Rusty's house.

Rusty and I went to high school together and have run on the periphery of the same social circle ever since. We bumped into each other, checking in at the D.O.C. office and again not long after at Celeste's house on Puget Street looking to score.

Rusty is a good cat; never makes me feel unsafe or insecure, so he becomes my go-to. He is the middleman for dope sales, which simplifies things for me. No need to meet anyone I don't already know or go anywhere I haven't been. I call him after work—after I spin my story to Merrick, of course—and by the time I show up at his place, he has a quarter gram ready and waiting.

We smoke dope together off burned and crumpled foil through a broken ballpoint pen and talk for hours in his room at the back of the derelict trailer where he runs his operation. No one else is allowed in the back room without permission; although, it's common to hear varied voices and activity from his roommates on the other side of the uninsulated wall. A lesbian couple with brash, grating voices; we usually drown out the sound of their cackling dope-fueled sex parties by blasting Metallica from Rusty's state-issue boombox.

Rusty's phone rings nonstop—typically someone looking to score—but every once and a while, he makes an outbound call. During those conversations, he counsels me into silence.

***

"Listen, homie. I'm gonna buzz Judd Knox, and he ain't keen on anyone bein' around when I call, so you gotta chill with the chatter, at least for a minute, okay?"

I sit up straighter and give him my full attention. "What if I don't wanna 'chill'? What if I want to meet him? Who's Judd, anyway??"

He chuckles. "He's my bro from way back. We did time together in the joint."

"What's he like? Would I like him?"

He shrugs and continues: "He's like…Judd. I don't know: long hair, leather jacket, Trans Am, cocky motherfucker. And like a grip older than us, too: almost 40, I think."

"Ooo! Now I *really* want to meet him!!"

"Uh, probably not a good idea, homie. Judd's pretty big-time. I thought you wanted to keep it where no one knew who you are, anyway?"

I cross my arms and pout. "Hmph. I can take care of myself, Rusty. I want to meet him! At least tell him about me and let him decide for himself."

Rusty smiles and shakes his head as he dials Judd's number. "You're crazy, girl. But it's your life; whatever you say."

He finishes placing the call and holds the receiver to his ear, tipping it slightly in my direction so I can hear both parts of the conversation. "Hey, bro; it's Rusty. I've got someone here who wants to meet you. She's a badass chick I've known for hella long."

A strong, confident voice carries easily through the receiver. "Oh yeah? I love me a badass chick. What's her name? Let me talk to her."

Rusty covers the mouthpiece and takes a deep breath. "You sure about this, homie? This guy is no joke."

I nod enthusiastically and grab the phone out of his hand. "Hey, Judd. How're you? My name's Rachel."

"Well, *hello*, Rachel. So, you heard about 'ole Judd, and just couldn't keep yourself away, huh?" He laughs, and his larger-than-life presence pours through the line—through me—the unadulterated arrogance in his voice is plain.

I giggle coyly. "I think if we meet, *you'll* be the one who can't stay away."

"Is that right? I guess we'll just have to make that happen, won't we?"

I laugh hard and blush, then glance down at Rusty's watch. "Oh, shit. It's getting late. I hafta go before my boyfriend gets home, or I don't know how I'm going to explain where I've been."

"Your boyfriend, huh? Hmmm, something else to take care of, it seems."

My whole body flushes, and I cannot stop grinning. "It was nice to talk to you, Judd; Rusty, will you walk me out to my car?"

"Fo sho, homie. Lemme wrap things up with Judd real quick-like."

Rusty says his goodbyes, promising to call later and arrange a meeting for us, then hangs up the phone. We both stand, and I start for the door. Before I can take a step, Rusty gently takes my shoulder and turns me to face him.

"You know I love hanging out with you all day and everything, homie, but have you thought about maybe buying a bigger bag?"

"Where did this come from all of a sudden? You trying to get rid of me, so I don't have the chance to meet Judd?"

He drops his arm back to his side. "Nah, I did my duty giving you a head's up. You're a big girl; you're gonna do what you want, no matter what I say. I'm just trying to save you some dough. It's a lot cheaper to buy a 'teener or an 8-ball than to keep coming back every day for a quarter."

"Hmm…I don't know. That's a big commitment, and if I bought *that* much, it'd mean I was really using again. This is, like, just to keep me going so I can work graveyard *and* spend time with the kids, ya know?"

Rusty smiles and shrugs. "Whatever you say, homie. I got you either way."

We head down the hall, passing his unsavory housemate's room, which—for one reason or another—has no door on its unfinished frame. Against my better judgment, I glance in and see a teenage girl standing in the middle of the floor flanked on either side by one of Rusty's roommates. One is clenching the girl's outstretched arm with a death grip; the other is repeatedly jabbing its inner crook with a full syringe, dark with what looks like coagulated blood.

"Uh, what the fuck," I say, stepping through the splintered doorframe. "How old are you? What's your name? Do you *want* to be doing that?"

She looks up, all smokey-sable mane and inscrutable eyes, and withdraws her outstretched arm to cradle her midsection in a protective gesture. "I'm Fiona. And, yeah, it's fine. I just don't think they are as good at hitting a vein as they say they are."

I glower at the couple, and they return in kind.

"Who fucking asked you?" one of them says, taking a menacing step in my direction.

I ignore her and continue speaking to Fiona. "Listen, you don't have to do that if you don't want to, and if you need a safe place to be, you just call me, okay? Rusty has my number."

She nods her head in the affirmative, and a faint smile appears. "I think I'm okay for now, but thank you."

I nod back, then turn and follow Rusty outside, and head home.

CHAPTER FIFTY-ONE

Expose

"WHERE THE HELL have you been, Rachel."

I stand next to the driver's side door just outside the carport and stare blankly.

Oh, shit. Merrick's home early.

I steel myself and toss my hair over my shoulders. "At work. Where the fuck else would I be?"

He watches me closely. "The kids and I came by for lunch. Your boss said you hadn't been there since 6 a.m."

"What do you mean 'you and the kids'? Why aren't they at school?"

"They had a half-day, remember? When you didn't show up to get them, the school called me. I figured you were working a double again, and we'd surprise you at work."

I grip my purse and keys tighter, my hands sweating. "Well, where are they now, then?"

He takes a step forward and leans in to search my face. "When we couldn't find you, I didn't want to freak them out, so I called your mom, and she picked them up for the night."

I toss my head again, snort contemptuously, and start for the front door. He takes my arm as I pass him.

"Look at me. Let me see your eyes."

I shake him off defensively. "Don't fucking touch me, Merrick."

His mouth drops open. "Rachel, what the Hell? What is going on?"

"Dude, seriously. Leave me the fuck *alone*." I push past him and sashay into the house. Before I reach the stairwell leading up to the bedrooms, he catches up with me and positions himself in front of the stairs, blocking my path.

"Rachel, I mean it: *Look* at me."

With hands like cashmere sheathed iron, he reaches out and turns my face. I try to avert my gaze but am drawn in by the tears gathering in his velveteen eyes.

"You're high. You're fucking high."

My jaw tightens and I shake my head to dislodge the tender sprouts of compassion and connection taking root in the storm cellar of my heart.

"So. Fucking. What? You're not my dad. I can do whatever I want."

A tear traces a path down his unshaven cheek.

I tense and dig in my heels. "I don't owe you any fucking explanations, Merrick." I shrug him off like a suffocating coat on a mid-August afternoon, straighten my back, and stomp upstairs.

A deafening crash reverberates through the duplex, stopping me in my tracks. I turn and see the phone ripped out of the wall, and amidst the tangle of cords and broken plastic is Merrick: collapsed in a heap, head in hands, sobbing.

"There. You're right: You *can* do whatever you want, but at least now you can't call your connection to get more dope," Merrick says, his melodic voice strained with emotion.

I drop my purse, its contents spilling on the landing, and take the stairs in one giant leap. "You don't get to do that. You don't get to lose your shit and stay. I won't have violence here; get the fuck out! Get *out*. Get the fuck out, right now!"

I shove him as he tries to stand, bewilderment clear on his face, tears streaming.

"No, Rachel! Please, don't do this! I'm sorry! I fucking love you!! You can do whatever you want; please, just let's talk!!"

I push harder, herding him through the entryway and into the carport, then slamming the door and locking the deadbolt. I sink to the floor and brace myself against the cheap, wooden frame—gears in my head tick, tick, ticking—as he pounds and cries for me to please, please let him back inside.

Fuck, fuck, fuck. Now what? I've ruined everything; I can't face him, and I can't fix this.

I stare at the pile of electronics at the bottom of the stairs.

Maybe it still works...

I stand, double-check the lock, and make my way across the room. It isn't that bad, after all. After a few minutes of tinkering—and despite a few scratches—it is operational again, and no worse for the wear.

"Rachel, *please*!" Merrick's incoherent cries are becoming fewer and further between.

I pick up the phone and dial the familiar number from memory.

Ring...ring...rin—

"'Sup?"

"Hey, Rusty. It's me again."

"Homie! What's good? Didn't think I'd hear from you 'til tomorrow."

"Yeah, I know, but things have changed."

The room is deathly still; the pleas and pounding have stopped.

I take a breath and hold it while I consider what to say next. "I'ma go ahead and do like you suggested; can you line up an 8-ball for me? And, get Judd over there, too? I, for *sure,* want to meet him."

"You got it, homie. Whatever you say."

CHAPTER FIFTY-TWO

Not Quite Brick-and-Mortar

JUDD KNOX IS GORGEOUS-FUCKING-PERFECTION—the epitome of hard rock—all long, dark hair; muscle cars; and loud music. He channels Billy Bob Thornton—a severe, quicksilver glint in his haunting, soulful eyes coupled with a slow-burning, knowing smirk—and positively drips with wit, sarcasm, and animal magnetism. It is love at first sight.

***

We sit on the cerulean-blue velour sectional my parents gave me as a housewarming gift when I signed the lease on the duplex, the last of the meth swimming in our veins and crashing through our nervous systems like moon-driven waves. Next to Judd on the plush couch cushion sits a giant serving bowl of half-eaten, soggy, off-brand fruity cereal. He flips through his little black book, systematically calling number after number, hunting for a connect to re-up our stash.

I'm curled up a few inches away, feet tucked beneath me—watching—spellbound by his dynamic swagger. His Levi's 501 jeans cling in all the right places; his bright-white wife-beater t-shirt highlights his olive skin—peppered with homemade tattoos and rope-like veins—and the inflated jail-yard muscles beneath. The room is without ventilation and sweltering hot. I tie my long—now dyed blonde—sweaty strands up and off my neck, and wait for Judd to make the call which will direct the rest of our day.

"*Hello*, my man! This is Judd. Yeah, Judd Knox. Who else? Me and my girl are looking; you holding?" A long pause. A look of consternation flashes across Judd's intense, craggy features, and he begins tapping the little booklet on his thigh. "No, not Jessica. That's over and done with. I got me a new one; she's a firecracker. I'm keeping this one all to myself."

Another pause, longer this time, and I gesture to get his attention. He sees and reaches over to stroke my jean-clad leg, his brazen smile sends shivers down my spine.

Judd listens for another minute or two, then hangs up. He nods to himself, sets the address book next to him, and turns to face me. "Guess it's time to go back into business! No one else seems to be able to keep up with what 'ole Judd Knox can sling in a day."

Another shiver passes through me. "You mean, like, *you're* gonna be the dealer?"

That sideways smile again, this time interrupted by a fiery, sensual kiss. "Yes, indeedy. If you want something done right, you gotta do it yourself, I always say. Put your boots on, girly, I'll meet you in the Trans Am."

***

Like convergent tectonic plates forming Pangea, the landscape changes. We are suddenly the top of the food chain; my house the axis of meth activity for the whole of the town. A team of people in our employ bring our every wish and whim to fruition with the mere wave of a baggie: gas, credit cards, cell phones, even a guy whose sole job is to daily procure new Levi's 501 jeans for Judd because who has time for laundry when you're delivering ounces of dope to all four corners of the county 24/7?

I secure Fiona as a nanny for Audrey and Nick and pay her in meth. With the kids under her supervision, Judd and I can make deliveries without leaving them alone after school. As the only one licensed and insured between us, I drive the car my mother loaned me for the kids' appointments and to get to work—a job I stopped going to weeks ago—so Judd can leave his Trans Am in the carport to work on the engine and update the stereo system.

***

Judd and I return from a drop to see Fiona at the front door, waving her arms over her head in distress. I shut off the car and hurry to her, envisioning vivid scenarios of death and destruction.

"What's wrong? What's going on? Are the kids okay?"

"That's just it," she moans. "I tried to stop them, but I—I didn't know what to do, and the kids wouldn't listen to me!"

"Tried to stop who? What are you talking about, Fiona?"

Judd comes up behind me and hands me a lit cigarette. I take an absentminded drag and give it back.

Fiona's chin quivers, and her shoulders slump in defeat. "Your family, Rach. They took the kids, and your mom is inside, waiting for you with some paperwork. I'm sorry."

CHAPTER FIFTY-THREE

On the Trading Floor

I DROP MY PURSE on the floor by the couch and plop down across from my mother. "What's all this? Where are the kids?" I demand. Judd stands in the opening between the living room and the hall, legs rooted in a warrior stance, hands in his tight jean pockets, ominous look on his face, his faded black leather groaning and creaking across his broad shoulders.

My mother shuffles a pile of papers from one flapping bird-like hand to the other and does her level best to avoid my eyes. "Can you have your *friend* sit down? He's making me uncomfortable standing there."

"First of all, he's not my "friend," he's my *boyfriend*, and secondly, don't worry about him; just tell me what the Hell is going on."

My mother stiffens, still refusing to make eye contact, and after several seconds of silence from her, I cave and nod to Judd, indicating he should take a seat next to me on the couch. In one swift movement, he is there, and I refocus my icepick glare on my mother.

"Well?"

More shuffling and an uneven, heavy sigh: "It's as simple as this, Daughter. You sign Nick and Audrey over to me, and I'll sign the title to the Saturn over to you. The alternative is I report the car as stolen and tell your parole officer you took it without my permission."

I sit back, stunned and speechless. "You mean, give you custody of the kids? Again? Why would I do that? And why would you turn me in for no fucking reason? Are you accusing me of being on drugs? 'Cause I'm fucking *not.*"

She sighs again. "Nobody is accusing you of anything, Rachel Kay. It's apparent you and your *boyfriend* need a vehicle; this is the perfect solution. The kids have only been out of my care for a few months, so it shouldn't be too big a transition for anyone. Of course, you can visit them anytime you want *if* you aren't on drugs. And, since you say you aren't, there shouldn't be any problem."

I turn to Judd and grip his arm in desperation. Internally begging him to have a solution. Silently imploring him to tell me what to say or do to make it all right.

He gives me a grim smile. "Go ahead, girly. Sign the papers. We'll get them back later."

I search his face for reassurance, and he pats my thigh in consolation.

"Promise?"

"Promise."

I turn and take the leaky blue ballpoint pen from my mother, and with shaking hands, sign the documents. My mother signs as well, then hands me the title to her car.

"Can I at least tell them goodbye?"

"I don't think that's a good idea, do you? They are already packed and home with your father, anyway."

My mother stands and morosely gathers the two school bags leaning against the living room wall, then walks out the front door, closing it behind her with a soft 'snick' of finality.

My hardened demeanor crumbles. My chin drops to my chest, and great heaving sobs reverberate from my core. Judd wraps his arm around my shoulders and pulls me to him as I wretch and moan, my insides splintering, my very soul wrenched from me.

A hesitant voice breaks through the din of my misery: "Rach? Are you okay?" Fiona, tense and unsure, stands in the middle of the living room like a jackrabbit in a field of wheat.

"She will be. We are going to fix her right up, aren't we, girly? Fiona, you stay here; get the rest of the kid's stuff cleaned up and out of sight. Rachel, you come with me. My brother is getting out of jail today, and we have a stop to make first. Then, the four of us will do the biggest, fattest hits you can fit into a rig, and you won't even remember this happened."

I sniffle, wipe my face, and look up at Judd through swollen eyes. He takes my chin in his calloused hand and kisses me, eyes twinkling.

"You ready, girly?"

I nod somberly, still sniffling.

"All right, then. Let's go!"

CHAPTER FIFTY-FOUR

Lamentation & Weeping

WE ARE BACK FROM the jail. Judd's brother, Marty—a near carbon copy of Judd, just with lighter hair and less charisma—is with us.

Like a jungle cat in pursuit of its prey, I race to the kids' room, Fiona hot on my tail. Everything has been collected and stacked out of sight in the far corner of the wall-to-wall closet they shared. The room is empty save for the pressboard toddler bed frame which this morning held Nick's mattress and a matching Mickey Mouse sheet and comforter set. I fall to my knees at the sight of it and sob inconsolably.

> *"...a voice is heard...lamentation and bitter weeping, Rachel weeping for her children, refusing to be comforted...because they are no more." (KJV, Jeremiah 31:15)*

Fiona follows me like a lost lamb as I hysterically circle the room gathering the remaining drawings off the walls and clenching them to my chest.

"Oh, Rach, Rach; I am *so* sorry."

I pay her no heed; all I see is the emptiness where my children once were.

A few broken colored pencils are strewn across the variegated brown-and-gray carpeting, and I swipe them up, setting down my children's creations oh-so-carefully. I balance on the edge of Nick's bedframe like a tightrope walker attempting to traverse the Grand Canyon.

I scribble moons and stars and wishes that this reality be a dream; symbols and spells of time travel and different decisions. Of babies back in my arms. I scrutinize the room, willing my intentions to manifest immediately, envisioning the space morphing around me, refilling with stuffed animals, books, and laughter.

There is nothing, though, but Fiona. Fiona, and an otherwise deserted room. I am prostrate, now, lying half across the scribbled, ineffective incantation, half on the floor. Fiona sits next to me, reaches out to rub my back, attempts to wipe my tears. I don't respond, even when Judd's just-off-the-shelf sneakers cross into my field of vision.

"Hey, chicky, why don't you go introduce yourself to my brother. He could use some company after his little vacation," Judd says to Fiona, his tone heavy with sardonic humor. "Leave our girl to me. I'll fix her up, then she'll be fit as a fiddle."

An air of indecision permeates the room as Fiona considers. "Wellllll, I *guess* so. If you're *sure*…"

A cold spot forms where her soothing hand was—forms and spreads—down, down, down to my epicenter. Through puffy, tear-laden eyes and bedraggled hair, I watch Judd cross the room. He opens the closet door and empties his metal locking briefcase onto the only other piece of furniture left behind: a white chest-high bureau wedged into the closet. A quart-sized sandwich bag filled to bursting with white crystalline shards, a glass bowl, a Thanksgiving-esque serving spoon, and a fresh pack of 28-gauge syringes litter the top of the dresser.

I watch—unfocused and unbound—floating somewhere in the ether, attached to myself by an insubstantial balloon string, as he nimbly measures and swirls his potion—the Wizard of Go-Fast—and fills four syringes. He makes his way back to me, kneels, and moves my hair out of my face. His characteristic smirk is contrasted by a flash of tenderness behind his wire-rimmed glasses. He holds the rig in between his teeth, rolls up my sleeve, and finds the sweet spot in one quick motion.

From the next room, I hear gasps, a thump, laughter.

Stirred from my despondent reverie, I tense and grab Judd's arm with my free hand. "Should we go check on them? Make sure Fiona is okay?"

"Marty's just blowing off some steam; I bet she's having a blast."

And with that, the plunger sinks deep, and the whole world goes away.

CHAPTER FIFTY-FIVE

Soliloquy

THERE ARE CAMERAS EVERYWHERE, now: one in the kitchen, one in the hallway at the bend by the stairs, one over the front door surveying the enclosed carport. A 24-hour feed displayed on a silver, 53-inch, CRT television—positioned in the corner of what used to be the kids' bedroom—shows all the activity in and around the duplex. Judd and I took over their room; it is much bigger than the other bedroom, and the window overlooks the road and driveway into the carport. Making it the hub of our operation was a no-brainer.

I lie back against the ruffled lace throw pillows on the queen-sized bed situated across from the closed-circuit feed, my body buzzing and mind racing as the most recent hit saturates my system. I watch the monitor closely as Judd tinkers away under the hood of his Gold Edition Trans Am.

I cannot talk, as per usual: The hits Judd gives not only take my breath away but my voice as well. I close my eyes and try to anchor myself to my surroundings, grasping the satiny sheets in my sweaty palms, in a vain attempt to ground myself.

Snippets of conversation

(and giggling; is that giggling?)

float in through the open window, and my eyes fly open and lock on the monitor. The television, with its sputtering lines over the black-and-white output, shows only Judd working alone on the car. The voices continue, though, clear as day. I grip the sheets harder, and will myself into a sitting position.

Who is here? Who is Judd talking to?

I inspect the feed intently, trying to reconcile what it shows with what I hear. The indistinct voices rise and fall, and black tendrils of foreboding shoot through my mind, raising gooseflesh and standing my hair on end. I grit my teeth and push myself off the bed and cross the room to the window. I sit in its frame, craning my neck to determine what is being said.

"…yeah, we've got her now…"

I am immobilized; the stench from my dripping underarms reaches my flared nostrils.

Is Judd plotting against me?

What is happening*?*

Get a fucking grip, Rachel. This is no good. You're not making any sense.

"…she's a goner…"

I may be in over my head here. Maybe I am doing too much dope. Maybe it's time to think about stopping.

Maniacal laughter—definitely Judd's—reaches my ears and is echoed by the unseen companion. I whip my head back toward the television. Still no change. Judd happily working away on his car, whistling to himself, no one else in sight.

Okay, this isn't actually *happening. And that's a problem.* But*, since I* know *this isn't real, then everything is* fine.

Right? Right.

The real *problem would be if I didn't* realize *this wasn't happening.*

When I can't distinguish between fantasy and reality anymore, then *I will stop.*

Until then, there's nothing to worry about, and everything is fine.

Everything is fine.

CHAPTER FIFTY-SIX

Hairspray & House Cleaning

"RACHEL! LET'S GET A MOVE-ON, girl! It's almost 2 o'clock, and we've gotta check in at D.O.C. before 4 p.m., or we are fucked!"

I scoff and roll my eyes at my reflection in the bathroom mirror. "I'm *coming*! I just hafta finish my makeup. I can't leave with only one eye done!"

I lean in closer and try for the fifth time to match the wing on my right eye with my left. The spray from the running faucet puddles on the edge of the sink and makes a wet spot on my skin-tight, ripped jeans. I push away from the counter in dismay, messing up my eyeliner again in the process.

Fuck. If my hand would just stop shaking, and my damned eyes would focus, this would be a lot easier.

"Rachel!"

"Dude, Judd. I *knowww*."

I turn off the faucet and look around the small bathroom in defeat. The contents of my makeup bag are strewn everywhere, a wet beach towel is crumpled on the floor near the shower, and my curling iron is on high and balancing perilously close to the edge of the draining sink. I stare again at my reflection: my pale, powdered face stares back under the harsh vanity lights hung above the medicine cabinet. My mid-back length hair—still wet—is tied back at the nape of my neck and lacquered with hairspray in an effort to corral my natural texture before taming the front pieces with heat. No way am I going to have time to finish getting ready before the office closes.

I sigh and unplug the curling iron, wet a Q-Tip on my tongue, clean up the black liquid eyeliner around my eye as best as I can, and rush down the stairs.

Both muscle cars are running in the driveway. Judd's Trans Am is a sight to behold. The work he put in over the last couple months paid out in spades. My white, T-top 1986 Camaro rumbles and purrs behind it. Marilyn Manson and Rob Zombie blare respectively from the custom stereo systems Judd installed.

Days after signing over custody to my mother, she rescinded on the agreement and collected the Saturn. Judd's solution was simple: trading a 'teener of dope daily for eleven consecutive days secured my dream car.

"Let's go, girl!"

"You have the shit?"

"Yup. It's in the trunk of the Trans in the lockbox. After we check-in, I'll go re-up, and meet you back here."

I plant a long, sultry kiss on his mouth and throw my purse in the passenger seat of the Camaro. "Well, what're you waiting for?" I smirk, blow him a kiss, rev the 350-block engine, and crank up "Living Dead Girl" all the way to the max.

His eyes flash impudently, and he winks and jumps into the Trans. We pull out of the driveway in unison, backing up and idling our cars like two racers on the Indy 500 track.

Windows down, music blaring, we throttle our gas pedals and grin at each other roguishly. A wink, a nod, and we are off: up the hill, through the residential area, bobbing and weaving like slippery silverfish in a too small pond.

The smell of hot engines and sunshine permeates the air—the speed of the Camaro is only topped by the adrenaline pumping through my veins—as we street race to the probation office for our mandatory drug tests.

***

As I step off the curb and open the driver's side door of my Camaro, I hear footsteps pounding behind me on the sidewalk. I turn to see a man in jeans and a button-up shirt sprinting out of the D.O.C. office.

It's my probation officer, Tom Mitchell, and he is heading directly toward me. A cold sweat envelops me despite the blaring heat of the afternoon sun.

Fuck, I thought they had to send the drug test out to the lab for results. Judd's gonna be so pissed! I'm screwed.

I slide into the driver's seat and slam the door behind me. I stuff my purse—full of syringes and rolls of twenty-and-hundred-dollar bills—under the seat, hoping it will be missed in the impending search, and I can at least avoid another charge added on to the looming probation violation.

He reaches the side of my car as I am sitting up, grasps the edge of the open window, and leans in halfway.

"Hey, Carter, you might wanna head straight home. Do a little house cleaning. Make sure everything is ship-shape if you know what I mean."

He gives me a long, knowing look, and I sneer, offended.

"I'm a lot of things, but a shitty housekeeper isn't one of them, Officer Mitchell," I say, cuttingly, gripping the steering wheel so tight my knuckles lose all color.

He stares at me levelly and says nothing.

As the seconds tick by, I gradually comprehend this is not an arrest, and my grip on the leather-covered wheel loosens. "Yeah, sure. House cleaning. Got it. Are we done here?"

He pauses again, then replies, "I got a joke for you, Carter. Wanna hear it?"

"Uh, I guess. Make it quick, though. I gotta go meet Judd."

"What's the difference between a porcupine and a Trans Am?"

"A porcupine and a—I have no idea."

"The pricks are on the outside of the porcupine."

"Holy shit, Officer," I say, flabbergasted. "That's harsh."

He holds the edge of my car a moment longer, then steps back.

"Really, though, Carter. Don't blow off what I said."

I nod, my adrenaline racing as I turn the key in the ignition and the engine roars to life. He is still looking at me pointedly as I whip the car out of the parking space and back onto the main road.

Whew, that was fucking close. *And, what was he talking about with that 'house cleaning' nonsense? What does that even mean?*

***

A few minutes later, I pull up to the duplex. It is eerily quiet—no movement, no lights—and the driveway is empty. I shut off the engine and stare through the windshield.

Where is everybody? Judd should definitely *be back by now. He was done way before me.*

I get out of the car, stroking its side panel absently as I walk toward the entryway. Once inside, I set my purse and keys on the kitchen table and inspect the room; the unnerving quiet causes the fine hairs on the back of my neck to stand on end. The new phone—attached to the kitchen wall and outfitted with a built-in answering machine function—is silent, and no messages are waiting. Unheard of. Usually, the blinking red number is in the double digits, and trying to catch a break between the relentless ringing is an exercise in futility.

I shiver and nearly jump out of my skin as my black kitten, Akasha, entwines himself between my ankles.

"Geez, kitty. Are you trying to give me a heart attack?" He meows in supplication, and I kneel to stroke his glossy fur. "You hungry? Did everybody leave and forget to feed you?" Another meow: I stand and go to the cupboard to get his food. On the way, I kick off my shoes and slip on my blue house slippers.

With Akasha fed and happily purring, I stand once again and study the empty duplex and silent telephone. Still nothing.

"Well, Akasha-baby, what do you think? I guess I'll check the mail while I wait."

With no response from my feline, I try to shake off the heavy feeling of wrongness in the room, and go out the front door to the mailbox at the end of the drive. Its joints creak as I open it and look inside. I grab a fat handful of bills and circulars. It's been a while since anyone thought to empty the old, leaky box.

I head back toward the house, hands full of water-stained mail; as I turn, I see a vehicle coast up the street and stop perpendicular to the driveway, effectively blocking the exit.

A white car.

With a lightbar across the top.

And Judd in the back seat.

Fuck.

I ditch the mail and run as fast as my slippered feet allow. Run back inside, slam and lock the door, and slide to the floor panting and sweating.

Fuck, fuck, FUCK.

I push myself up to a standing position using the door as leverage and try to cross the dining room and make it up the stairs.

Our bedroom.

I have to clear out our fucking bedroom before it's too late.

I make it about three steps before the door splinters open in its frame, and the house is filled with shouting, warrants, and uniformed officers. At the tail end of the melee is Tom—my probation officer—still in plainclothes, but now outfitted with a bulletproof vest over his chambray shirt, and holding handcuffs.

"That's far enough, Carter. You can stop right there. Hands behind your back; face the wall."

I halt, shoulders slumped, and follow his instructions. As he snaps the handcuffs closed on my bony wrists, Akasha runs out the now destroyed front door.

"Dude, you guys! My cat! Please, don't let him get out. He's just a baby."

Tom sighs and calls out, "Hey, Officer Reynolds! Get Carter's cat back in here and put it in a room with food and water, and close the door."

His colleague gives him a quizzical look, but does as he is directed.

With the handcuffs securely in place, Tom leans in and, in a hushed tone, says: "Your cat is the last thing you should be worried about, Carter. I hope you took my advice and did some house cleaning."

I twist sideways to make eye contact over my shoulder, and comprehension hits me like a meteor colliding with the desert floor.

Clean the house, Rachel. Jesus H. Duh. *He didn't mean dust or vacuum. Clean the fucking house!*

***

We are back at the duplex later that night: Bailed out before we can even be processed out of our street clothes and assigned to our respective units. Bailed out at the full cash amount with a signature and promise to return for our court date. The truck waiting to pick us up is driven by a stranger, likely muscle employed by our connect to keep everyone nicely in line.

As we pile into the front seat, the driver gives us a sly smile and a snarky, "The big boss can't have his cash cows sitting in jail, now can he?"

We are back at the jail first thing the next morning, although neither of us have slept. I prance up to the reception desk—dressed to the hilt in platform suede heels and a skin-tight sparkly silver skirt, fake fur-collared coat, and full face of makeup—with forged documents stating the cash seized in the raid was earned legally through lawn care and babysitting. I pass the papers through the small opening in the glass encasing the officer on duty, then hold out my French tip, press-on-nail-bedazzled hand expectantly. I grin salaciously as he scoffs at the paperwork's legitimacy—but unable to prove it—is forced to count out $2,000 into my outstretched palm.

I wink, a smirk plastered across my face, my pupils fully dilated from the hit I did in the parking lot, and flounce insolently out the glass double doors to join Judd in the Trans Am.

"Got it, babe!" I lean over for an impassioned kiss and reach between his legs for a quick squeeze. "Let's go pay the connect, re-up, and get this show on the road."

"You read my mind, hot stuff," he says, grinning.

He cranks the stereo to full volume, filling the air with the heavy bass riffs of Seether's "Gasoline," and speeds away from the police station.

CHAPTER FIFTY-SEVEN

Target Run & Done

HOLDING COURT IN THE LIVING ROOM engaged in a convoluted, philosophical discussion—the bedroom is off-limits for mixed company when Judd is off handling business—the illegal police scanner crackles in the background. *Aenima* by Tool plays on repeat on the portable CD-player.

Rapid-fire activity begins over the loudspeaker of the scanner, drowning out the instrumental solo of "Stinkfist."

"Head-on collision at the Target off Sleater Kinney Road; 1986 Camaro; stolen plates."

I stop mid-sentence and hush everyone in the room. "Hold up, guys. Listen."

Feedback screeches through the speakers. "Repeat, vehicle crashed into the side of Target department store. Attempting to make contact now."

"Yo, Rach, wasn't Judd doing a deal in the Target parking lot? In the Camaro?" one of the guys asks.

I nod, my heart pounding in my chest.

A crackle, then a bleep.

"Vehicle has collided with store wall a second time. Repeat. Vehicle reversed and drove directly back into the building. Please advise."

I look around the room for reassurance but receive only silent stares in return. "This cannot be happening, can it? That's not Judd; I mean, he *has* been known to sleep-drive, but he wouldn't drive into the side of a building *twice,* would he??"

Bam! Bam! Bam!

The front door.

Someone is at the front door.

"Charlotte! Marissa! Someone! Quick; run upstairs and check the video feed. Tell me who's out there!" I hiss through my teeth. "Everyone else, be fucking quiet."

Charlotte, a frequent flyer and one of my favorite members of the dope circle, jumps into action taking the stairs two at a time. I stand uneasily in the middle of the room, waiting for the all-clear.

The knocking at the front door grows more forceful. "Hold on! I'll be right there!" I call out in my best customer service voice. And, then, quieter, "Charlotte! What do you see?"

"Uh, Rach…it's for sure the cops. There's a sheriff and a cruiser out there," she calls in a strained voice from the landing.

Fucking great.

More pounding, louder now.

What do I do? What do I do? They know *someone is here. And that's a brand-new door; I don't wanna hafta explain why we need* another *new one to the landlord.*

Shit, okay.

"I'll be right there, Officer!"

I cross the short distance to the door and open it, leaving the chain lock engaged. A uniformed officer stands on the stoop, a displeased look on his face.

"Ms. Carter? Rachel Carter?"

I purse my lips and shake my head. "Nuh-uh. Nope. Definitely not. That's not me."

"Right, okay. You care to explain how you knew there was an officer at your door before you opened it?"

I tilt my chin and affect a doe-eyed look of innocence. "I don't know *what* you mean! How can I help you?"

He grunts and pulls a folded sheet of paper from the day planner he is holding. "I need your signature here, Ms.—what was it?"

"Ummm—King. Charlotte King. Yeah, that's it."

"Okay, 'Ms. King.' This is an official eviction notice from the county; you've been served. It is your lawful duty to ensure 'Ms. Carter' gets a copy of this documentation; do you understand?"

I smile sweetly and bat my eyes. "Eviction notice? So, you mean, like, you're not here to arrest me—I mean her?"

He scoffs and shakes his head. "Not today, 'Ms. King.' All I need is your signature."

He holds out the official document on top of his notebook, along with a pen emblazoned with the Thurston County Sheriff's Department logo on the side.

I unhook the door chain and open it enough to take the notebook and pen, sign it with a flourish, and hand it back. "Is that all?"

"That's all. Enjoy the rest of your day, 'Ms. King.'" He stares intently for another minute before he turns to leave.

I slam the door, reengage the lock, and whoop with delight. "That was fucking *close*!"

Charlotte peeks around the corner of the stairwell. "Is it safe to come out?"

I press my palm to my heart. "Yeah, everything is golden. Where is everyone else?"

She steps onto the main floor and glances back up the stairs, while twisting her hands. "Welllll, when I saw the cops were here, we all kind of panicked. I didn't want you to get in trouble again, so Marissa stuffed the shit."

I jerk my head back; positive I heard her wrong. "S—she what?"

"Stuffed it. Like, the rigs; the dope. In her biological purse."

From overhead, Marissa bemoans pitifully, "Yeah, you're welcome. This shit is uncomfortable as fuck; can someone please come and help me get it out of my pussy? Charlotte's fingers aren't long enough, and I'll be damned if I have some dude digging around inside me."

I throw my head back and roar with laughter. "That's fucking great, dude. Yeah, I'll be right up."

***

I'm crouched in the bathroom between Marissa's open legs—one balanced on the toilet lid, the other braced firmly on the floor—my fingers trying to grasp the slippery bag of dope and syringes hastily hidden in her nether regions, when I hear Judd behind me.

"Well, *hello*, Nurse. What do we have *here*?"

I turn at the sound of his voice, just as I catch the edge of one of the squirreled away rigs. "It's a long story, babe. I'm a lot more interested in what happened to *you* today. The chatter on the scanner had me worried."

"Well, girly, you *did* tell me to run into Target for you." A look of unrestrained mischievousness breaks across his face: the mythical boy who refuses to grow up.

"Jesus, Rachel, watch what you're doing; that pinches!"

I look from Marissa to Judd and laugh and laugh and laugh.

CHAPTER FIFTY-EIGHT

It's Nothing Personal

MOVING DAY. A U-HAUL BOX TRUCK is in the driveway, filled to the brim with the fixings of normality: blankets, pots and pans, baby pictures. The Camaro is parked at a safehouse, hidden away along with Akasha while we figure out a plan. I'm wandering, forlorn, through the empty duplex tracing my fingers in melancholy over the blank walls.

Judd opens the front door and hollers, "Come on, girl. Let's go! The truck's full, and one of us needs to get to the Motel 6 before our dude gets impatient and jets."

I clench my jaw and let out an exaggerated sigh. "I'm just double-checking that we got everything, Judd. Hold your horses."

His eyes flick from side-to-side, and he lets go of the doorknob and speed walks across the room, wrapping his arm around my waist, and steering me toward the door. "Nah, girl. Everything is out. I told you. It's all good. Our crew took care of the whole ball of wax, just like 'ole Judd promised. Now be a good girl and get in the car."

I dig in my heels and cross my arms. "Geez, Judd. Quit it! I've checked every other room; I just want to make sure the downstairs bathroom is empty, too. It's easy to miss, tucked away in the corner by the front door."

A flash of undefined tumultuous emotion rolls across his face as I shake out of his embrace, and he takes a step back, hands up in surrender. I straighten my shoulders, turn, and slide the pocket door to the small bathroom—a closet really, barely room enough for the toilet and sink—open. For a moment, I cannot compute what I see, what is in front of me. I take a step back, shake my head, and look again.

Sitting on the closed toilet lid is a long-haired beauty of about 19; on her lap, a coloring book and pencil case full of pastel gel-pens. Her shining blue eyes echo the color of the pen in her hand, and she stares, her face a perfect imitation of the cat-who-ate-the-canary.

"Are. You. Fucking. Kidding. Me. Right. Now."

Judd swoops his arms around my waist again, more firmly this time. I scream, hit, and thrash like a rabid raccoon. He is stronger, though, and effortlessly ushers me outside and into the passenger seat of one of our runner's vehicles.

I let out a guttural roar. "I knew it! I fucking *knew* it!! You fucking ass-fucking-hole; you're cheating on me!!"

"Calm down, girl. Don't trip." He takes a deep breath and holds it before continuing in a sharp tone. "Just go drop off our stuff at the storage unit, and Matt here will bring you back to the motel. We can talk then. After you've regained your senses."

"Regain my *senses*? Calm *down*?? I'm supposed to 'calm down' when you've got some young piece of ass hidden away in my fucking bathroom??"

He grabs my chin, despite my clawing and scratching hands lunging for his face, and stares at me levelly. "Don't take it personal, girly. It's just business."

***

Judd is already settled into the motel by the time I finish supervising the unloading of my boxes and keepsakes into the storage unit on the other side of town. One of our associates—who not only possesses a valid driver's license but is also free of warrants—secured us the big, corner room on the second floor. The perfect spot: tucked away from the main balustrade. From that vantage point, the unmarked police car which periodically cruises the area cannot see the comings and goings of our customers. Matt—who was tasked with driving me all afternoon—eases his boat of a car into the parking lot, and I am out of the vehicle and up the stairs before he can turn off the engine. The motel room door is cracked open; a signal to those coming to buy our wares.

I barrel in, slamming the doorknob into the cheap drywall. "I'm so fucking pissed at you, Judd! Sending me off, so you don't have to deal with the consequences of your actions; it's total bullshit!"

Furious tears obstruct my vision; Matt—a few steps behind me—hesitates, keys in hand, when he reaches the doorway.

Judd sits on the edge of the bed, the accouterments of the dope trade strewn across the cheap bedspread in front of him: rigs, baggies, a scale, at least an ounce of white powder.

Judd freezes as I enter, and his shoulders stiffen. "Heyyy, guys. This is my girl, Rachel. She's had a long day, haven't you, Rachel? Why don't you be a good girl and come sit next to me? Meet our guests."

Across the room, sitting in the two garishly upholstered armchairs is a couple I have never seen before. Although they do not speak, their animated body language parodies a silent film in its intensity. Their obvious amusement in reaction to Judd's anger and embarrassment at my entrance only amplifies the mounting tension.

"Fuck our guests, and fuck you, Judd. You can't fucking tell me what to do!! You owe me a Goddamned explanation!!"

The unfamiliar visitors look from me to Judd, their amusement transforming into scorn.

"Might be we should do this another time when you've got your bitch in order, man," the male counterpart says, sardonically.

"His 'bitch'?? I'm no one's fucking 'bitch.' Judd, are you going to let him talk to me like that? Do something!"

Judd rises and casually flips the edge of the faded orange-and-purple comforter over the works. "Now listen: Everyone just chill out. I'll walk you two down to your car, and we'll set up a time to finish this later. Rachel, go wash your face and wait here. We'll talk when I get back. Matt; keep an eye on her 'til then."

I don't budge. As the three of them leave the room, the woman catches my eye and snorts in derisive laughter. Matt moves aside to allow them passage, then steps in and closes the door behind him.

I plant my feet on the floor. "I don't need a fucking babysitter, Matt!"

He shrugs and sits in one of the chairs and jiggles his keys.

I survey the otherwise empty room and screech in frustration.

"You might wanna tone it down a bit, or Judd'll be pissed."

"Fuck you; fuck that; fuck Judd."

I stomp to the bathroom, deciding washing my face isn't such a bad idea after all. I am gripping the counter and crying when Judd comes back inside.

"Rachel."

I try to subdue my sobs and rally, unsuccessfully. I straighten, let go of the counter, and face him, barely holding myself together.

"You've gotta quit with this. Nobody likes you. I can't keep the business running if you are acting crazy in front of customers."

My chin quivers, and I stumble and reach for the edge of the sink again to steady myself. "How can you talk about business right now! I don't give a fuck about all that. That girl in my bathroom: Who was she? Tell me the truth; don't fucking lie to me! You are cheating on me, aren't you? How could you?!"

He steps closer—there is almost no space between us, now—and looks me dead in the eye. "I am *not* cheating on you; I would never lie to you, Rachel. I *love* you."

I search his face for some indicator of deceit. His eyes, though enlarged from the dope running through his system, are bright and do not waver.

Inside my head, things that should be anchored in place begin to fracture and free fall.

If he's lying, I'm in trouble here. Nothing is safe, and I can't trust him.

But he looks *like he's telling the truth; there's no way he could look me straight in the eyes and lie, right?*

If he's not lying, then I must be crazy.

And, if I'm crazy, then I can't trust me.

A howl then, circling, circling, rising to the cracked ceiling, drowning out all thought.

"Hush, girl, hush. Come sit by me." He directs me across the room and sits me on the bed. "I'll fix us a hit before I head out to clean up the mess you made with our visitors."

I am pliant now, and mute, although the disharmony inside contradicts my outward exterior. I am peripherally aware of the incessant jangling of Matt's keys from the other side of the room.

Judd works his mixology magic, dumping a quarter ounce of dope into a container and filling three syringes to the brim. He finds a vein in my arm with ease and pushes the mixture in. I cough and fall back on the bed before he is done. Prone, and riding the rush to near oblivion, I watch as he takes a second syringe—the syringe meant for him—and instead, shoots it into my arm, piggybacking off the first hit.

From somewhere outside my body, I hear, "Stay here, 'til I get back; here's a rig full of shit to make it worth your while." And then, the sound of the door shutting behind him.

CHAPTER FIFTY-NINE

Confirmation Bias

R*ING…RING…RING…*

The rotary dial phone on the scratched and dingy bedside table rings with the urgency of a malnourished seagull demanding french fries; it's shrill, jangling tone rouses me from the darkness I succumbed to after the double hit of dope. I open eyelids made of broken glass from a body dipped in cement and see only water-damaged, acoustic ceiling tiles, and a broken light fixture with one burned-out bulb.

"Matt, dude, make yourself useful. Can you make the phone stop ringing, please?" I growl, the words like crumbling cinderblocks in my mouth.

No response. Nothing but the relentless ringing.

I push myself up; the cheap bedding bunches and puckers beneath me. The room is empty save for me. A discarded rig—orange safety cap nowhere to be seen—is on the end table, and Matt's chair is empty: toppled on the grubby carpet, as if he left in a hurry.

"Fuck that guy, anyway."

Ringgg…

"Jesus; fuck, okay!" I say, gaining my bearings bit-by-bit. I grope for the tan, plastic receiver, finally pulling it off the cradle on the nightstand and bringing it to my ear with a stilted, jerking movement, then fall backward onto the bed with the effort.

"Hello?" I work to untangle the long, spiraled cord as I wait for a response. I am met with static. "Hel-*lo*? Is anyone there?"

More static, then distant laughter.

I drop the phone cord and lurch back into a sitting position, my hackles up. "Who is this??"

More laughter—female—then a masculine voice. Broken and intermixed with feedback, but clear enough.

"We are *freee*! …evil bitch…gave her…double shot; she'll be down for…come here, girl…kiss…no, not on the mouth…"

Giggles carry easily through the line. The blood drains from my face, and I press the receiver closer to my ear: trying to hear more, to hear less, to hear nothing at all.

A sudden jarring *SCREEE* of feedback—then silence.

CHAPTER SIXTY

Jagged Edges

HOW MANY DAYS HAS it been? We've been awake for so long, I've lost count. The world has a dreamlike quality, an insubstantial feel. The edges: They are crumbling. I am floundering, laid bare, adrift upon the sea.

"I can't take this anymore, Judd. It's too much. I need a break. Can't we go away somewhere? Take the weekend off? I'm so tired; I don't even remember the last time we slept. And my heart feels like it's breaking."

I am showered and in clean clothes, my makeup done, my freshly dyed hair yellow fire in the sun. We stopped at my mother's peeling doublewide on the way back through town—three weeks since I'd been by or called—and Nicholas, 6 years old now, met me at the door.

My heart swelled at the sight of him. I dropped to my knees, arms spread wide for a hug. He stared at me—unmoving—his face reminiscent of one of the stone heads littering Easter Island. His words play over and over in my mind.

'If you're going to just leave again, maybe you shouldn't even come home at all.'

Judd twists in his seat to face me and pats my arm. We are parked outside some glass-fronted government office buildings, the Trans Am idling, Powerman 5000 turned down to a respectable level so we can talk.

"Business is business, girl; we have a daily commitment. It doesn't work like that; we can't just take a day off. People depend on us," Judd reasons.

My chin drops to my chest and I fiddle with the handle on his metal briefcase. A tear traces a course down my face and drip-drops onto the corrugated surface of the lockbox.

'I'm homesick, Momma. And do you know what the saddest part is? I don't even know where home is anymore.'

"Listen, as soon as we are done delivering the shit for the day, I'll take you on a shopping spree, okay? You can get whatever you want."

I sniffle and wipe my face. "Promise?"

"Promise. Can you hold it together for the rest of the day?"

"Yeah, I guess. I love you so much, Judd."

"I love you, too, girl. Now, let's get back to work."

CHAPTER SIXTY-ONE

High-Quality Supplements

We are at Ralph's, the fancy drugstore situated at the top of the hill above the downtown core. The one where they sell all the hippy-dippy supplements and dietary aids. Judd is looking through the bottles labeled 'MSM,' and considering them at length.

I pace behind Judd, flipping through our planner, trying to devise the schedule for the rest of the day's deliveries.

"What do you need that weird vitamin for, anyway?"

He winks, grabs my waist, and kisses me so fervently I forget where we are.

"It ain't a vitamin; it's high-quality cut. Way better than baby powder or laxative. This'll make the rush even better, so we are doing our clients a *favor* by adding it in."

Judd's crooked, cocky smile melts my insides, and his caramel eyes smolder with desire behind his glasses.

"Come on, girly. Let's get settled into the new motel room and take care of business, so I can take care of *youuu*," he says, with a lusty grin.

***

"Grab the works, girl. We'll *make* time for a hit and some hanky-panky before our next appointment shows."

I reach into my purse and pull out the faux tortoiseshell planner; the perfect implement for storing phone numbers and orders. It's fitted with a side pocket the exact size necessary to tuck away the two ounces of dope we are fronted daily: one ounce from each of the county's two competing suppliers.

The pocket is empty.

I bite my lip and my hands start to sweat. "Uh, Houston, we have a problem."

He turns from setting up the mixing station, rig in hand, his brawny muscles gleaming under his white t-strap undershirt.

"Huh? What're you talkin' about?"

"The dope; it's gone." I sit down hard and shy away from his gaze.

"How the fuck is it "gone"? Haven't you had it on you the whole time??" His free hand clenches and unclenches.

"Yes, I've had it all day. I never even set my purse down once. I swear," I say, eyeing the exit.

"Jesus, FUCK. This is a serious problem, girl; you do know that, right?" His face darkens as he throws the empty syringe on the bed.

"Of course, I do," I paste on a smile, then straighten in my seat, and meet his eyes. "We'll find it, though. We have to. Let's check the car; maybe we left it in the lockbox in the back?"

He shakes his head: a perfunctory snap. "No, the lockbox is here, see? I was going to make us hits, remember?"

I flush with embarrassment and stand. "Oh, yeah. I forgot. Okay, let's just retrace our steps."

We tear through the room, turning over tables and ripping the bedding apart.

Nothing.

We scour the ground from the motel room to the Trans Am, then tear that apart, too.

Still nothing.

We stand together—a dope show version of Hansel and Gretel—in the dirt parking lot, all the car doors open, including the trunk and hood.

Him: hand on hip, the other raking through his long, hickory-brown hair; me, twisting my purse strap and scrutinizing him for signs of an imminent explosion.

Like the famed two birds, it hits us both at once.

"Ralphs!!" We shout in unison.

***

We are back at the drugstore in record time. My lithe, gazelle-like legs give me an edge, and I make it to the supplement aisle before Judd is barely out of the car.

Laying on the patterned vinyl in front of the green MSM bottles is a quart-sized Ziploc bag four-finger-widths filled with white shards.

I swipe our bread-and-butter off the floor and stuff it into the day planner; I am triple-checking the zipper as Judd comes sliding around the corner like a ballplayer stealing second base.

"Well?" he says, the resignation in his voice unmistakable.

I shrug and give him a cheeky smile—my apprehension a fading memory—and lift the now full planner in victory.

CHAPTER SIXTY-TWO

Back Roads & Backpedaling

TWO-LANE ROAD ON THE FAR END of the county. Not sure how we got way over here, or where exactly we are heading. Judd is in the Trans Am going breakneck speeds, taking corners on two-wheels. I follow behind him in my father's old, beaten up, red panel van: The usually empty cargo area is filled to the brim with what we've deemed too essential to leave locked away in the storage unit.

Boxes and bags of clothing, keepsakes, and wires (always so many wires) are stacked Tetris-like to shoulder height of the two captain's chairs in the front. On top of our belongings is a heavy metal toolbox. It slides from one back window to the other as I attempt to maneuver the turns. The van has a shaky front suspension, a hole in the radiator I tried to plug with a container of black pepper, and is held together by a wish and a prayer. The chairs long ago lost their headrests.

"Shit, Judd. Slow down!" I mutter under my breath as I grip the worn and peeling steering wheel tighter, trying to control it as it swings wildly under my sweaty palms.

There's a sharp turn ahead, and Judd speeds up to take it. I floor the gas and pull the wheel as far to the left as I can. Although the gas pedal responds, and the speedometer is now buried somewhere past 80MPH, the steering wheel does not. The front of the van drops like a breeze-block tied to a mobster and tossed into the sea—drops into the ditch—bounces once, and plows headlong into a telephone pole. The large metal toolbox changes its side-to-side trajectory and speeds full force into the back of my skull, slamming my head into the dash.

***

Judd is in the doorway of the van, pushing my hair out of my face, his eyes wild, his leather jacket crinkling and shining in the sun.

"Rachel. You alive? *Rachel.*"

Through a curtain of haphazard tangles, I see his head whip around comically as he surveys the deserted road.

I grunt something incomprehensible and lift my forehead from the steering wheel.

"Ahh, fuck, my head!" I reach back and gingerly examine the massive goose egg forming at the base of my skull.

"Ok, good. You're not dead. I gotta *jet*! Cops'll be coming any minute now." He makes a break for his idling vehicle, parked a few car lengths ahead with its nose sticking into the road.

I catch him by the scruff of his neck and scoot out onto the pavement to face him. "You're going to leave me here? On the side of the road? With all our stuff? After I just almost *died*?"

He vibrates like a high-voltage power line through the tough leather, and I can see him internally backpedaling, scrambling for a response: a rabid badger caught in a snare.

"No, no, '*course* not. Not *you*. I didn't mean *you*. Come on, get in the car, but you better hurry. I'm gonna be pissed if they get us *and* our stuff."

CHAPTER SIXTY-THREE

Say Cheese!

SAME RUN, DIFFERENT DAY; still haven't slept.

We pull into The Oleander Motel—the last stop on skid row—a line of sagging, run-down stucco rooms rented by the week, the day, the hour. Our few belongings not left behind in the van are shoved in the back of the Trans, pushing the seats forward, leaving almost no legroom.

Judd parks under a gnarled and crooked tree in front of room six. The accident was several days ago, but my mind is stuck, galloping wildly, careening from thought to thought—two distinct voices—vehemently arguing.

He wasn't going to leave *me by the side of the road. There's no* way *he'd do that. He* loves *me.*

And:

Oh, yeah? Are you fucking blind or just stupid? He was so fucking outta there, it's not even funny.

I whimper, shake my head to dispel the escalating internal debate, and follow Judd out of the vehicle and into the room. It takes a couple of trips to collect our meager belongings; we pile the haul on the sunken mattress in the middle of the room. I get busy cataloging the dope supply on the dresser to the left of the door while Judd grabs the shower bag off the bed, tossing his cell phone down in its place.

"I'm gonna go clean up. It's been a Hell of a day," he proclaims.

My shoulders tighten, but I do not respond. The shower turns on, and the air fills with the smell of Aussie 3 Minute Miracle and Garnier Fructis: his holy grail of hair products.

I continue itemizing our stash, making sure to keep personal separate from business, all the while muttering to myself.

Are we safe now, like he said? For how long, though? What if someone saw us pull in here? What if this is a trap?

And:

More importantly, why were we going so fucking fast *before I crashed? Did we outrace the cops?* Were *there even cops?*

My rambling cascade of thoughts is interrupted by a muffled jingle. I reach into my open purse and grab my phone, but no indicator lights are flashing.

The jangling continues.

I glance over my shoulder onto the bed; Judd's phone, half-hidden under his cast-off clothes, is lit up and vibrating.

I look at the bathroom door, expecting him to come out to answer it. The spray from the shower continues, and I hear him singing off-tune.

I stare at the phone intently, considering.

Judd always says if he's not around, people can deal with me directly. And, technically, *he's not here, so...He wouldn't want us to miss out on a deal just 'cause I was too scared to answer the phone, would he?*

The ringing continues. I steel myself in my decision, swoop up the phone, and answer it.

"Hello?"

CLICK.

I must notta grabbed it in time.

I turn back toward the dresser, and the phone begins vibrating and ringing in my hand, startling me. I looked down at the Caller ID; it reads 'Private Number.' I push the 'Talk' button in the middle of the second ring.

"Hello? Who's there?"

Silence, then another CLICK.

No, fucking way. *We are not doing* this *again.*

I launch the phone back onto the bed and start pacing the short distance between the dresser and the far wall, the voices in an uproar, my blood boiling.

The ringing begins afresh as Judd steps back into the room. He gives me a sidelong glance as he answers it, listens for a moment, then turns away from me.

"No, not right now. I told you not to call this number," Judd says in a hushed tone.

I lean against the dresser, eyes narrowed, watching him. He snaps the phone shut, turns, and smiles broadly, then navigates around the bed and comes in for a kiss.

I comply. The kiss is hot and wet and passionate. Content he has effectively placated me, he leans back—a smug, self-satisfied look in his eye—and turns to walk away.

"Wouldn't do that if I were you," I say, my eyes flashing.

"What're you talking about? Wouldn't do what?"

I tip my head in the direction of my left hand, down near the fold of the once-white bath towel wrapped around the damp skin of his chiseled waist.

He instinctively turns in the direction I indicate, his eyes broadening with understanding when he sees it's not my hand pressing into his side in a loving embrace.

It's his bowie knife.

"Your phone. I'm not stupid; I know it's that girl again, Judd. I'm not going to put up with your bullshit for another Goddamned minute," I say coolly, smiling all the while. "I'm fucking done. *You're* fucking done."

I grin like The Joker and lean into him, the edge of the blade indenting his bronzed skin.

An onslaught of emotion rolls furiously across his visage, but joviality is what sticks, that cocky smile of his settling firmly in place.

Never breaking eye contact, he grabs one of the disposable cameras we always have on hand off the dresser and holds it out, capturing us both in the viewfinder. "Well, if today is the day and it's time to die, at least let me get one last picture of us for you to remember me by."

I look from him to the camera just as the flash goes off—the knife drops to the ancient, rust-colored shag carpeting and laughter peals from an untapped pit inside me.

"You are *so* fucking *lucky* you're funny, Judd."

CHAPTER SIXTY-FOUR

Semi-Famous

WE MISSED COURT AND ARE officially listed as 'Western Washington's Most Wanted' for bail jumping, failure to report, our original possession charge, and who knows what else. There's a Crime Stoppers reward for us, and we can't trust anyone for fear of being turned in. I've dyed my hair red in hopes of not being so easily identifiable.

Judd is passed out, finally, but we must find somewhere to re-up. I'm driving, and the shit we do have is in the lockbox under his seat. I know there's dope at Celeste's house, but Judd has forbidden me from going there.

I go anyway, thinking I'll just pull up around the corner, and go in the side door; no one will even know we are there. At the stop sign a block away from Celeste's house, I see a cop cruise past, do a double-take, flip a bitch, and come up behind us with lights flashing.

"Judd; Judd! Wake up. There's a cop behind us. I think they recognized me! Wake *up*."

He opens his eyes just enough to see the street sign in front of us. "Puget Street?! Fuck, Rachel! I said, *don't* go to Celeste's!"

Loudspeakers, now, and more cop cars. A gun is shoved through the open window and pressed against my temple. I look at Judd out of the corner of my eye, afraid to turn my head and get a bullet for my trouble.

There's a gun to his head, as well.

The game is up—nothing to do but call it now.

CHAPTER SIXTY-FIVE

Interior Door

I'M OUT, BUT JUDD IS NOT. Doesn't look like he will be any time soon, either. The show must go on, though, and that leaves me in the metaphorical driver's seat.

I don't know how to drive this big rig, though. Don't know how to shift all the complicated, multitudinous gears; don't know how to balance my sea legs with steering the ship.

Without Judd, I'm shipwrecked: free-falling to depths not yet plumbed. Nothing has meaning anymore. I am flailing, falling, failing, and the day comes when the connect—the big boss—suggests a ride in his fancy whip.

Time to have a heart-to-heart. Suss out the problem. Formulate a plan.

He prattles incessantly as he drives—out of town, out of the county, out of cell phone range—drones on and on about the importance of follow-through, of loyalty, of trustworthiness.

I don't know where we are going, and I am too high—too petrified—to ask.

He parks in front of a nondescript Craftsman house in an unremarkable neighborhood; indicates I should follow him inside. There is business to be dealt with here, and it's time I understood the enormity of the situation. The necessity of my daily success as a businesswoman. The magnitude of the role I've been jettisoned into by default.

We don't knock; the door just opens when we step on the concrete stoop. A Hispanic man with hard glinting eyes stands inside; he nods once then ushers us in.

The space is simply appointed: couch, chairs, lamps, kitchen off to the left.

There is a tense, serious exchange between the connect and our host—nonverbal, but easy enough to pick up on.

The taciturn occupant of this unassuming little bungalow turns, reaches behind an armchair, and—in the baseboard near the floor—grabs an until now hidden lever.

Grabs the lever and rolls up the entire back wall, and like an articulating garage door, it disappears into the ceiling.

Behind the cleverly disguised artificial wall is a warehouse populated by a conglomeration of floor-to-ceiling metal drawers.

The connect steers me in behind our mute emcee: We stand shoulder-to-shoulder; I'm sandwiched between them in a narrow corridor of a giant depository of post office boxes. I watch as the clean-cut Latino unlocks a drawer with a key from around his neck and pulls it open wide.

Crammed inside are several shrink-wrapped, brick-sized packages of white powder: at least two pounds in each bag; at least four bags in the drawer; at least two-hundred drawers in this aisle alone.

Our benefactor in distribution takes two bricks and holds them out to the connect. The connect smirks, shakes his head, and tilts his chin toward me.

Unsure what else to do, I hold out my hands; they drop slightly at the weight of the haul.

I cannot breathe. I cannot move. I cannot run, even if I fucking want to.

The breadth of business complete, we turn and leave; drive back to town. The entire exchange is completed without a single word from anyone.

CHAPTER SIXTY-SIX

Rigged

THE APARTMENTS ON SCHOOL STREET may as well have 'Welcome to the Actual Ghetto' spray painted across its broad, disintegrating clapboard siding. A short, squat u-shaped arrangement of dirty-gray, one-level, one-bedroom low-income flats—sparsely furnished and smelling of cat piss and stress sweat—the occupants wander from one open door to the next: trading sex for drugs, paranoia for inclusivity.

I am in the bedroom of the far-right corner unit with Abraham Baptiste, an older Black gentleman with an air of sophistication, unlike most of the guys in the circle. Although he makes it clear he won't say no to any burgeoning extracurricular activities between us, he isn't lascivious about it—respects my 'no thank you' with genteel ease, in fact—and as such, I feel safe with him. Safe enough to settle in—cross-legged on the bristly carpet while he sits on the corner of his mattress on the floor—and share my rambling, convoluted, conspiracy theories along with my dope.

"I don't fucking know, Abraham. Like, I'm trying here; but slinging a bag on my own is fucking *hard*. People just don't take me seriously without Judd, and I feel like I can't I trust anyone. Everything is spinning out of control, and I'm not sure how much longer I can hold it together." I lean forward and talk even faster. "And, then, like, there's the whole Judd being shipped off to prison thing, which is honestly even worse! I don't understand *why* they kept him and not me."

"Hmmm," Abraham ponders, sympathetically. "That *is* unusual. What exactly happened after they picked you two up? Go on, and give me all the details. Have you seen or spoken to Judd since?"

I sigh and drop the half-mixed hits on the floor. "I mean, I *did* get to see him once in passing before they released me. In the visiting area; we were both being escorted in handcuffs in opposite directions. I was going to meet with our lawyer. I think Judd must have just met with him, 'cause he yelled out as I walked by."

"Well, young miss, what did he say?" Abraham replies, thoughtfully, with his regal, Deep South inflection.

"Something like, 'You get her outta this place, you hear? I won't have my girl locked up.' Which is super cool and all, but since they let me out after only nine days, and Judd's on his way back to the joint, I am pretty sure the higher-ups think I rolled. Things have been…sketchy since I got out. I think someone is trying to set me up or something. The connect's goons came and collected both cars—he says I still owe him for the last front before we went to jail—and—and…let's just say shit's been getting real fucking *deep*."

The words tumble out of me in a rush of emotion, and I sit panting and shaking in fear and exhaustion. "I'm so scared, and I don't know how to convince people I didn't do anything! Like, I would *never*! I went to prison last time they asked me to talk, and I'd do it again in a heartbeat!"

Abraham pauses for a long moment, then replies with an air of seriousness: "Word around town is you have a price on your head, dear girl. That you've seen too much, and without Judd to keep you in line, you've become a liability to the powers-that-be."

I gasp and scoot backward on the floor. "Oh, fuck! That's worse than I even imagined! A price on my head? Do you mean, like a…a hit?"

Abraham nods and offers silent commiseration while side-eyeing the dope in front of me. "Yes, and it's a considerable dollar amount, from what I gather. But don't worry about that nonsense right now, young lady. Just put all this drivel out of your head. I bet you'll feel as right as rain after you do yourself a hit. How long has it been since you've bumped, anyway?"

I shrug and sigh in despondence.

"Right, then," he continues. "Let's both get our speed on, then we can strategize in earnest."

I purse my lips, draw in a ragged breath, and let it out, then turn my full attention back to the task at hand: mixing up thick hits, Judd-Knox-style. Once the concoctions are complete, I pass a rig to Abraham, and we both imbibe and fall backward—almost in unison—in a surge of amphetamine and adrenaline.

The room is not quite steady and solid yet when I register a loud, repetitive thumping.

"Is that…is that my imagination?"

Abraham sits up and claws the corner of the bare mattress, fingers like hooks, eyes feral and rolling furiously in his head.

"No, girl, NO; it's the door. Oh, Goddamn it! I think it's the cops!!"

Shouts carry easily down the narrow hall—one of the neighbors, squatters, fellow highflyers—sounding the alarm: a schism of panic, stomping feet—madness—in all directions.

I jackknife from my prone position on the floor and sit ramrod straight, arcs of tension and paranoia cascading through my overloaded system. Abraham treads in an exaggerated mime to the opposite wall, sticking his head out past the blanket thumbtacked over a small window.

"Oh, no! Girl, they are everywhere; hide the shit, hide the shit!"

I gather the nearly full pack of syringes, scramble to find the orange plastic lids to recap the two we just used; and take the whole bundle—along with the dope—push aside first my skirt, and then my panties; and shove it all up and out of sight.

"Fuck that fucking *hurts*!" I whisper, gritting my teeth in misery.

Abraham grips my shoulders, his face etched with primal fear and solemnity. "Girl, you have *got* to make it work. Just stay as still as you can, and we will get through this, all right?

I nod and try to adjust my private hoard by shimmying my hips.

The barrel of an AR-15 held by a SWAT team member in a black mask sweeps aside the window covering. In through the bedroom door waltzes another officer—this one in plainclothes, a bulletproof vest, and a smirk—accompanied by several others in full riot gear.

"Well, well, well; what do we have here?" the officer quips, voice dripping with snark.

Abraham straightens his back with aristocratic poise and grace. "I don't know what you mean, Officer, but I sure do know my rights; I demand to see your warrant."

"A warrant? Nah. Don't think I need one of those. Do you, Ms. Carter? It *is* Ms. Carter, isn't it?"

My mouth drops, and I grapple for a response. "I-I've never seen this man before in my *life*. What are you talking about?"

The plainclothes sheriff snickers and grasps my bicep—taking note of the bruises in the crook of my arm and clucking his tongue in mock concern—and pulls me out the bedroom door and down the hall. "Right. Why don't you come with me? My friends here will keep Mr. Baptiste company, won't you boys?"

"Let me fucking *go*! I don't know you! I don't know what you are talking about!"

He drags me down the hall—the smirk still plastered on his unyielding face—and out the front door. Once we are positioned in the middle of the courtyard—where everyone can see us through their bent and broken Venetian blinds—he lets me go and stands facing me, arms crossed, grinning.

I glare at him and take a step back. "What the fuck is this all about?"

"You and I, we are just going to have a little chat. Your friend there, Abraham, is it? He's going to jail."

"What? Why? He didn't do anything. Neither of us did!" I retort caustically while trying to discreetly adjust the incriminating items stuffed away out of sight.

"Oh, that doesn't matter. That doesn't matter in the slightest. What *does* matter is what people will *think*. And, wouldn't it just be *terrible* if everyone saw you out here talking at length to the SWAT team while your compatriot got locked up, and you didn't? Again?"

Comprehension seeps in through the chaos, then.

The game is rigged. And I am outgunned.

"You wouldn't dare! That's—that'll get me killed!"

He chuckles—a glint in his eye—shrugs with cavalier indifference, and hands me his business card. "Let me know if you want to make your life a little easier."

CHAPTER SIXTY-SEVEN

Clear as Mud

BACK SEAT OF A FLASHY red convertible, top down; hair whipping and catching at the corners of my eyes, my mouth. It's hard to hear over the gusting wind and roaring engine, but I make out enough of the conversation to follow along.

In the driver's seat, on supple dove-colored leather with pristine stitches, sits the connect; my father rides shotgun.

"So, once I sign the title to the motorhome, the lien will be lifted, and—"

"And we'll call it even," the connect says in a rush, finishing my father's sentence.

My father continues grimly, not bothering to make eye contact. "You understand if you go back on your word; if my daughter has any further trouble for any reason, there will be consequences."

The connect gives my father a furtive, sidelong glance. "Yes, sir. I do. I understand completely. She has the golden ticket."

"And, I don't want to hear any more of this B.S. about her talking to the police; are we clear on that subject?"

"Yes, sir. Crystal."

The engine revs louder as the discourse between them ends. We ride on in silence, the fancy car weaving from one lane to the next, mirroring the course of my thoughts.

CHAPTER SIXTY-EIGHT

Super Fuckin' Hot

THE SHAKY FRONT SUSPENSION of the old panel van—reclaimed from the tow yard easily enough with a flash of the legitimate ownership papers from my father—vibrates under my hands. My bare, dirty foot is propped on the dashboard, the window is halfway down, and dappled sunlight forms abstract patterns on my leg as I traverse back roads, no specific destination in mind.

The speedometer hasn't worked since the crash, but it is safe to say I am way over the limit by the way the loveseat wedged across the wheel wells shudders and bangs into the van's metal frame. Akasha, collected from his temporary home after Judd got locked up, meows plaintively and paces from the passenger seat to my lap.

My breath is labored, and my skin splotchy. Chills roll through me, and my vision is unsteady and blurry. My lower back aches inexplicably, and I bend over the wobbly steering wheel to catch my breath through the mounting pain.

"*Fuuuck*. I don't feel so great, Akasha. What should we do? Just let the van lead us? 'Cause, I'm not sure where to go."

Akasha meows again and rubs against my arm, begging for attention. I caress behind his ears distractedly while doing my best to successfully manipulate the unwieldy vehicle into the public access area of the Nisqually River.

I navigate the turn, just barely, and stomp on the persnickety brakes with all the force I can muster with only one foot on the floor. The van stops just short of the embankment, skidding sideways on the balding tires, and shooting up a spray of loose gravel and sand in its wake. The engine shimmies and shakes and sputters to a halt. The loveseat slams violently to one side then tips forward before falling roughly back in place.

I look around circumspectly as the dust settles. Sweat pours out of me, and with the violent stop, the pain in my lower back is amplified to a bright, burning agony.

Now what?

I turn the rearview mirror toward me and give myself a once over: my hair is frizzy and lifeless; my eyes so dilated I can barely see the blue-green of my irises; my eyeliner—applied several days ago—is smudged and crusty in the corners; my otherwise pallid face sports two spots of brilliant, flushed color high on my cheekbones; and my stomach clenches and gurgles loudly.

I can't *be hungry. I downed a 20-ounce Diet Pepsi and an* extra-large *Symphony candy bar on, like, Tuesday, so what gives?*

I wet my finger on my tongue and do my best to wipe away the smudged eye makeup. I give up after a few unsuccessful swipes. My skin feels like fire. I sigh in frustration, push the mirror away, and lean back in the ripped leather seat.

The river running in front of the van has a calming effect, and I turn my attention out the bug-covered windshield, hypnotized by its eddies and swirls. I light a cigarette from the dashboard lighter, roll the window the rest of the way down, and fall into a sort of meditation: stroking Akasha's soft fur as I smoke and watch the river follow its endless course.

A sharp rapping snaps me out of my trance.

Akasha hisses, hackles up, and I jump as the ash of my cigarette lands on my thigh and burns me. Sure it is the cops, or worse, I turn and see a face framed in the passenger side window.

"Yo, Rach! What're you doing down in the valley? And, how come you didn't come say hi if you were gonna be in my neighborhood?"

The pulsating tension leaves my body as I recognize my unexpected company. Cooper. Cooper is fine. Harmless, even. He works for the higher-ups, sure, but isn't a mindless thug. He has always been partial to me, in fact. Even if the price on my head *hasn't* been lifted, it is unlikely Cooper will be the one to collect.

"Fuck, you scared me! How did you know I was down here?"

"I didn't. I was just out and about dropping some dope off to my dude and saw your van. You gonna let me in, or what? I've got some shit if you've got works."

I smile broadly—the searing ache in my side forgotten—and lean over to unlock the door. Akasha gives me a sour look as he loses his seat on my lap.

"Yeah, yeah, I totally do. Come in; get in, Coop."

Cooper hops into the seat, and in the blink of an eye, we are high, high, high, and rolling around—sweaty and entangled—on the loveseat in the back.

"Oh, God, girl, you are so hot!"

I shake my head, perspiration dripping and spattering on the streaked windows. I *am* hot. My vision is doubling, and I can barely move. He grabs my hips and pulls me closer, and I yelp in pain and squirm away.

"I can't…it hurts so bad. My back. Ah, fuck. Something is really wrong."

I sit on the edge of the small sofa, doubled over in pain, and trying to catch my breath—Akasha mewls with concern and paces the oil-stained floor.

Cooper props himself up on one elbow: bare from the waist down, Raiders jersey tucked behind his neck, but still on his arms. "Aww, come on! You felt so *good* wrapped around me. You're super fuckin' *hot*."

I rock back-and-forth, clutching my sides in anguish, the pain cresting and crashing in torrential waves.

He strokes the base of my neck, attempting to coax me back down onto the crude love nest. "Oh, shit, girl. You're burning up! You need to see a doctor."

I lean away and stiffen. "I can't see a doctor. I've got warrants; they'll report me, and I'll go back to jail."

"Man, do what you gotta do, I guess, but I ain't gonna sit here and wait around for you to die." He jumps up, pulls on his wrinkled basketball shorts, adjusts his shirt, and scoops up what is left of his bag of dope.

Hand on the sliding door of the van, he turns, his expression a mixture of concern and alarm. "Rach, you really should go see a doctor."

CHAPTER SIXTY-NINE

Cold Tile Floor

OKAY, OKAY, JUST BREATHE.

The air in the van is solar-level-hot, each breath akin to breathing fire straight from the dragon's mouth, and only serves to make the pain more pronounced. I fix my eyes on the ripped and faded captain's chair in front of the steering wheel, gathering all my will. Akasha sits to the side and watches.

"Okay, kitty. We can do this. One step at a time."

Deep breath and stand.

I collapse onto the ridged floorboards, scraping my knee in the process. A weak cry escapes from my cracked lips.

It's just a few feet. I can do this. I can do this.

Inch-by-inch, I crawl across the van, cradling my side with one hand and propping myself up with the other, leaving spots of blood on the metal floor from my insulted knees. At last, I reach the driver's seat and pull myself up into a sitting position, using every ounce of determination I can amass.

My grip on the physical realm ebbs and flows like the river in front of me. I close my eyes and claw internally for a life raft to cling to as the whirlpool of my sinking consciousness threatens to drag me under.

After several infinite moments, the world solidifies. The dark spots in my vision fill in, although the pain does not abate.

Water. That's all I need—some water.

A cursory glance around the cab tells me there is none to be had here. I start the engine, back out of my reckless parking job, and drive back toward town.

"Come on, Akasha. We'll just hit a fast-food joint and get a free cup of water. Then, everything will be fine."

***

I pull into the parking lot of a Jack in The Box and turn off the engine, out of breath and grimacing in pain. The sun is beating down through the open window, but the passenger side of the van is positioned under a lofty Bigleaf maple giving Akasha plenty of shady spots to rest.

"I'll be back in a few minutes, okay? Just wait here."

The door squeals and groans as I swing it open, and the blacktop scalds the bottoms of my bare feet. I ignore it and race across the parking lot to the glass door marked 'Entrance' and into the air-conditioned foyer of the burger joint.

The line is long, but I don't care. I cannot wait. I circumvent the customers and go straight to the counter. "Can I…can I get some water, please?"

The girl working the register glares at me and tosses her lank, greasy hair out of her squinty eyes.

"You'll have to wait your turn, ma'am," she retorts, looking down her nose and snickering to her coworker.

Knives, then. Swords, even. I double over and howl like a wolf at the moon.

A hellish orchestra of clamoring voices:

"Is she even wearing shoes?"

"What is *wrong* with her?"

"Get her out of here!"

Piercing, unbearable, torturous pain; I collapse onto the cold tile floor, screaming.

"Hey! Stop it! You can't do that here! You're disturbing the guests."

"Call 911; stop screaming!"

"Are those *track marks*? Eww!"

I am undone; there is no barrier between me and not me. In the distance, I hear sirens; in the foreground, muttering and scoffing. There is nowhere to escape; my vision melts and morphs into a swath of visual snow, and the world goes black.

CHAPTER SEVENTY

Apt Statements

WIRES, TUBES, BLOOD PRESSURE cuff. The narrow bed to which I'm strapped jumps and jolts over curbs and around corners. Baby blue scrubs, gloved hand holding up drip bag. Disdain, disgust.

"Enough with the screaming."

"…definitely track marks."

"Drug-seeking…"

"…dramatics…"

Blackness, again.

***

White room, faded curtain; different faces, voices: same straps. And so much pain. Writhing, sobbing, all-consuming pain.

"If you don't hold still, I'll just leave you until you can control yourself."

"No one in *real* pain screams this much."

A stern-faced nurse with brusque hands checks my saline bag, grabs my wrist, and sneers at the bruises in the crook of my elbow; drops my arm in revulsion as if I am contagious.

"What did you expect? …IV drug user…did this to yourself."

Scene falls to the cutting room floor.

***

Beeping monitors. Tubes taped to hand. Cheap, prison-esque, basketweave blankets. Blank TV in the far corner. Same restraints.

In the doorway, a shadow. My vision wavers, clears, wavers again.

"Officer Mitchell…? Tom, is that you?" I ask in a small voice.

No longer in the door, but sitting next to me in a plastic chair, now. Dark hair, crinkly eyes, D.O.C. badge clipped to his belt. It is Tom; my probation officer.

"Tom, what are you doing here? How'd you find me? Am I going to jail?"

He wraps my hand in his own and shakes his head briefly. "Your fever has been hovering around 104° for the last few days; your kidneys have all but shut down."

The doorway is darkened again, this time by an imposing figure in black; a small white collar the only break to his monochromatic look.

"Pardon me…Ms. Carter? I'm here to offer my services if you are so inclined."

I look from Tom to the figure in the doorway, trying to make sense of what he means, my head pounding, my vision swimming in and out of focus. "What services? What is he talking about? What's going on?"

"Your last rites, Rachel," Tom says, his face gray and still, his eyes turbulent pools of concern.

"My-my what? No, I don't want that. Go away. Send him away!"

Tom nods and grits his teeth, gesturing for the clergyman to leave.

"I'm not dying. I'm *fine*. I just—I just needed some water."

"Your chart says you weigh 92 lbs. What are you? Five-ten? Five-eleven? I honestly don't know how you're not dead right now. You've got to stop, or you most certainly will end up that way. Rachel, this life: It's not for you. Don't you see you're better than this? You have so much potential; you could be anything you put your mind to if you could just love yourself enough to walk away."

He pats my limp, cool hand, and everything fades to black once more.

CHAPTER SEVENTY-ONE

State Names are Code for

I'M IN A SPORTY LITTLE car, in the passenger seat. I'm not sure how I got here. The sun is setting behind the cotton candy clouds, and I am tired, so tired.

Next to me, in the driver's seat, sits Tennessee: a bull-dyke who showed up on the outskirts of the circle some weeks back. Her close-cropped curls and knee-length cargo shorts contradict her delicate frame. She is speaking at a rapid pace, and I am struggling to keep the thread, to nod in the right places, to maintain coherence.

"So, you up and left? Against medical advice? That's some moxie you've got there, girl."

She reaches across the console and rubs my thigh, a grin spreading across her elfin features. I register the smile and attempt to affect a similar expression, but only manage a weak grimace.

"It's okay, you're okay. Just sit back and relax. You're safe with me now. No one can touch you when you're with me. See? Look." She lifts her hand off my leg and reaches around the back of my seat, wrestling with a configuration of straps and buckles.

I turn, craning my neck to see what she is doing, and get an eyeful for my effort. In her slender, freckled hand is the black, metallic butt of a Glock 19.

Shockwaves lurch me into acute awareness despite my depleted energy stores. I shrink back, pressing my frame into the door, its handle digging into my still-tender lower back.

"Uhhh, why do you have a fucking cop-fucking-gun?"

She shrugs, smiles conspiratorially, and reholsters the weapon. "It's pretty standard issue…like I said, you've got nothing to worry about as long as you're with me. Even with the hit on your head supposedly quashed, some hot-rodder may still try to come and collect. And, if they do, they'll have bigger things to worry about than my sidearm. Pretty fortuitous it was me who picked you up, isn't it?"

My tenuous grip on self-possession washes away in a murky swell of dread and confusion at the implications of her statement. I pull back farther, willing myself smaller, envisioning I can disintegrate out the window, scatter out the door into the void.

Tennessee turns her attention back to driving, and I catch sight of the antenna of a small flip phone wedged between my seat and the door. I casually reach down and grab it while she is turning the car into the driveway of an expansive, Contemporary-style house at the back of a cul-de-sac. The lights are on throughout the residence, and the windows are without blinds, showing bare, open rooms seemingly devoid of furnishings.

"Where are we? Whose house is this?" I probe, as I slip the phone into the pocket of my jean shorts.

"This is my partner's place," she says, distracted by both my questions and her efforts to park under the motion sensor floodlight mounted on the edge of the garage. "For the time being, anyway. We've kinda set up shop here.

"Come on; let's go in and get you cleaned up, then we can all have a nice long chat."

I inhale, gathering all my will and strength in hopes of maintaining some semblance of a poker face. The weight of the squirreled away phone pressed against my leg offers some small comfort.

"Yeah, okay. Sounds good. I could use a shower, for sure."

I follow her out of the car and around the walkway to a beveled-glass-inset front door. A man I've never seen before opens it as we approach. His oversized frame takes up the entire entrance, and he is on high alert, dripping with sweat, eyes pinpointed.

"What're you doing bringing her back *here*?" he fumes, eyes darting and head craning in and out of the opening in an exaggerated prairie dog impression.

"Where are your manners? Can't you see we have a guest? Kindly do the courteous thing and step out of the way."

He glowers and holds his stance for another moment before conceding and shuffling to the side.

All my senses are thrumming as if I might vibrate clean out of my skin at the slightest provocation. I trail close behind Tennessee, and once inside, her imposing male counterpart snaps the deadbolt closed.

I survey the interior and confirm what I ascertained from the uncovered windows: The space is almost entirely empty. Our footsteps echo down the tiled hall to the kitchen/family room combo. A brown microfiber sectional and a glass-topped coffee table sit in the middle of the room like the top of an iceberg jutting out of a cold, barren sea.

On the table: two gallon-sized freezer bags of white powder; a crackling, high-tech police scanner; an oily, black 12-gauge shotgun; and some sort of reinforced laptop displaying a black-and-white feed of the interior of somewhere obviously other than here.

I can feel the hair lifting on the nape of my neck. "You—you guys get *high*?"

They look from one another to me, and Tennessee shrugs. "Sure, of course. Isn't that what you do as part of 'The Circle'?" she says, using actual air quotes. "My friend here will *happily* mix you up a hit; give you back some of the spirit and pluck you seem to be lacking currently. How's that sound?"

"Umm, good, I guess. Yeah, great. Could I—could I use the bathroom first, though? I'd like to wash my face—clean up a bit—like you mentioned earlier."

"What am I thinking! Of *course*, you can. Here, I'll show you the way while my partner gets your refreshments ready. And, I'll stay right outside the door the whole time, so don't you worry your pretty little head about running out of toilet paper or hot water," she says with a paper doll cutout smile; a smile invalidated by her foreboding, ominous eyes.

She leads me down a short hallway to a bathroom on the first floor; with each step, I scramble to maintain my slipping and sliding composure.

Her eyes bore into mine as she holds the door open. "Remember, I'll be right here."

"Great, thanks," I proclaim, in a strained sing-song voice.

I step into the stark, empty room, and look around. The tub is free of toiletries save for a sliver of cracked, orange soap, and the sink is covered in water spots and men's whiskers.

(what now; what now?)

I spot it, then: across the grubby, echoey space is a small window high above the toilet. In a flood of adrenaline, I lock the bathroom door and turn on the sink faucet.

I tiptoe across the grungy terra-cotta floor and climb onto the closed toilet lid—gripping it with my bare feet and willing it not to be loose—and hoist myself up to the windowsill.

It is unlocked. With one hand, I slide the window to the side and pop the screen from its tracks, watching as it falls into the bushes below.

My arms—shaking with the effort—begin to give out, and I lower myself back onto the toilet. The lid shifts sideways under my sudden weight and makes an unnervingly loud CLUNK.

Sound carries easily through the empty house. I hear a muted, yet still distinct, male voice, "You better not let her out of your sight, *Tennessee*. She's seen us, and we don't need the hassle of the fallout that'll bring."

"You're paranoid. Where would she go? She's in the *bathroom* for Christ's sake!" And then, a constrained voice directed toward me, "You okay in there, Rachel?"

My pulse gallops like a thoroughbred rounding the last corner in the Kentucky Derby. I pause—not breathing—until I am sure I can respond evenly: "Yeah, I'm good! Just finishing up. I'll be out in a few."

I force myself back up into the windowsill, and with all my strength, foist myself through the constricted square. My hips aren't quite slim enough to move smoothly through the space; a belt loop catches on the levered handle, and the phone slips out and into the night.

An audible moan escapes me.

Bam! Bam! Bam!

Ignoring the sounds from the hall, I wriggle and shimmy through the opening, scraping my thighs on the rusty aluminum frame in the process. Fresh pain—and the metallic taste of pennies—floods my senses as I bite my tongue to stifle my cries.

"Rachel? It's about time you open the door and come join us."

(just keep going, just keep going)

And then, suddenly, I am free: free like the old, incorrigible bear popping out of a knot in a tree after a month of fasting from honey. I drop soundlessly, arms first, into a ground-hugging rhododendron bush; somersault into the underlayment of cedar bark, covered in scratches and scrapes; and search the dark in desperation for the phone. The cedar penetrates my hands with a thousand tiny splinters, but I don't care.

At last, behind a shadow cast by a shifting branch, I see it, lunge for it, make it mine again, and take off running into the night. The bathroom window is a square of cold yellow light floating in the darkness—ever-smaller—behind me.

CHAPTER SEVENTY-TWO

The Valley of the Shadow

I SPRINT THROUGH THE DARKENED suburban neighborhood, my feet slapping pavement still warm from the afternoon sun. I twist my neck backward like a barn owl, sure I'll be found out, they'll give chase, I'll be caught. I zig and zag through side streets and yards, feeling my way by intuition and fear.

On the outskirts of the residential area, I cry out, a stitch in my already abused side bringing me to a halt. I stand panting and wincing in agony, covered in a sheen of sweat. I have crossed over into the Nisqually Indian Reservation and am at the base of the solitary two-lane road, which cuts up at a steep incline out of the valley. There is only a sickle moon to keep me company.

The valley is not a safe place: not in the daytime, not in a car, and sure as fuck not all alone at night in my bare feet. But I'm convinced behind me is imprisonment, certain death, or worse.

A cool breeze tickles my skin; I sweep my hair off my brow and pat my pocket for reassurance the phone is still there.

Okay, then. Let's do this.

***

The way is narrow—not quite a dirt road, but close enough—and the uneven pavement bruises my tender feet. The winding lane is treacherous in the dark. The lack of streetlights only adds to the ominous angles and shadows cast by the waxing moon. The air is hazy; a kind of crackling visual static shrouds my vision, blotting out the true shape and meaning of things.

My breath is quick and unsteady; the stitch in my side is magnified the harder I push. My head snaps from side-to-side at scuffling in the vegetation, at low animalistic noises from the swaying evergreens—silver and tangled in the moonlight. I am catapulted into hyper-vigilance as my mind fills with visions of stalking, insidious humanoids: circling, surrounding, closing in.

A shriek cuts through the night: *Is it me, or my stalker?* I dive into the undergrowth at the side of the road and try to pinpoint the sound, assess the danger. I fumble for the phone with shaking hands, feeling the numbers by touch: There isn't enough ambient light to illuminate the number pad.

Ring…ring…ri—

The call is dropped.

"Damn, fucking dead zone Reservation Road, anyway." I push the buttons again, praying I'll get them in the correct sequence.

Ring—

"Hel…Who's th…" Sputtering, distant, nearly imperceptible, but there: My daddy.

"Daddy, help! Please, come save me! Something is following me, and—and I don't know if I can make it!"

"Daughter? Is…that…? Hello?"

"Daddy! It's me! There are bad things in the woods, and I'm all alone!"

Suddenly, the connection strengthens, and I hear him as clearly as if he were standing right beside me. "Listen to me, Daughter. I am here. Just keep walking, one step after another."

The shriek comes again, and I crouch lower in the scotch broom, internally pleading for it to stop. "But—but to where? I'm so scared!! I can feel things—bad things—all around me. Where do I go??"

"Where exactly are you, Daughter? I'll come to you."

A shape swoops out of the night and glides over my head. "I—I'm coming up out of the Nisqually Valley. About halfway up Reservation Road. In the bushes on the right." I choke out a sob and whimper in abject terror.

"Listen to me, Rachel. Stand up. Do it now. Stand up, and start walking up the hill. I'm on my way."

"But Da-ad-dy," I sputter, my throat clenching shut. "I don't think I can! I'm so *scared*, and it's going to get me!"

"We'll do it together; I'll stay on the phone with you until I get there, and I'll pray the whole time."

I press the phone to my ear with a slippery, sweaty hand. The shadows circle closer, and the air is heavy with menace, but I cannot just sit and wait for the inevitable.

"Okay, Daddy." I stand—my legs unset gelatin beneath me—and step back onto the road still clutching the phone to my ear; take one step, then two, then sprint despite the staggering pain radiating from my kidneys.

"Just focus on my voice and ignore everything else, Daughter. I'm almost to you."

I run—ignoring the panic, ignoring the shadows, ignoring the fear—my father's prayers in my ear with every step I take until, at last, I reach the crest of the hill—the end of the road—all in one piece.

Waiting there, with the passenger door of his big rig truck thrown open, is my father: just like he promised.

"Come on, Daughter, get in," he says over the running engine. "How 'bout you take a break from all this nonsense and come out over the road with your old man for a while."

CHAPTER SEVENTY-THREE

Middle America

DINNER IS A CHANCE TO SIT face-to-face, but usually, the conversation consists of light, surface-level topics. That is until we firmly settle into the day-to-day rhythms of this month-long excursion over the road. Then my father is finally ready to talk, to break the ice, to get down to the nitty-gritty.

"What's your plan, Daughter? What are you going to do now?"

I sigh, toss my hair, and try to avoid the question, but he levels his gaze pointedly; refuses to be put off.

"I don't know, Daddy. I just don't know."

"Well, you better figure it out, Daughter. This is getting old."

I swirl the remnants of my coconut cream pie on the small serving plate in front of me with the tines of my fork. I've lost my appetite and my ability to meet his eyes.

After an interminable strained, weighty silence, he claps his hands together and says with forced cheer, "All right, let's get this show on the road."

And we are off again to the plains and prairies of middle America.

***

I am silent this leg of the journey—we both are—I curl up on the seat, lean against the window, immerse myself in music, and watch distractedly as the farmhouses and windmills whip by on the other side of the glass.

Daddy is right; this is *getting old. I can't keep doing this forever. It's all too much.*

What was it, Officer Mitchell said? I'm better than this? I have potential? I don't know about all that, but I do *know I'm tired. Tired of running. Tired of spinning around the fucking circle. Tired of hurting my babies, myself, every-fucking-one.*

I mull things over and twirl a lock of my faded unnaturally red hair, condensation from my breath fogging the window and obscuring my view of the passing fields. I sigh and adjust the foam ear covers of my headphones and continue ruminating.

I want so badly to be a good person—a good mommy—for my kids to know they are safe and loved, and when I come home, I'm there to stay. I want to be trustworthy again. To be a whole person. To find peace.

I wish there was a way to cement a new path in my mind—something to remind me of the life I so desperately desire.

The proverbial lightbulb—this one the 5,500-lumen variety—goes off. I burst out, my words splitting open the silence like a ripe watermelon on a summer day.

"Daddy, I need a new tattoo! Will you get me a new tattoo?"

He gawks, surprise and amusement unfurling across his features and settling into the creases at the corners of his aviator blue eyes. "A tattoo? What in the world do you need that for?"

"You know, like, something tangible to signify a fresh start," I counter, my eagerness building as I work to convince him.

He pauses, then in a voice tinged with humor, says, "Daughter, if you can find a tattoo parlor I can pull this rig into, you got it."

"We'll find one, Daddy. I just know it!" I bounce in my seat and clap my hands.

He chuckles to himself as I turn to watch the billboards roll by.

A mile—maybe two—down the road, and there it is:

TRUCK STOP
& TATTOO SHOP
NEXT EXIT

We read the words aloud in unison. Me, utterly thrilled; him, utterly shocked.

"Well, I'll be damned. I've never heard of such a thing!" He downshifts, laying on the Jake brake, and maneuvers the big rig toward the exit.

"See! I told you we'd find one!" I exclaim, my enthusiasm bubbling over.

He chuckles again and shakes his head in good-natured disbelief. "You sure did, Daughter. You sure did."

The semi rumbles to a halt, and I race ahead of him into the shop. I've picked what I want by the time the door jingles announcing his arrival.

A dragonfly. A small flash tattoo to cover the '27' etched on my right bicep—and the skin of so many others—the summer Aleister died. A symbol binding our circle together.

"See Daddy? Dragonflies symbolize freedom. I wanna put all this behind me, liberate myself from all it represents. Create, like, a whole new beginning."

He ponders thoughtfully, then nods, giving the okay to the bearded, biker-type to proceed.

There's barely time to get settled before the simple line drawing is complete. The artist does a superb job of camouflaging the stick-and-poke number from lifetimes ago.

I am thrilled and crane my neck to see my decision signified in blood.

I float happily around the foyer, perusing the keychains and other souvenirs while my father pays the bill. I gravitate to a display of postcards on a rotating metal rack, pick a few up, and shuffle through the pictures.

"Hey, what state are we in, anyway?" I call over my shoulder.

"Ohio," comes the amused response from the tattoo artist.

"Ohio, huh?" I turn back toward my father with my hands full. "Hey, Daddy, can I get one of these to send home?"

He smiles and nods. “Sure, Daughter, whatever you want.”

I settle on the most striking one—a wheat field under a dead, stormy sky—and make my way over to the counter.

“Can I borrow a pen?”

The biker reaches under his impressive gray beard and into his leather vest pocket and pulls out a blue BIC. I take the pen, turn over the glossy image, and scrawl the address of the house on Puget Street.

“Could you mail this for me, please?” I ask, handing both the pen and the card to the shop proprietor.

My father takes note of the blank greeting portion and raises a questioning eyebrow. “You didn’t write anything, Daughter. Don’t you want to send a message?”

“It’s time for a new beginning, Daddy. What is there left to say?”

POCO A POCO

(Epilogue)

CHAPTER SEVENTY-FOUR

Kintsugi

MY SECOND TIME IN PRISON was different. I turned myself in as soon as I learned there were warrants for my arrest. I did my sentence clean. This time, my mother refused to bring my children to visit, and I was down for eight months, the longest I'd *ever* been away from them.

This was the most beautiful gift, though: a profound miracle, in fact.

Without this display of TOUGH love, I would have never fully comprehended the deep, abiding pain and loss my continued use was causing not only me but my precious children, as well.

When I was released, there were two roads in front of me: go back to using, back to the circle, back to a life of crime and insanity, or go home to my children.

I chose the latter and continue to do so every day.

I am devoted to breaking my family's generational curse, NO MATTER WHAT it takes. The cycle of trauma and abuse ends here—it ends with me.

SURRENDER is the key. I finally let go of all attempts to self-medicate, to find healing outside myself, to fix something internal by external means. I finally faced my traumas head-on; the only way through, after all, is THROUGH.

There was an entire lifetime of packaged up, stuffed down, hidden away emotions to address. I wish I could tell you I just waved a magic wand, and everything was suddenly better, but that's not how it works. Recovery is an INSIDE job. It is living life on life's terms. It is a daily commitment to honesty, to open-mindedness, to the willingness to keep doing the next right thing regardless of how I feel.

I MUST continue the work of healing for the rest of my life. All the beautiful gifts I've gained in recovery—restored relationships, self-love and self-acceptance, forgiveness, and trust—can only be KEPT through vigilance. This includes making amends even when forgiveness isn't offered, taking accountability for my own behavior—my own pain—and not projecting my internal chaos on those I love.

And speaking of love, I began to learn to love MYSELF when I discovered I was neither as virtuous as I pretended, nor as defective as I feared. I am more than the sum of my suffering, more than the sum of my misdeeds. We all do bad THINGS—all of us—but that does not negate our inherent worth or make us bad PEOPLE. Letting go of shame is a pivotal part of healing.

The decades-long pendulum swing between good girl and rebel is finished. The truth of who I am lies somewhere in the middle. Keeping things right-sized and telling myself the truth, no matter how badly I want to maximize or minimize any given situation is the secret to freedom.

The road to healing isn't easy; it isn't quick. I've failed. I've floundered. But the alternative? Holding on to the pain and using it as an excuse to hurt others? I'm done with that. My relationships today are too-fucking-important to destroy by refusing to do the work to heal.

Because LISTEN: The opposite of addiction? It's connection.

Connection to Self: Seeking outside approval was just a complicated, convoluted, contrived way of lying about who I actually am. The only validation I need today is my own, and I find that in authenticity. I don't have to be the prettiest, the funniest, the most successful girl in the room anymore; I can just BE.

I don't need to impress you to prove to myself I have worth, go against my morals and values to find acceptance, become a caricature of myself to fit in. I already fit into this Rachel-shaped space I was given at birth. I am exactly who I am supposed to be: ME.

And, today, I choose to embrace and accept every single part of me, including and especially, my sexual orientation.

(And, spoiler alert: I'm apparently gay! Who fucking knew??)

No longer do I labor to hide this core element of who I am from you, from someone else's contrived, dogmatic concept of God—from ME—in fear of eternal damnation.

How did I get here, you ask? Well, check it out, yo:

> *"But the fruit of the Spirit is LOVE, joy, peace, forbearance, kindness, goodness, faithfulness, gentleness and self-control; AGAINST SUCH THINGS THERE IS NO LAW." (Galatians 5:22-23 NIV)*

No law.

There is NO LAW against love.

None.

Not a single-fucking-one.

And as such, I stopped silencing this central piece of myself with a perpetual cocktail of poison and slow suicide. I know way down deep—no matter what ANYONE says—who and how I love is pure and beautiful and sacred. This fundamental truth is an intrinsic part of what makes me ME, and I am acceptable, whole, and worthy precisely the way I am.

Connection to a Higher Power: Since birth, I was spoon-fed the rhetoric that any spiritual path not rigidly adhering to a legalistic set of rules was wrong, unacceptable, the antithesis of all that is pure and holy. As a result, I ran far and fast from any manifestation of my genuine spirituality.

I no longer swallow this concept wholesale; I am not required to conform with any list of rules or fit into a predefined box. It is not an either/or situation. Integrating my spiritual gifts into my faith has given me a freedom I never knew possible.

Today, I have a relationship with a loving Higher Power that is not fear-based. I stopped attempting to win God's favor or punishing him when I felt unworthy. I realized—fully internalized—this simple truth: I. AM. ENOUGH.

Connection to Others: Today, I am not a victim or a victimizer. I work hard to make amends when I cause someone pain, to take accountability for my actions instead of placing blame—on others OR myself. I am not always successful—but even so—I strive to participate in healthy, balanced, nontoxic relationships and behaviors.

Today, I get to be present in my family's lives, and they *want* to be a part of mine because I dove headfirst into the arduous labor of rebuilding the bonds I destroyed while running from my traumas. My family chooses to be here because *I* choose to be here.

Today, I do my part to develop and maintain healthy, healed relationships with my now-adult children. I have reconnected with the child I gave up for adoption—he is creative and quirky and intelligent and looks JUST like me—and I am blessed beyond measure to have collected a passel of other kids who call me Mom.

A few years ago, I married a generous, committed *woman* of integrity, who is also in recovery. On that most precious of days, my strong, independent, passionate daughter—who is also my dearest friend—stood beside me as my Maid of Honor, and my kind, thoughtful, witty son walked me down the aisle.

***

This life I've worked so hard to build would not be possible without the love and support so freely given by those around me. If my family, friends, and community at large hadn't seen me as human—instead of just an addict, just a felon—if they hadn't taken a chance on me and afforded me the opportunity to succeed, I would *never* have made it out of the cycle of trauma, addiction, and incarceration no matter how badly I wanted a new way of life.

If this support system had existed decades ago, if it had been culturally appropriate to talk out loud about sexual identity, mental health issues, addiction, abuse? This book might not exist. As a society, we MUST provide empathy and assistance to those struggling, humanize our fellow man through every iteration of trauma. We must LOVE. When we fall into the trap of us versus them, when we create a divide of otherness, we lose our way, and all of humanity suffers.

And, when things get hard—and they still sometimes do—when things begin to slip and slide back into unmanageability, when my character defects and old coping mechanisms start to resurface? I reach for my support system. I use my voice and share my struggles out loud; I bring the darkness into the light.

Because dark plus light? It ALWAYS equals LIGHT.

People like me? We are everywhere. We could be working right next to you, in line with you at the grocery store, our children playing with yours at the park. You would never know us if we weren't pointed out.

Anyone can change; anyone can reach their potential if willingness is met with love. If biases are set aside, and a fresh start is offered, any-fucking-one can heal.

***

Since leaving that world behind I have regained custody of my children, fought with my parents, earned a college degree, participated in unhealthy relationships, owned a business and had a successful career, struggled with parenting, bought a house, survived an almost fatal illness, come out of the closet, and was the last one to hold my father's hand before he died.

The long and short of it is this: Life happens whether you choose to be present or choose to be loaded.

And, you guys, today I choose LIFE, and fuck:

I hope you do, too.

The lie is dead. We DO recover.

And so can YOU.

THE END

Grateful, Grateful, Grateful

Entire oceans of eternal gratitude to the following:

My beloved family for their incomparable love and support, and for patiently listening to me speak of nothing but this book for eons

My first-born daughter for taking the maiden voyage through the muddled, mucky first draft, and imparting invaluable insight

My dearest friends Joyce Kilmer, Dan McNeil, John Edgerton, Sabrina Helton, Donna Peeples, and Erin Appel for moral support and thoughtful perspectives

Sage Adderley-Knox for diving into the depths of my story and offering guidance and direction

Maynard James Keenan, and the rest of the TOOL crew, for creating the inspirational soundtrack to my book and my life

Erin Adams-Chase for reading and reading and reading again, and being my ultimate champion and cheerleader

My unnamed here, yet ever-prized and present, soul connections

This book, and life as I know it, would not exist without you

Resources

SUICIDE PREVENTION
National Suicide Prevention Lifeline
1 (800) 273-8255
suicidepreventionlifeline.org

LGBTQ+ SUPPORT
LGBT National Hotline
1 (888) 843-4564
glbthotline.org

The Trevor Project
Saving Young LGBTQ Lives
1 (866) 488-7386
thetrevorproject.org

DOMESTIC VIOLENCE HELP
National Domestic Violence Hotline NCADV
(National Coalition Against Domestic Violence)
1 (800) 799-7233
thehotline.org • ncadv.org

CHILD ABUSE EDUCATION & PREVENTION
Prevent Child Abuse America
1 (800) CHILDREN
preventchildabuse.org

Childhelp National Child Abuse Hotline
1 (800) 4-A-Child
childhelp.org

MENTAL HEALTH & SUBSTANCE ABUSE DISORDER SERVICES
NAMI Helpline
(National Alliance on Mental Illness)
1 (800) 950-6264
nami.org

SAMHSA's National Helpline
(Substance Abuse and Mental Health Services Administration)
1 (800) 622-HELP
samhsa.gov

Narcotics Anonymous
1 (818) 773-9999
na.org

SEXUAL ASSAULT SUPPORT
National Sexual Assault Hotline
1 (800) 656-HOPE
rainn.org

REINTEGRATION AFTER INCARCERATION
Legal Services for Prisoners with Children
(All of Us or None of Us)
1 (415) 255-7036
prisonerswithchildren.org

The Lionheart Foundation
1 (781) 444-6667
lionheart.org

Printed in Poland
by Amazon Fulfillment
Poland Sp. z o.o., Wrocław
14 September 2021

9de2b740-d861-4610-b1e7-009df0b35016R01